How to Select a Network Marketing Company

How to Select a Network Marketing Company

Six Keys to Scrutinizing, Comparing, and Selecting a Million-Dollar Home-Based Business

Daren C. Falter
Revised 6th Edition
www.NetworkMarketingBook.com

How to Select a Network Marketing Company
Six Keys to Scrutinizing, Comparing, and Selecting
a Million-Dollar Home-Based Business

NetworkMarketingBook.com
PO Box 8607
Lacey, WA 98509-8607
(360) 790-8571
daren@networkmarketingbook.com
http://www.networkmarketingbook.com
http://www.facebook.com/DarenFalterFanPage
http://www.twitter.com/DarenFalter
http://www.youtube.com/NetworkMarketer

Original Copyright 1998 1st Edition
Copyright 1999 Revised 2nd Edition
Copyright 2000 Revised 3rd Edition
Copyright 2003 Revised 4th Edition
Copyright 2007 Revised 5th Edition
Copyright 2012 Revised 6th Edition

This specific book is the
Revised 6th Edition, Version 6.11

Daren C. Falter
www.networkmarketingbook.com

ISBN: 978-0615605272

Printed in the United States of America

This book is dedicated to my beautiful wife and business partner, Sandy, who has given me a wonderful life, six beautiful and talented children, and has sacrificed in every way to support my crazy dreams and endless ambitions. Sandy, you define support.

This book is also dedicated to the thousands of independent distributors in MLM who, like myself, never gave up on network marketing and ultimately made it a way of life.

"Never give up, never surrender."
Commander Peter Quincy Taggart
Galaxy Quest

Acknowledgments

I would like to recognize the following individuals who inspire me every day.

Special love and appreciation goes out to my wife and children who not only support me, but have even been and continue to be my stamp lickers, photographers, videographers, chauffeurs, roadies, groupies, and social media managers in our family business. I must take the time to express my love and thanks to my great friends, and traveling buddies, Robby and Kimi Fender who fuel the fire and inspire me daily. I'd like to acknowledge my good friends and business partners, Michael "Sugar Daddy" Prichard and his wife Trina for your support of my book and career. I want to thank the amazing Corey Citron and his wife Paloma for his amazing talent and dedication to our common dream. I want to thank and acknowledge Bobby Jones for his vision, knowledge, and experience and for believing in me. I must recognize my parents and my in-laws for their unfailing support and love, David and Margaret Falter, and Gerald and MaryKay Belnap. Thank you to Chad Luke for his amazing illustrations in the book.

I'd like to acknowledge Len Clements for his dedication to fact-finding and truth-telling. I consider Len to be one of the most knowledgeable and intelligent consultants in network marketing today. I'd like to thank my mentor Robert Allen for teaching me about book promotion, transformational marketing, multiple streams of income, and self-promotion.

I'd like to recognize the leadership and members of the ANMP (Association of Network Marketing Professionals) and the MLMIA (Multi-Level Marketing International Association) for their dedication to network marketing issues and the individuals and companies they represent. I'd like to acknowledge the DSWA (Direct Selling Women's Alliance) and the DSA (Direct Selling Association) for their valuable contributions to network marketing.

Contents

Foreword by Len Clements

I read the first edition of Daren's book *How to Select a Network Marketing Company* back in 1998—and I wasn't impressed. Oh, I was impressed with Daren, and I still am. I'm a fan of anyone who adores statistical analysis and pragmatically researching MLM and its companies as much as he does. Unfortunately, that's a very short list. This business needs more Daren Falters.

But back to 1998.

The first thing that struck me as blatant hyperbole, which Daren is otherwise loathe to practice, was the first line of the fourth paragraph of the Foreword, back then written by Daren himself. He had the audacity to exclaim that, by reading his book, you would learn how to "pick a winning network marketing company every time." The theme is original and, I thought back then, optimistic at best, delusional at worst. But now it's 2012. Daren's been in the biz two decades now—and he's not only picked a winning network marketing company every time as a distributor, but now he has cofounded one of the most promising network marketing companies in operation today!

That same paragraph went on to promise the reader they'd learn how to evaluate and select a network marketing company based on "facts, not hype." This was around the time I was conducting my "Facts & Myths of Network Marketing" seminars and running my "Anti-Hype" ads throughout the MLM media. How could I not at least admire and respect his intentions? After all, this is an industry where, as unfortunate and cynical as this may be to admit, we often put ourselves at a marketing disadvantage by telling the truth. In offering an honest, realistic presentation of our products and opportunity, it becomes increasingly difficult to remain competitive with promoters who indulge in hype and propaganda. We can't simply ignore these competitors who use this unfair advantage to sway the masses; we have to fight back! We have to expose them. Like revealing how a magic trick works, we have to reveal the illusion and thus eliminate its power to persuade. That's why the majority don't like guys like Daren. What he does takes guts.

But what really stuck in my craw back in '98 was Daren's "Top MLM Companies" list, based on his "objective" analysis. This was the first time that Daren listed them in descending order of preference (they're usually alphabetical). And lo and behold, the company he was a distributor for was first on the list! What a surprise. But Daren's credibility loss was short-lived. Not long after, by popular demand, I rated all the best companies in the industry and published my own Top Ten list on my Website. And lo and behold, the company I was a distributor for was number one on the list. I was also challenged for not being objective and displaying bias in choosing the order of my picks. I would always respond, quite sincerely and confidently, that I wasn't rating my company highly because I was in it; I was in it because I rated it so highly. After all, I would rhetorically ask my challengers, doesn't it make sense that I would join the company I thought was the best one?

Hmmm.

Okay, but then there was the issue of due diligence. I spent years of genuine full-time research on this business, and had surveys of over 5,000 distributors (over 7,700 now), a meta-analysis of many other industry surveys, interviews with dozens of MLM company CEOs and thousands of prospects, thorough reviews of hundreds of companies and pay plans, and years of practical experience to back up my findings. Surely no one else had done that, or was even capable of it (or so I arrogantly thought at the time). So, after finishing Daren's book, my ego and I were faced with the possibility that perhaps Daren's statistics, analysis, theories, conclusions, and company ratings were almost identical to mine, due to a series of literally hundreds of amazingly accurate wild guesses.

Or maybe he actually knows what he's talking about.

Len Clements
Author of Inside Network Marketing
Founder & CEO, MarketWave, Inc.
www.marketwaveinc.com

Introduction

Before we get into the main content, I want to make sure that everyone reading this book understands the basics of network marketing, and that you've been briefed on the purpose behind this book. For those who are veterans of the network marketing industry, you can skip to the second half of this introduction entitled *For the MLM Veterans*. But if you're new to network marketing, you'll want to make sure you absorb the following terms and explanations so you don't have trouble with these concepts as they appear in the book.

I'd like you to pretend, for a moment, that you're an entrepreneur and you've just purchased the marketing rights to an all natural, whole food nutritional supplement that naturally and healthfully helps people feel more energetic. Your marketing research shows that most customers will reorder this product after they purchase it for the first time. You're convinced that it has multi-hundred million dollar potential, so you drop all other projects and commitments and you dedicate yourself to marketing this product. The first thing you must decide is the method by which you'll take this product to market.

As an entrepreneur, you have several different choices on how to get this product from the manufacturer to consumers. The traditional path involves raising millions of dollars and launching a corporation with a large headquarters building, hundreds (maybe even thousands) of employees, and thousands of retail locations worldwide supported by local, regional, and national warehouses.

An alternative to starting a large corporation is franchising your business. You'll still need start-up capital and employees, but now you can share the risk and the wealth by allowing other entrepreneurs to invest in your retail locations throughout the world. The franchisees share in the risks and rewards. Still, another option is to simply sell the marketing rights to a giant national or worldwide retail establishment like Wal-Mart or Costco. You'll sacrifice some of your profits in exchange for a ready-made distribution machine, but it might just be worth it. However, if you really understand the model of network marketing, you might consider this form of distribution as the perfect alternative to the others mentioned. Network marketing was made for distributing products that have great *word-of-mouth* (sharing person-to-person) appeal.

Everyone is choosing network marketing

Considered twenty years ago to be the domain of the housewife and blue collar worker, network marketing has now come of age. Network marketing or multi-level marketing (MLM) is now considered a white collar industry by the millions of people who are bold enough to look past the stereotypes and see this enterprise for what it is.

Network marketing has become the business model of choice for those seeking extra income, or those wishing to completely replace their full-time income in a short period of time. With extremely low start-up costs, and extremely high income potential, home business hopefuls are turning to network marketing as an alternative to the expenses and hassles of traditional businesses or franchising.

In the past, network marketing was considered by many to be the last resort for people down on their luck who refused to seek traditional solutions. To others it was a social club for people who enjoyed adult interactions, camaraderie, and recognition. Today, network marketing is a high-tech, sophisticated, and professional business model. According to the Direct Selling Association, it's now a $100 billion per year industry worldwide. Pep rallies, prayer meetings, and the all too common "ambush" approach of "old school" network marketers has been replaced by webinars, Facebook chats, and video conferencing.

With all of these advancements in network marketing in recent years, it's no wonder that top business consultants, authors, and celebrities have good things to say about network marketing. Just ask best-selling authors Robert Kiyosaki, Robert G Allen, Mark Victor Hansen and Jack Canfield, T Harv Eker, Denis Waitley, Brian Tracy, Paul Zane Pilzer, Richard Paul Evans, Tom Hopkins, Anthony Robbins, and even Donald Trump what they think of network marketing. MLM is going main stream and now is the time to find out if it's right for you. Before we can know if network marketing will work for you, it's important to understand just how this business model works.

Network marketing defined

Network marketing is part of what is often referred to as the direct sales industry. Both network marketing and direct sales are often referred to as industries but they're really a method of distribution where instead of selling a product through a retail store, products are retailed or sold by *independent business owners* who are usually called *distributors* (or sometimes reps, agents, consultants, or members). These distributors don't earn a salary and they're not employees of the companies they represent. Instead, they're independent contractors who have signed a legally binding *distributor agreement* giving them the authority to represent a company's products or service.

In direct sales, distributors earn commissions mainly on the products they sell. Sometimes there are some bonuses that can be earned by distributors for recruiting and assisting other distributors, but this is not the emphasis of direct sales. In network marketing, a form of direct sales, distributors are paid on the number of *retail sales* they generate, but they're also paid special *bonuses* on the sales produced by the distributors that they recruit or *sponsor* into their sales force. Not only are they paid commissions on the sales produced by their own independent distributors, but they're also paid bonuses on the selling activity of distributors their distributors recruit for several generations. Independent distributors can make money retailing products or sponsoring new distributors who purchase and sell products.

Affiliate programs are another form of direct sales which usually indicate a one or two generation compensation structure. Though similar to network marketing, affiliate programs are mostly promoted and maintained on the Internet, and they generally do not offer substantial *full time* or *six figure* income potential like network marketing programs based on only paying one or two generations of commissions.

Recruiting an independent distributor into a network marketing business is called *sponsoring*. As a sponsor, you're responsible for the training and support of your new distributors. Sponsors ideally work hard to help their new recruits learn everything they need to know about starting a successful distributorship. The more distributors you help to be successful, the more money you'll make.

The mathematic formula for paying distributors is commonly referred to as a network marketing *compensation plan* or *pay plan*. Although distributors can earn commissions when they purchase product wholesale and sell it retail, they can earn even more commissions as they sponsor a sales force of other independent distributors, or what is referred to as a *downline*. Commissions earned from your downline distributors are called *bonuses*.

There are usually special bonuses and recognition associated with the sponsorship of new distributors and helping your downline grow. As you accumulate more distributors, generally you will produce a larger *group sales volume* and with that comes a larger commission check. As mentioned previously, you're ultimately paid not just on your own personally sponsored distributors, but on the distributors they sponsor, and on the distributors they sponsor, and so on for multiple generations. The number of generations or levels paid and the percentages paid on each of those generations are determined by the company's compensation plan. Distributor leaders can even earn special *override bonuses* based on top performance.

In order to qualify for commissions in network marketing, you generally must be an *active* distributor, which indicates that you've agreed to receive an *automatic order of product* every month. When you're active, you qualify to earn *residual income* (income that will continue to flow month after month) from your *downline's* (sales organizations) monthly purchases of product. You can earn commissions from the *personal consumption* of your distributors, from the products they purchase to sell to customers, and from the purchases of customers direct from the company who were originally introduced to the product by someone in your downline. The automatic reordering of product every month is generally referred to as an *autoship* or *auto order*. This autoship is usually around $50-$300 with the average being around $100 per month (or per 4-week cycle depending on the pay plan). Sometimes you can earn larger bonuses based on the level of autoship you've committed to. In modern day network marketing, all autoship orders are generally *drop-shipped* from your company's warehouse so independent distributors don't have to inventory or deliver products to their downline.

Your *upline* is the key to learning how to build your business. The word upline refers to distributors positioned in the compensation plan above you including your sponsor, and their sponsor, and so on. Your *downline* is the key to your profits. The word downline refers to everyone below you or your sales force. Your upline will teach you how to *prospect* (attempt to sponsor) and *recruit* (to sponsor) new distributors into your downline and how to maintain a high level of *retention* (to maintain or retain active distributors or customers), so you don't experience customer and distributor *attrition* (inactivity or fall-out rate).

Throughout the chapter on compensation plans, we'll be referring to terms such as *back end* and *front end*. The back end of a compensation plan usually refers to the advanced stages or the long-term money that can be earned over time. The front end usually refers to the beginning stages of a compensation plan and what you're earning during the first several months of activity.

I know I've introduced a lot of terms here. Hopefully this has helped those new to network marketing pick up on some of the basic jargon and nuances of this business. Please note that if you read anything in this book that is difficult to understand, don't hesitate to contact me with questions at daren@networkmarketingbook.com.

Creating this Book

Creating this book was no easy task. It took years of study, careful thought, and application. Obviously I wouldn't have accepted this challenge if I didn't have some compelling reasons to finish this book. I actually have three reasons.

First, I'm tired of reading and listening to self-proclaimed network marketing gurus review moneymaking opportunities. These so-called experts generally have strong opinions founded on nothing but their own personal experience, or worse, opinions. Most of these experts have done very little research, and many have little or no background in business or in building a successful long-term network marketing business. I'm committed to telling the truth about how to scrutinize and select a winning network marketing company. I'm committed to taking a closer look at the criteria for selecting the best companies. I'm committed to keeping my sleeves rolled up and staying in the trenches, actively building my next successful MLM while still maintaining total objectivity when reviewing business ideas and opportunities for others. To validate my research and conclusions, I have quoted some of network marketing's most universally respected authorities throughout the book.

Second, I feel that too many people are selecting business opportunities without doing enough of their own research. Most people simply don't have the time or the resources to effectively evaluate and compare many ventures. So they accept and follow the advice of someone not qualified to give it, like a fellow employee or even an inexperienced friend or family member. Or they follow the first charismatic mentor or business coach they meet, without really scrutinizing their backgrounds or character. I decided to do most of the research myself and then provide an objective resource for my readers so you won't have to spend months, or even years, selecting a top home-based business.

> "Too many people are selecting business opportunities
> without doing enough of their own research"

And finally, I have a passion for helping people succeed in business. This book allows me to share the information that I have gathered over the past decade with others who have the potential to be great in network marketing but are striving to find a good company and system. By following the principles and criteria outlined in this book, I have been able to make excellent, informed choices that have truly paid off for me. Every time I've failed to apply these principles (and believe it or not, sometimes I have failed to follow my own advice) I've failed to select a good business vehicle. Now it's your turn to do your *due diligence* (or diligently research something on your own). Find out if my strategy for selecting a business opportunity makes sense to you. If it does, jump on board, hold on tight, and prepare for the ride of your life as we explore the secrets to selecting a million-dollar network marketing company.

For the MLM Veterans

The rest of these introductory comments are targeted specifically to those who are not beginners to network marketing, but have been around the block a few times. Are you among the beaten, and the battle scarred? Are you one of those distributors who never really earned a check that reflects your true potential, but you never gave up trying? You may be like I was before I applied the principles in this book. The knowledge I gained in the process of researching and writing this book changed my life. I know it can change yours if you let it.

Getting Serious

This book is designed to teach you how to make money in network marketing - a lot of money. It's designed to teach you how to keep that income for a very long time. I make no apologies for its contents. This book was mainly written for those who are choosing network marketing as a career or as a life-long source of substantial residual income. If you're only looking for a few hundred extra dollars every month, just about any network marketing company will do as long as it stays in business. But if you're like me, you probably won't be satisfied until you're creating substantial monthly cash flow. For the big buck, you need the best company. Learn to just say "no" to the good, or even the great, to say "yes" to the best.

Ego vs. Income

The opinions and recommendations I share in these pages are designed to teach you how to become wealthy in network marketing. You can have all the best intentions in the world, but if you don't agree with the information and choose not to do what is recommended, you'll be horribly disadvantaged in your MLM business and you probably will never be successful. But if you want the best chance at achieving massive success, I'd recommend that you get rid of your ego and all of the things you think you know about network marketing, and study every word with an open mind. Why am I so confident in my content? Two reasons:

1. Most of this is not my material. I didn't dream up the contents of this book and then write it out on paper. Although I feel some portions of it are inspired, it did not come to me in a vision. My recommendations are the result of interviewing dozens and dozens of network marketers who make between $300,000 and $3,000,000 per year in network marketing. This book is an extensive compilation of their recommendations. I don't pretend to be the world's greatest authority on network marketing success; I just have a passion for interviewing people who are proven leaders and top money-earners in this business. In this book, I humbly present to you multi-million dollar advice offered by those highly qualified to give it. And keep in mind that if you disagree with the philosophies in this book, you're not just disagreeing with me. You're disagreeing with most of the top authorities in the network marketing industry.

2. As I learned how to shed my ego and forsake my own crazy ideas, I gained the knowledge and wisdom that I desperately needed from these top authorities in network marketing. I started applying these principles myself, and now I'm among these top earners. I feel I have now earned the right to at least contribute to the commentary. I also stopped reading books written by phony networkers, broke networkers, or network marketers who don't have what it takes to maintain large, successful organizations. Again, I implore you, from this day forward you must only take advice from people who are qualified to give it.

Are You a Career Network Marketer?

If you consider network marketing to be your career of choice and the only occupation you're interested in pursuing for the rest of your life, then we're on the same page, literally, and you qualify to keep reading all of the pages in this book. After all, why wouldn't you want to be a pro networker? If you knew what I knew about the incredible lifestyle, relationships, growth opportunities, travel, and other perks associated with a successful networking career, you'd be just as enthusiastic as I am. However, if you have reservations about starting a network marketing distributorship, I'm afraid that this book may not help you feel any better about participating. It's not designed to. There has been concern expressed by some of my editing staff that this attitude of exclusivity could hurt sales of this book. I'm not concerned. According to the Direct Selling Association, network marketing is a thirty billion dollar per year industry just in the US alone. The industry continues to grow annually unhindered by the rise or decline of the economy. I'm confident that millions of people who have never heard of it before will be turning to network marketing soon. But it's important to gain a belief in network marketing as a viable and honorable business model before this book will have a profound impact on you. For those still wondering if network marketing is for them, try seeking books that will help you build your belief in MLM first. Consider this book a sequel.

Success is a choice

Before you can succeed at anything worthwhile, such as a home-based business, you must be able to see yourself achieving this success in your mind's eye; you have to experience the thoughts and feelings this success brings. You must take on the attitude and the mindset of a serious career MLMer. I realize that you might be in a situation where you'll need to keep another job or business going while you're building your MLM career. Almost everyone does. But we must all make that choice to be a pro, and make that choice immediately. Are you in, or are you out? It would be best to decide right now.

Are you still on the fence? What are you afraid of? After all, there's no schooling or certification necessary to consider yourself a MLM professional. You don't need anyone's permission. Becoming a successful network marketer is a choice. If you haven't made this decision yet, now is the time. Whether you've made the commitment or not, please humor me for a moment. I'd like you to put your hand over your heart and state, "I, (say your full name), choose network marketing as my lifetime career. Today, and for the rest of my life, I'm a professional network marketer. I commit to doing whatever it takes to succeed in network marketing, which includes learning and applying the contents of this book." If you're on a crowded plane, in a busy lunchroom, or otherwise confined to some public area with lots of people around, you can whisper so people don't report you to the authorities. Okay, go ahead. Are you finished? I'll wait.

Good. Now don't you feel better? Welcome to the rest of your life! I'm looking forward to helping you change your life and grow in ways you've never thought possible. By the way, I'll be holding you to your commitment. Sorry I digressed there for a few minutes, but these kinds of commitments are absolutely necessary for you to get the maximum value from this book. This book is worth its weight in diamonds, if you're committed to applying its contents in the process of selecting your next MLM venture. Now you're prepared to select a network marketing company.

PART I

Finding Your Purpose

Before we get into the meat of the book, I felt it extremely valuable to relate to you the circumstances that led up to the creation of this book, as well as my zero-to-hero story, which was a direct result of applying the information I gained from my study of literally hundreds of network marketing companies. Over these first few chapters, not only will you discover my reasons for selecting a company, but I'll try to help you identify the reason that you're studying this book in the first place. Understanding your purpose in reading this book will help you get the most out of it. Once you've completed this book, try reading it again with a different purpose and see what new information you can acquire.

Chapter 1

Zero to Hero

Father Knows Best

It's funny. My father was, and still is, an armchair entrepreneur and, to my mother's vexation, has been affiliated with more home-based business opportunities than you can shake a protein shake at (that was an attempt at home business humor). While I was growing up, my brothers and sisters would fight with each other over whose privilege it was to check the mail. Every week was like Christmas at the Falter household because we were always receiving mysterious new packages filled with miscellaneous merchandise. Everything from nutritious food tabs, to mini-trampolines, to waterless car wash sprays, to face-lift creams, to concentrated soap, to water filters—and the list goes on. Although I was always interested in all these cool products, and used or consumed more than my fair share, I never wanted anything to do with the businesses associated with these products. What can I say? I was a kid! When Dad was giving opportunity presentations in the living room, I was sneaking quietly out the back door to go play basketball with my friends. If he caught me trying to sneak out, he'd make me give a testimonial.

It's funny how something I had so little interest in as a youth became my passion as an adult. Eventually network marketing would support my family, my extended family, and a variety of other worthy causes and concerns. Ironically, I didn't become interested in network marketing until I actually moved away from home and was approached by a complete stranger. What this stranger said to me made sense and, suddenly, I put down the basketball and I was all ears. After I was converted to network marketing by a total stranger, I then started calling my father on a regular basis to compare notes from my armchair, of course. Thanks Dad.

The Hook

I became officially involved in network marketing during my first year
of college. While enjoying a delicious plate of chicken cordon bleu at my
dormitory cafeteria, I received a compelling sales pitch from a fellow
student. He invited me to a product and business opportunity
presentation and even offered to arrange to pick me up since my only
form of transportation was a hand-me-down Schwinn 10-speed with
half the gears missing and semi-flat tires. That night, my soon-to-be
business mentor, Paul, rolled up in his brand-new fully loaded Pontiac
Grand Am purchased with home biz cash. The temporary license plate
was still in the back window. Paul proudly displayed and demonstrated
all of the features and high-tech bells and whistles as we rolled through
the 'hood on our way to the business opportunity meeting. One thing
that impressed me about Paul was that he was not much older than me,
but he really seemed to have a handle on his finances. He was a former
hairdresser turned businessman. And he was one of the first guys I'd
ever seen with a portable cell phone—you know, what we used to call
the Motorola "brick" phone. Back in the day, this was the symbol of cool,
especially to a college freshman. Paul really knew how to throw out the
"broke college student" bait. I was caught - hook, line, and sinker.

At the time I was a full-time student in my first year of college,
volunteering many hours with my church and working a minimum

wage job that I didn't like in order to pay for school expenses and, of course, dates with my soon to be bride. Needless to say, I was very open to suggestions on how to make more money in less time so I could enjoy the things I liked to do with the people I enjoyed doing them with. Being open to any ideas, and having nothing to lose and everything to gain, I agreed to attend my first opportunity meeting.

The Road Less Traveled

Not to be over dramatic, but this meeting changed my life in every way. I wish I could go back and thank the people who first addressed me at that meeting and lit a flame in my heart. Little did they know, this flame would never be extinguished and would grow to become a towering inferno of purpose and passion. Even though I was attending college at the time and just deciding on my major, I knew from that day forward that my formal education was not going to help me find an opportunity with this much potential.

Over the next few years, I was foolishly enticed into several different network marketing and home-based business opportunities, one after the other. Although I had nothing to show for it after several years, these were the years when I earned my PhD in the school of hard knocks. What kind of education could be better? So where was the turning point? How did I pull myself out of this failure slump?

Here's my story…

Motivation through desperation

Flash back fourteen years prior to the printing of this book. Picture a young married couple just starting out in life. We were blessed with twin daughters about a year and a half after we were married. For a while, we struggled with entry-level jobs consisting of everything from shift manager at Burger King, to secretary at a steam plant, to assisting in the office of a Japanese sports academy and trade school. Neither one of us had a college education, though I was trying to squeeze a few classes in here and there while working full-time and attempting to start a successful home-based business. After a few years of swapping childcare responsibilities and working opposite schedules, we both found ourselves working as state government employees at a large agency building in Lacey, Washington. Sandy had the fancy job working as an administrative assistant in the press office up on the third floor where all the executives were hanging out. I, on the other hand, was confined to the front desk working as a receptionist for the entire building of several thousand employees. We were forced to place our twin daughters in daycare while we tried to figure out how we were going to get Sandy home full-time to be the homemaker and nurturer of our babies.

It was interesting to hear the conversations that went on in Sandy's office when we started talking about families and future plans. It was common to hear things like, "My salary barely covers my daycare bill, but I'd go crazy if I had to be home with my children all day long," and, "Wow, you had twins? Now you really have your hands full with work and babies. At least you have your entire family over with in one pregnancy!" My personal favorite was, "I can't believe you're considering more children. What are you going to do about your career?"

These comments always hit my wife really hard because all she ever wanted was to be home with her babies. Even though twins were quite a handful, we were not finished with our family yet, even though some thought we were crazy throwing away her "career". The only career my wife was interested in involved being a stay-at-home mom and raising a family.

Although many of the individuals we worked with were fantastic people with incredible family values and meaningful lives, most of them were working on second and third marriages, complaining about delinquent children, suffering horrible health problems, and experiencing financial meltdown. Most of them would accomplish little at work while complaining about their work conditions and taking a free ride on the taxpayers' dollars.

"My wife and I were both terrified at the prospects of being employees for the rest of our lives. We knew something had to change."

Time for a change

As we worked in this government job, we began to gain a better vision of what we could expect if we made this our career. We knew the pay scales and benefit plans. We were very concerned about how long it might take to climb the agency ladder and start experiencing the benefits of upper management. From the vantage point of our entry-level jobs, this did not look appealing at all. I began to realize that it might be like this in corporations or government agencies everywhere, throughout the entire country. My wife and I were both terrified at the prospect of being employees for the rest of our lives. We knew something had to change.

You see, my wife and I both come from large, traditional, religious families. We were raised in one-income households where Dad provided for the family through a job or business, and Mom was always home to nurture children, prepare meals, and manage the household. We desired the same lifestyle, but realized as adults that not very many families could afford that traditional life anymore—especially families with no college degrees and no prospects for any jobs that could provide a decent living. Sandy became very discouraged as she realized how long she would have to work before we could even afford to purchase a small starter home.

The last straw

I think the boiling point came when I realized how much we were spending on daycare and then suddenly we were expecting our third child. Now we absolutely planned for and eagerly anticipated the birth of our third child. But at the time, our twin daughters were starting to crawl and talk and do all of those wonderful things that babies do. Dropping off and picking up our girls from daycare was a daily reminder that we had missed their precious first steps and first words that every parent cherishes. We had missed comforting them when they got hurt and caring for them the way only parents can. Now we were starting to imagine putting a third child into daycare, and we couldn't figure out how we were going to squeeze out more money at the end of the month when we weren't making it in our current situation. How were we going to be able to afford a bigger apartment with another bedroom? How could we ever dream of purchasing a home? How could we bear to now leave three children with caregivers while we went to jobs that we didn't want to be at in the first place?

Suddenly, something snapped in me, and I changed. I suddenly took full responsibility for getting my family into a better situation, and fast! I had already been dabbling in home-based businesses for several years with sketchy results. But this time, it was different. I knew it was now sink or swim.

I did something that year that still stirs up controversy among people who know my story. I dropped out of college. I just didn't have the time to pursue school and my new business commitment at the same time. Now I'm not condoning this or encouraging anyone to drop out of school. But I was sure I was making the right choice for me at the time. You see, I had to remove all of my excuses and all of my escape routes. I was committed to my dream, and there was no turning back. Maybe I can explain it in an allegory.

In 1519, the Spanish explorer Hernan Cortez sailed his fleet of eleven ships into the harbor of Veracruz, Mexico for the purpose of occupying this land and claiming it for Spain. It was common practice in those days to leave guards with the ships, as they might be needed to return to the Old World for supplies or, if necessary, to retreat from the enemy. But Cortez came for victory. He didn't care about having options. He didn't want his soldiers to have any doubt about their mission, so he gave the orders to burn the ships. Cortez ensured that conquest was the only means of survival by providing no possibility of retreat. Failure was not an option.

I knew that if I wanted to be successful in my business, I had to start burning my ships, and maybe even a few bridges. I remember people telling me, "Even if you think you want to build a business instead of finish a degree, you should get your degree so you have something to fall back on." My feeling was, if I had something to fall back on, I'd fall back. Though it seemed foolish to many of my associates at the time (and probably still does) I feel it was one of those moments of truth. Again, it wasn't the act of leaving school that was significant; it was the act of total commitment to my purpose and the shedding of all excuses for failure.

The agreement

Now let me introduce you to my next challenge, the network marketing stigma. Most people have been approached by various home-based business ideas and opportunities over the years, and they either love them or they hate them. I was no exception, and I fall into the "love it" category. I was so excited about the idea of leaving full-time employment behind and building my own future in my very own home-based business that I ate, slept, and dreamt home business. I got giddy just thinking about it. However, my wife was the exact opposite, and for good reason. While she was just as excited as I was about our first home business idea, she soon became very disillusioned as I proceeded to max out all of our credit cards with business supplies and product inventory. I was also spending most evenings and Saturdays giving meetings and presentations. By the time I was ready to make a real commitment to building my home business, my wife was about to put me in the doghouse, and we couldn't even afford a doghouse (or a dog).

We floundered for several years in network marketing, spending quite a bit of money that we didn't have to spend.

Facing the problem

Several things were very obvious in my home-based business career at that point. First, it was crystal clear that I didn't understand the criteria for selecting the best company. Second, I didn't know the most effective and efficient ways to manage and build a home business. And finally, I didn't personally know anyone who was enjoying tremendous success who was willing to mentor me and teach me the true principles of business success. I was floundering. Every dollar spent on home business products or supplies was wasted. Every business or product presentation I gave was ineffective. As I failed miserably at my sixth attempt to start a home-based network marketing distributorship, I knew that if I wanted to stay married and keep my children sheltered, clothed, and fed, I needed to take a new approach. This time failure was not an option.

The talk

That's about the time my wife and I had "the talk." My wife has always been supportive of me and she really did believe that I could do anything I committed to, but she finally put her foot down and developed some ground rules. She told me that she knew that I could be successful in building us a home-based business in network marketing. She knew that I had network marketing in my blood and the only thing that would get it out of my blood was embalming fluid. She was doubtful that I'd ever be happy doing anything else. But she finally came up with what I affectionately call *The Ultimatum*. She said, "Honey, I'm going to support you in your attempt to build a home business for us, under the following conditions. First, this is your last chance. Number seven had better be your lucky number because I can't keep going through this. So choose well, *Skywalker*. Second, we're flat broke, so you're going to have very little money to invest. You're going to have to keep the spending under control and get the cash flow rolling fast, *comprende*? Third, I thought the idea of a home-based business was that you worked from home, not that your files were at home, your family was at home, your computer was at home, but you were never home. I'd like you to work from home as much as possible. No more leaving the house several nights per week to meet with customers and distributors. And finally, I don't want you to take this personally, but ... I don't want to be involved in any way. This is your business. Build it!"

Wow, I love it when she talks sexy. I think that's one of the things that attracted me to my wife. She's a no nonsense kind of woman, and I'm nothing but nonsense. So we kind of balance each other out. Anyway, I accepted her terms ... in writing ... in triplicate. I don't know where she found the carbon paper, but it was obvious that this was premeditated. But, seriously, all nonsense aside, I agreed to her wishes and went to work. My first task was to find my last company.

Last chance

Having been given one more chance to make something of myself in life, I decided that I could not afford to make the wrong choice again. As I explained previously, I needed to find three things: the best network marketing company, the best system for building a distributorship with that company, and a mentor who was already successful and who was willing to help me duplicate his or her success. So I immediately put all of my energies into taking the first step: finding the best company. I'll be writing about the other two topics in future books.

In seeking out the best network marketing business, certain challenges immediately come to mind. Anyone who has ever investigated a lot of different companies could tell you that hype and propaganda are alive and well in the business opportunities industry. I'd like to share a story that relates to this idea. You may have heard this one before, but it's worth telling again.

Hell has its charm

A good man died and went to the pearly gates. There he met St. Peter, who greeted him by saying, "Sir, I know you're expecting to go to heaven, but based on new celestial regulations, I must, in all fairness, allow you to view both heaven and hell before allowing you to make your final decision as to where you would like to spend the rest of eternity."
The man said, "Well, I see what heaven looks like; lots of puffy clouds, angelic music, peace, and happiness. This would be fine, but I guess if it's your policy, you might as well show me hell."
So St. Peter escorted him into an elevator, and they both plunged down to the depths of hell. Finally, the elevator opened into a banquet room filled with live music, dancing, delicious food and drinks of every kind, and thousands of charming and sophisticated people welcoming him. "Wow, I never expected it to be like this!" the man said.

After sampling the food and mingling with the guests for a few minutes, St. Peter escorted the man back onto the elevator and the doors closed. St. Peter inquired, "Well, have you made your choice?"

The man replied firmly, "You know, the fluffy white clouds, angelic music, and peace and happiness stuff was great, but I have to say, I really, really liked that hell place. If I have to make a choice now, I guess I'd really rather to go to hell."

St. Peter looked at him with skepticism, and said, "Is that your final answer? Alrighty then. As you wish!" Instantly St. Peter snapped his finger and disappeared. The elevator opened again at the bottom floor. The man stepped out, and the elevator closed behind him and ascended to heaven without him. Suddenly the room became dark. All of the food, dancing, and music dissipated and was replaced by evil pipe organ music. The room's temperature instantly climbed thirty degrees and it started hailing fire and brimstone. Hooded demonic guards flooded the room with chains and shackles to bind the ankles of all the partygoers. The atmosphere had become depressing and hopeless.

A demon approached the man with a pitchfork to force him into line with the others. The man spoke up and asked the demon, "I don't understand. Just a few minutes ago, I saw a banquet room filled with music, dancing, food, and fun. What's all this?"

The demon laughed heartily and relied, "Oh, you must have visited during our twice-weekly Hell Opportunity Meeting. It's back to business as usual."

The first time I heard this story, I fell off my chair laughing. Anyone who has been through the experience of trying to evaluate a home-based business venture by attending an opportunity meeting can relate to this. All they want to show you is "all of the good, and none of the bad." In other words, it's a completely unrealistic look at what the company is really like. It can take new distributors as long as six months to figure out whether or not that initial opportunity meeting was truly accurate or not. I must admit that I was suckered into many different opportunities with this kind of hype and fluff, only to feel my dream slipping away from me after a few months. The song and dance was replaced with frustration and regret, not to mention wasted time, effort, and money. Without some kind of objective and highly professional system for eliminating the flimsy programs and focusing on the winning opportunities, one could spend a lifetime bouncing from company to company, trying to find something of lasting value and creating a truly hellish business.

Picking the best

I decided that if I was going to be successful in a home-based business, I had to select the *best* home-based business. And if I was going to select the best home-based business, I was going to have to review every home business available and then make an objective decision based on the facts. No more opportunity meetings. No more hype. I knew that if I was going to truly be successful, I had to look at every opportunity from the inside out. So that's exactly what I did.

Homework

Over the better part of a year, I dedicated myself to searching the world over for information on every available home-based business opportunity. I found lists and lists of distributorships, franchises, network marketing companies, home-party plan programs, and Internet-based affiliate programs. I wrote hundreds of letters requesting detailed information. I sent e-mails and faxes, and made hundreds of phone calls to the founders of every kind of business concept imaginable. And then the responses started pouring in.
At the time, I was borrowing some space in my parents' basement to run my research office. Luckily, I was able to intercept the mail every day before my mother saw her oversized mailbox filled to capacity with company literature, videos, distributor kits, product samples, and who knows what else. I began filling large boxes and storing these materials under my father's four large drafting tables, in the closet under the stairs (move over Harry Potter), and in other storage locations throughout the house. It took me most of the year to go through all of the material carefully and gather the data for my home business study.

Research and Evaluation

In 1994, during the time I was gathering information on all of the companies in direct sales and network marketing, I was also reading every book on the subject, interviewing consultants and top distributors, and attending as many MLM seminars as I could afford. By the end of 1995, not only had I developed a solid understanding of what it takes to build a successful business in network marketing, but I had compiled a list of over one thousand MLM company names. Later, in Chapter Three, I'll explain the six criteria I used to eliminate companies from my consideration. As I started using these six key criteria, I was successful in narrowing this list of over one thousand down to no more than two hundred of the top home-based business programs. Still too many companies to consider, I began applying the six criteria to eliminate more companies and continue to narrow this list down to include only the best of the best.

Using mainly the second of the Six Keys (selecting the best product industry), soon I had narrowed this list down to just fifty popular programs. These finalists had to be in business for at least two to three years, and they had to have a stellar track record. Later in Chapter Eight, we will go into great detail on how to examine the track records and backgrounds of the company and its founders.

From these fifty, I chose my top twenty, then my top ten, and then I narrowed it to only five companies. I accomplished this by applying the last four of the six success criteria explained at the beginning of Chapter Three. I can honestly say that I could have chosen any of the final five programs, because not only were they good choices then, but they're all still in business today and thriving in the marketplace. Yes, my study really works!

When the dust settled, I selected one of these top five programs, and the rest is history. For the first time in my career, I launched a successful business and earned a solid income that provided financial security for my family for years. This income and the time freedom provided by my network marketing distributorship allowed me to publish the first version of this book in 1998. I initially sold tens of thousands of copies of my book without the help of a single publisher or bookstore. Realizing I could help more people by researching, training and consulting outside of my current company, I stopped actively building my network marketing distributorship in 1998. During this time, I also spent a lot of time on the Internet, learning how to build a network marketing business using the Web. Incidentally, because of the purchasing activity of my customers and distributors, I still earn weekly income from the network marketing company I selected in 1995 using the criteria outlined in this book.

Because of my success in selecting a top network marketing company and building it for a few years to a substantial income, I had the opportunity to travel all over the world, sharing my network marketing knowledge with the founders and distributors of multi-million dollar companies. I also worked with aspiring network marketing pros of every creed and nationality. My research and writings threw the door of opportunity wide open and allowed me to experience an extraordinary life of discovery and fulfillment.

Even though I took a break from active participation as a network marketing distributor, based on the residual nature of network marketing commissions, today I still receive a weekly income from the efforts I put forth over a 15 years ago. This is one of the key messages I want to get across in this book. Are you ready? Here it is. If you select the right company, you could work hard for a few years and generate income for the rest of your life! I did it. And if a college dropout working as a receptionist can do it, imagine what you're capable of.

Chapter One Review

1. For many people, network marketing becomes a solution to many of life's challenges. Once I discovered the power of network marketing, I couldn't shake it. I, like many others, was willing to endure several years of selecting and working with bad companies to ultimately discover the success principles outlined in this book.

2. Although my first network marketing meeting changed my life in many ways, this first company was not the company that led to my success. As a matter of fact, I went through half a dozen companies before picking a winner. Don't be discouraged if you've made poor choices in the past. That's all about to change.

3. Even though I was attending college at the time that I was first introduced to network marketing, I knew that my formal education was not going to help me find an opportunity with the kind of potential that network marketing had to offer. Earning a PhD in the school of hard knocks can ultimately lead to more career satisfaction and financial security than any doctorate degree.

4. To me, network marketing represents a streamlined business-building system, complete with competent leadership, easy-to-sell products, and a lucrative compensation plan. Most importantly, it provides unlimited free training and mentorship.

5. In my mid-twenties, I found myself in desperate circumstances. When your back is against the wall, you have two choices. You can compromise and settle for whatever existence you can scratch out, or you can use your frustration and failure as a springboard to launch a successful network marketing career. I chose the road less traveled (as Frost's poem describes), and that has made all the difference.

6. You may be forced to build your business without much support from friends, family, and co-workers. Don't let anyone steal your dreams. Once you select the right company, you must believe in your company, believe in your product, believe in network marketing, and most importantly, believe in yourself. Once you're successful, even those who were initially negative will come around in the end.

7. If your family is not supportive of your dream to build a successful business, you must communicate your desire and commitment in terms that are unmistakable. No one has the right to hold you back from success. However, you may need to play by rules that are mutually accepted. Work together with your family towards success, even if they're not directly involved at the beginning.

8. No one is responsible for your success but you. Your parents are not responsible; neither are your children, friends, partners, spouse, church leaders, or even your MLM sponsor or company leadership. You must develop the attitude that claims, "If it's to be, it's up to me."

9. Once you have the tools for success, all you're missing is the "do or die" attitude of total commitment. As illustrated in our previous story in this chapter, sometimes you have to "burn the boats" or remove all possible retreat options in order to make the commitment necessary for total success. Don't be afraid to take a chance with full purpose of heart, mind, and soul. These are the risks worth taking. Total commitment is the foundation of total life transformation.

10. Don't sign up for an opportunity based on attending a dynamic opportunity meeting. Be sure to take the time to research and scrutinize the company before getting started. Allow your emotions to settle down before signing on as a distributor.

11. By the end of 1995, I had compiled a list of over two hundred top home-based business programs. Using my list of Six Keys that I'm going to teach you in Chapter Three, I started scrutinizing and eliminating companies from my consideration. I literally used the principles in this book to select my network

marketing vehicles. I chose two winners as an independent distributor, and now I used these principles to co-found my own MLM – a company that has already survived the challenging start-up phase and is now in momentum (very rare). When I follow the advice offered in this book, I pick a winner every time.

Chapter 2

Quest for Truth

I want, more than anything, for you to experience great success in network marketing. However, I've discovered through sad experience that most people can be led to water, but, for whatever reason, they still refuse to drink, even when they're very thirsty. It seems so silly, but I continue to observe this behavior in people to this day.

If this book is going to have maximum impact on you, it's critical that you understand *why* you're reading it. In fact, you could study this book for one purpose the first time you read it, and then come back and read it again for another purpose and learn a completely different set of lessons. So where are you in your career this time? Why do you need this information? If I were offering a private consultation, I would ask you to try to identify with one or more of the following "reasons" for reading *How to Select a Network Marketing Company*.

Bracing for a Breakthrough

1. Some readers have been casually dabbling with different ideas for creating cash flow and are now ready to get serious about making money.
2. Some readers may already be involved with a home-based business, and they're curious to see how one business vehicle compares to another business vehicle.
3. Still, some readers are already successful network marketers who have suddenly found themselves without a company or they're in a company that is having problems. They need to pick a new company ... and fast!
4. Others have never been involved with a home-based business, and they're in the process of evaluating various opportunities in order to select one.

5. Finally, some have given network marketing their heart and soul. After spending more time, effort, and money than they could afford, they have little or nothing to show for their trouble. These people simply want to know how to avoid the pitfalls and finally select an opportunity that will not only survive but will become the vehicle that drives them to financial freedom.

Before we continue, let's address each of these motivations so we can become crystal clear on how this book can help. Don't be offended if some of these comments hit a little too close to home. They did for me. Instead of getting angry and quitting, I used my frustration as rocket fuel to propel me towards a solution. Your propellant may be just a few words away … keep reading!

1. The Dabbler Gets Serious

The *Dabbler* is commonly referred to in network marketing circles as the *MLM Junkie.* I agree that it's not a very flattering label. But for some wannabe networkers, sadly, this label fits like a glove. MLM Junkies move from company to company with the greatest of intentions but no long-term commitment. They stick with one product until the newness and the excitement wears off, and then they move on to greener pastures. The trouble is, MLM Junkies don't know what to look for in a great network marketing company, so they keep picking losers, and walk away from some of the winners before they hit their momentum. I absolutely believe, as everyone should, that our past does not equal our future. Why? Because I was a MLM Junkie for a few years, and I know how it feels. My commitment level was higher than most, but it wasn't strong enough to provide me with any lasting success. The research I did for this book was my rehab process. Now I know what it takes to overcome this costly addiction. That's why I refuse to give up on many of the lost souls in network marketing and home-based business who, to this point, have never made a solid commitment to one company for any length of time.

If you have the tendency to jump from company to company on an annual, quarterly, or monthly basis, this book will not do you any good until you reverse this trend. All of the science and statistics in the world cannot help someone who is a member of the network marketing *Flavor of the Month Club.* Once you're ready to make a true commitment, or you're so sick and tired of failure that you'll do anything to build your business, it's time to study this book inside and out so you can pick the program that will allow you to succeed in network marketing.

There is hope for MLM Junkies. I know dozens of Junkies, including myself, who have been "clean" for years now, even decades, and they didn't have to join a twelve-step program. If you have tendencies to bounce around, use this book to help you nail down a top company and ride it out. Simply put *blinders* on (like the ones you see on horses to keep objects in their peripheral vision from distracting them) and start building a business.

2. Going Undercover

I should actually call this person the *Undercover Agent.* Your purpose here is reconnaissance. You're learning how to collect intelligence on the other companies in your industry. Spying on the competition is something that I encourage networkers to do, even after they've committed to a company long-term. Without a fundamental grasp of the entire industry and the companies and products that make up that industry, you'll never be a top recruiter. Unfortunately, most network marketers don't know how to spy properly. Most distributors will gather just enough information about their competitors to try to manufacture half-truths designed to exploit their weaknesses and make their own opportunity look better through unfair comparisons. If you really want to know how your company or product compares to another, you must be willing to open your mind and let go of any preconceived ideas. Half truths and prejudice can easily be planted in distributor's heads by non-objective MLMers who may have an axe to grind with the company you're investigating.

Sometimes the best information I've ever collected has come from people who are currently involved with a company, but no longer actively building that business because they're semi-retired or they're having some reservations about continuing to build for any number of personal reasons. These distributors still have an emotional connection to the products and some kind of special bond with the management, but they're more prone to speak frankly about what is going on with a company. If they don't have an axe to grind, generally this is a premium source of information. If they do have an axe to grind (they'll usually deny this), their emotions may be clouding their judgment, and the information may be unreliable. Only people who have been with a company in the past and left on good terms can provide objective and accurate insights. Remember, you're looking for the good, the bad, and the ugly presented with fairness and balance. People possessing total objectivity are harder to find than diamonds and rubies. Find them, and keep them handy while researching.

If someone is trying to tell you a company is all good and has no bad qualities, or if someone is trying to sell you on the idea that a company is all bad and does not have a single redeeming quality, then you know their opinions are worthless. Their emotions are clouding their judgments and their views are warped, distortions of reality. If you plan on going undercover to investigate companies and products, do it right. Be fair. Give credit where credit is due. Your product is not the only product doing people good in the world, and your company is not the only game in town. You shouldn't be looking for dirt on a company so you can expose them or trash them to make another plan look better. We all need to play nice. Once you really adopt the principle of fair play and start peacefully cohabitating with the other network marketers in the industry, not only will you master the art of selecting the best network marketing company, but you'll be much more effective in recruiting intelligent leaders into your company of choice. Top leaders can see right through the hype, and they will know after a five-minute conversation if you've really done your homework or if you're just another immature, unintelligent distributor groping and scratching your way to success.

3. Is Your Ship Sinking?

For its time, the *Titanic* was the largest, most impressive ship on the ocean. Everyone wanted to sail the seas on what appeared to be the best luxury liner ever built. However, if you were congregating with all of your business associates on the deck of the *Titanic* while it was sinking, you'd really want to find another seaworthy vehicle to get you out of icy waters fast.

When your ship is sinking, you don't have time to lose. You must choose a new ship, and choose quickly, before your business associates and friends start jumping ship and are lost forever. This is a time for you to show leadership. Don't jump into the first lifeboat that comes along without any thought for your friends and associates. You have to find a boat big enough for everyone. At the very least, you have the time to quickly read this book two or three times and then seek a company with the qualities described herein. If you choose the right rescue ship, you may save every single person on your sinking boat. Transitioning from a failing company to a thriving company may be extremely stressful for several days or even a few weeks, but it can also be extremely profitable. Select the right company and those who are leaving the sinking ship will have forgotten all about their misfortunes within a couple of weeks. All they'll be able to think about is arriving at their desired destination in safety and in style.

Be courageous. Take action. Choose well.

4. The Comparison Shopper

If you really want to learn how to compare apples to apples, and even watermelons to raisins, you're reading the right book. Keep in mind that this book was prepared to help you select the *best* network marketing company, not to help you justify a hasty decision, and then use it to rationalize your choice after the fact. To make the correct choices in business, you must push away your emotions and your impressions and focus on the facts. You must learn how to find and verify truth on your own so you don't have to rely on someone else's propaganda. You must resist acting on your emotions before you have all the facts.

This book allows anyone to objectively break down and evaluate the criteria for selecting the best company based on real data, real facts, historical documentation, and real-life success stories. Our process has been proven over and over again, time after time. Those who obey the company selection process in this book will always be able to make proper comparisons and, in the end, will be able to make a great choice.

5. Your Last Shot At Success?

Although I've found myself in all of the previously mentioned situations, this is the one I identify with the most. If you've been beat up in network marketing for several years but have not lost your dream, this information is long overdue. This is the book you should have read before you started on your MLM journey. If you've been in the industry as long as I have, it may not have been around when you started. And if you're a new comer, you may not have known it existed.

So many distributors who would otherwise be thriving in business are trying to build a long-term MLM organization with a company that will not be around in a few years. Sometimes top distributors will stay with an inferior company because they're not able to recognize the danger signs. They're so wrapped up in their vision of success that they don't notice even the most conspicuous warning signs.

Still, other network marketers are involved with companies that will not necessarily go out of business, but they're companies that don't have the capacity to support top distributors. There's nothing more common in network marketing than wasted talent. I know at least a dozen distributors who are among the greatest network marketers of our time. However, they're involved with companies that can't market their way out of a paper bag. The distributors in any company are limited by the vision, ambition, and growth capacity of that company.

If you're willing to make a commitment to do whatever it takes to find a winning company and build it big, I know you're going to have an experience similar to my own. Your next opportunity could be the one that really explodes. There's nothing more exciting than watching an aspiring network marketing superstar on a rocket ride to the moon. Anyone who has been in a lot of network marketing companies that just have not worked out will eventually find a winner, as long as they refuse to quit searching for the best company. But if you're ready to shorten the learning curve substantially and find that winning opportunity faster, keep reading.

Right Here! Right Now!

No matter your reason for seeking network marketing knowledge, you're finally in the right place at the right time. All of your experiences in life, home-based business, or independent distributorship, good or bad, have been preparing you for what I'm about to share with you. What you're about to read may change the way you think about network marketing forever!

Doing Your Due Diligence

Before you become a successful network marketer, you need to pick the right vehicle for the right reasons. The key to selecting the right business is doing your due diligence. This is a popular phrase that has caught on in the last decade as people have started to realize that not all business opportunities are created equal. People are beginning to understand that the smart way to select the best MLM business venture is to thoroughly scrutinize a business vehicle before getting involved.

Better to Have Loved and Lost ...

Right now you may be thinking, "But I've already tried and failed at network marketing." You may feel like I did several years ago, like you are doomed to failure in your own business. Believe me, I have been there, done that, bought the T-shirt, and have even lost that shirt more than once. I know what it feels like to refer friends to a business venture that goes out of business, or a product that is pulled off the market. I have walked on eggshells with my spouse when she didn't see the dream of business ownership, while I struggled not to spend more than we made each month. I know what it feels like to be alone in a business with no support. I know what it feels like to pump hundreds, even thousands of dollars into a network marketing business that doesn't seem to be going anywhere.

A Better Way

I'm going to invite you to do something very different. I'm going to invite you to give network marketing another try, or, as the case may be, one last try. However, this time, before you choose a company, I want you to first understand the principles behind selecting the best network marketing company. After all, this isn't a roulette wheel ... this is your financial future! Don't throw a dart to select your opportunity. Learn how to choose a business and a support system based on the facts. I want to teach you how to avoid the pitfalls and pick a company you can really get behind. You can't imagine the feeling of selecting a company that is truly the best. Building a distributorship is no longer hard work, it's a passion.

> *"The awesome power of absolutely knowing your product and opportunity are the best (at least for you) can be an incredible, life-changing experience. When you reach this point, you will be amazed at how easy it will be to sell it to others."*
> --Len Clements, Author of *Inside Network Marketing*

Everyone Claims to be the Best. Who Can I Trust?

Here's a fitting quote from one of the world's most famous writers and humorists, Josh Billings. He once wrote, "As scarce as truth is, the supply has always been in excess of the demand."[1]
There are so many voices out there; it is hard to know who is telling the truth. Don't take information at face value. Don't believe something because it's in print. Don't listen to the opinions of people who are unqualified to give those opinions. Learn to verify, quantify, and validate information. Hypothetically speaking, Dad may give great advice on how to be honest, and Mom on how to be compassionate, but that doesn't necessarily qualify them to give you stock market tips unless they have the background to do so.

Stop listening to hype and learn to do your own research. Once you have all of the facts, study them, meditate on them, pray about them if your faith dictates, and then trust the answers that come to you. You're the only person who doesn't have a hidden agenda. You're intelligent enough to find and research the facts, objectively review the data, and even call on divine help when appropriate. Only then can you make an intelligent business decision. Only then can you make the correct decision.

Chapter Two Review

1. Take the time to evaluate your reasons for reading this book. Why are you reading?
    a. You may have been casually dabbling with different ideas for creating cash flow and are now ready to get serious and make some money. Don't join the MLM Flavor of the Month Club. Find one company using the principles in this book, and then focus on and commit to building that distributorship to the top of the pay scale.
    b. You may already be involved with a home-based business and you're curious to see how your business compares to other business vehicles. Learn how to objectively evaluate each company and you'll be much more effective in recruiting intelligent leaders into the company you ultimately choose.
    c. You may be a successful network marketer who has suddenly found yourself without a company. You must quickly select a new company! When your ship is sinking, you don't have time to lose.
    d. You may have never been involved with a home-based business and you're in the process of evaluating various opportunities in order to select one. This book was prepared to help you select the *best* network marketing companies, not to help you rationalize your way into a company and product that you think is great.
    e. You have given network marketing your heart and soul. After spending more time, effort, and money than you could afford, you have little or nothing to show for your trouble. You want to know how to avoid the pitfalls and finally select an opportunity that will not only survive, but will become the vehicle that drives you to financial freedom.

2. All of your experiences in life and business have been preparing you for the information held in the pages of this book. What you're about to read may change the way you think about network marketing forever.

3. Stop listening to hype and learn to do your own research. Once you have all of the facts, trust your instinct and act upon them. You're the only person who doesn't have an agenda.

PART II

Preparing For Success

These next two chapters are an introduction to the criteria we'll be using to find the best company. We will also focus on some of the tactics, tools, and attitudes you'll need to select a successful company. This is where the Six Keys will be introduced and then the first key will be explained in detail. Don't skip these steps. They're vital to your success. Here we'll introduce our master list of network marketing names which is growing every week. We'll also teach you to start thinking and acting like a network marketing professional.

Chapter 3

The Study

"To know if something is the best,
you have to look at all the rest!"
-Daren Falter

Before we get too far into this chapter, can I ask for a commitment from you? Can we start the research off with a mutual agreement to keep an open mind and look at the facts first before making any final decisions? Let's agree not to pass judgement until we understand the criteria for evaluating a network marketing company and the principles for selecting the best company. If you're currently in another network marketing company, or if you're leaning towards a specific company, try to detach yourself emotionally so you can make an objective evaluation of your company as well as others. I want your company to be the *best* because it *is* the best, not because some guy in a fancy suit at an opportunity meeting said it was.

The Six Criteria for Selecting a Top Distributorship

Rather than simply running through the criteria I used for selecting the best company in network marketing, I want to walk you through the evaluation process, step-by-step. It's valuable for network marketers to understand the importance of each criterion. You can use this system to rate any network marketing business venture.

Listed below are the *Six Keys* or criteria we will review in this book. Associated with each key are some of the critical questions that this book will answer. Don't worry if you don't understand the question before reading the chapters associated with each criterion or key. But keep in mind that eventually understanding these questions and their answers is critical to your long-term success in network marketing.

Key #1: Profit Mindset – How to Think Like a Marketing Pro

In order to be able to recognize a good opportunity, you must be thinking with a marketing mind. This section will help you understand how successful home business owners think about success and money. Adopting these same beliefs and philosophies is your first step in selecting the right company. Chapter Four will answer these questions, and many others you might have about what it takes to have the mindset of a millionaire.

- What is your main reason for starting and maintaining a successful business?
- What is the difference between business ownership and self-employment?
- Would you rather be *right* or *rich*? Is ego more important than profits?
- What message is the marketplace sending you every day?
- Are you coachable enough to effectively apply what you learn in this book?

Key #2: Product Industry-What to Sell, and Why

The term product industry refers to the type of product or service you will be selling through your independent distributorship. Chapter Five will answer the following questions in detail.

- Should I select a product company or a service company?
- Which product or service will produce the largest income for me?
- Should I go with a new idea or go with something proven?
- Which industries are absolutely not viable this year?
- What role do trends play in selecting a product industry?
- Should I choose a Baby Boomer industry, or does it matter?

Key #3: Timing-When to Join a Company

Many distributors learn how to think like marketing pros, and how to pick a winning product industry, but they fail when it comes to selecting the right time to join a company. Getting started too early or too late can be detrimental to your success. Find out the best time to get involved in a company's cycle of success in Chapter Six.

- During which phase of growth should I join a company: the start-up phase, the momentum phase, or should I wait unit the company is mature and stable?
- Should I get involved with a ground floor opportunity?
- Is there such a thing as market saturation?

Key #4: Compensation-How to Scrutinize a Pay Plan

There are many different ways to be compensated in network marketing, but not all distributor compensation plans are created equal. Discover the differences between the different plans, which plans to look for, and what to watch out for. All of these questions will be answered in Chapter Seven:

- How much commission should I earn as a distributor?
- Which distributor compensation plan is the best, and why?
- What is the difference between the breakaway, binary, unilevel, or matrix plan?
- How can I identify these different plans and how do they compare?
- Which plan has the best track record? Which plan has the worst?
- What is a hybrid or a 2-Up compensation plan? How do they work?
- Can a comp plan pay out too little or too much?

Key #5: Company Leadership-Who are You in Business With

This could be the most important topic of this entire book. You must learn how to investigate a company's ownership and management team before you get involved. In Chapter Eight, you'll find answers to these questions and more.

- How can I tell if a company's management team has high integrity?
- Is it important for the company to be debt-free?
- Is it important for the company to own its own products and facilities?
- Is it an advantage to be involved with a publicly traded company or a private company?

- How can I find out if the management team is experienced, competent, and committed?

Key #6: Product Integrity-How to Scrutinize a Product

We've already covered the different product industries available through network marketing and which ones are the best. Now we'll go into detail on how to scrutinize a specific product. This will make up the contents of Chapter Nine.

- What makes one specific product or product line better than another?
- How can I select the best product for my home-based business without having expertise in that product industry? Which of the four hundred scrutinized products ranked among the top twenty?
- How can I find the time to study and compare all of these products?
- How can I find out if a product is dangerous or controversial?
- Which product is right for me?

Have you asked yourself the questions in this survey? If not, go back and ask each question and really think about the answers. Read every bullet point. Can you honestly answer these questions right now without doing any additional research? Do some of the questions confuse you? Did you know that if you select a company without knowing the answers to these questions, you'll likely fail within months? *All* of the answers to these questions are buried right here in this book. It's time to start digging.

The Blind Men, and the Elephant

You may remember hearing the popular folk tale from India about the six blind men and the elephant. It's not only a powerful tool for teaching us not to judge something based on limited knowledge, but it gives us a perfect analogy for the importance of these *Six Keys*.

In the story, six blind men approached a large elephant and each of them touched the animal at a different place on its enormous body. Not seeing the big picture, each blind man imagined a totally different image of what they were actually touching. The first blind man touched the side of the elephant and announced, "It's a wall." The second, feeling the tusk, said, "It a spear." The third felt the elephant's trunk and proclaimed, "It's a snake." The fourth reached out and felt the leg and said, "It's a tree." The fifth, touching the ear, said, "It's a fan." And, the sixth seized the elephant's tail and declared, "It's a rope." Like the blind men, if you focus on just one part of the elephant, you'll be deceived. A company is just like the elephant. It's not whole and complete without all six of these vital parts or keys. Make sure you understand the importance of all of these criteria and how they make a company complete.

You're Just a Few Chapters Away from the TRUTH!

The rest of this book will break down and explain in detail the *Six Keys* for selecting a company. After each chapter, I've included a review. At the end of the book, I even have a rating system for testing and scoring any opportunity you're evaluating.

Based on my evaluation and test results, I have prepared several lists at the back of this book detailing my findings and recommendations on how to select the best network marketing company and which companies scored the highest. However, don't skip any of the chapters in between. All of this information is vital to your success. Remember, don't take my word for it; you must gain your own knowledge and make your own business decisions based on your educated intuition. Enjoy the process, and good luck!

Ready to Throw a Dart?

With all of the choices, you'd think aspiring business owners would spend more time evaluating an opportunity before joining. Unfortunately, most new distributors simply select a company at random. They spend more time and effort selecting a used car than they do selecting a business vehicle that could lead to financial independence. It's like throwing a dart to choose your destiny. Well, if you're going to throw a dart, I'd like to provide you with a *great* dartboard!

The following few pages contain a condensed list of the most popular network marketing companies that have launched over the last several decades. This only represents a portion of the companies that have been in existence over the last century, and it does not include many of this year's start-up companies. Some of these companies are less than one year old, while others are more than one hundred years old. I have looked into all of them.

Most of these companies are not even worth evaluating because they'll be out of business within months. Also keep in mind that *many* of these companies have been out of business for some time or have gone out of business since this book was printed. If you are going to throw a dart to select your company, you might have to throw a few more times before you pick one that will last through the end of the year. I've purposely left some of the more prominent MLM failures on the list as reminders of the mortality rate of all business start-ups.

I have a very important question for you, and I want you to think about it before you answer. Repeat this question five times. Here it is. Unless you've carefully reviewed *all* of the companies on this list that are still in business, how do you know the company you've chosen is the best? Okay, now repeat it five times. Are you starting to understand the true meaning of the word *objectivity*? Are you starting to get a feel for what I went through to create my conclusions in this book?

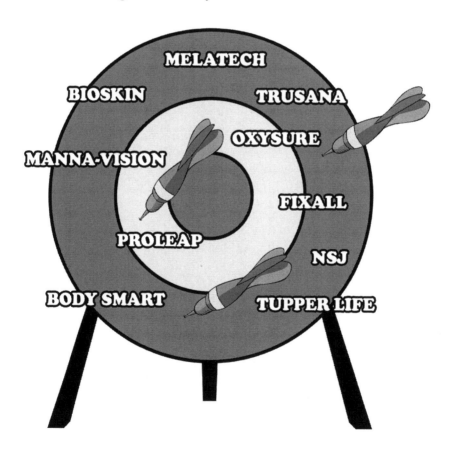

Some of the Network Marketing Companies in My Database:

1-800-PartyShop
1st Family
1To1Everyone.com
1Voice Worldwide
2 by 2 Net
2Xtreme
21st Century Collecitbles
21st Century Global Network
21st Century Nutriceuticals
21stNetwork.com
360 Solutions
4 the Good Life
4-Life Research
5 Star Auto Club
5Linx
8 Point Communications
A Better Chance PTY
Acceris Communications
Achieve Success Team -AST
Achievers Unlimited, Inc.
AcoMark Concepts Pvt. Ltd.
Act II Jewelry
ACTIS Global Ventures Active Life Plus
Ad-Net
AdJuice
Advantage International Marketing
Advanced Internet Solutions
Advanced Marketing Concepts
Advantage Marketing Systems, Inc.
Adventure International
Adverworld
AdvoCare International, LLC
Aerus Electrolux LLC
Affinity Just-2
Affinity Lifestyles
Agent Nation
Agloco
AIM International
Airlume, Inc.
Alive
AliveMax
All That's Natural
Alliance
Aloe Vitality
Alpine Ecoquest
AlpineV
AL Williams
Altitude
Amazon Herb Company
Ambit Energy
AMC Corporation
Amega Global
American Longevity

Amera
Americall Network, Inc. (ACN)
American Bio Labs Inc.
American Communications
American Dream Nutrition
American Freeway 100
American Gold Plating Eq.
American Gold Reserve
American Longevity
American Post
American Travel Network
American Image Marketing
American Benefits Plus
America's Team Inc
AmeriKare
AmeriLat
AmeriPlan USA
AmeriReach
AmeriSciences
AmeriTalks, Inc.
Ampegy
AMS Health Sciences
Amsoil
Amway
Anew International
Anise Cosmetics
AOL Select
Aprise
AquaGenus
AquaSource
Arbonne International, Inc.
ARIIX
Art Finds International, Inc.
Art of B. Living
Artistic Impressions, Inc.
Ascential Bioscience
Aspire Worldwide
Assured Nutrition Plus, Inc.
AtHome America, Inc.
ATX Inc
Australian Body Care
AutoPlus Window Stickers
Avalar Network, Inc.
Avon Products, Inc.
Awareness
Awesome Specialties Int'l
AyurVida
Aztech Financial
BabyCrazy
Baby Signs
Baby Splendor
Bazi
Beads of Hope
BeautiControl
Beauty Counselors

Benchmark
Better Wellness
Beverly Hills
Beyond Organic
Big Bang Infonetwork
Big Planet (See NuSkin Enterprises)
Big Yellow Box (by Crayola)
Bimini
BIOPRO Technology
Bio Tech Neutriceuticals Inc
BioCrave Health Products
Biogime
BioGreen Systems, Inc
Biometics
BioNovix
Bizarre Promotions, Inc.
BizKonnect
Blue Strawberry Bath & Body Products Inc.
Body Alive
Body Electric Inc
Body Extreme
Body Systems
Body Wise International, Inc.
Bodyguard Technologies
Books and Beyond, Inc.
BookWise
Boresha Coffee
Brain Garden
Bright Minds
Builders Referral Incorporated
Bulletin Board
Cabouchon International
Cajun Country Candies
Calculated Couples
Calls For Kidz
Cambridge
Cambridge Direct Sales
Candlefun
Cantralliance
Capital Crafts
Carco
CardLink International
Care Entrée
Carico International, Inc.
Carino Nurseries
Carolina Fine Cookies
Carprofit
CD Express
CDI Telecom
Celadon Road
Celestial Harvest
Cell Tech
CenterSource Life Systems
Changes

How to Select a Network Marketing Company

Changes International, Inc.
Chantal B. - Paris
Charitable Partners
Charmelle
Charter Financial
Chef Selections
Cherish Designs
Chesapeake Bay Company
Chews 4 Health
Chez Ami
Chicken Soup for the Soul
Chic Pursenality
Clean Easy
Clearbrook
Clever Container
Close To My Heart
Cognigen
Colesce Couture, Inc.
Color Me Beautiful
CommonWealth
Communications oncepts
Conklin Company, Inc.
Consumer First, LLC
Consumer's Buyline
Cookie Lee
Corlink Communications
Country Bunny Bath & Body
Country Charm
Creative Financial Options
Creative Memories
Creative Network Int'l
Creative Photo Concepts
Cruise to Cash Vacations
Custom Corner
Custom Telecard
Cutco Company/Vector
Marketing Corporation
CyberWize
Dare2BU Records, Inc.
Daystar
Debt Free
Delphin
Designer Fragrances
Designer Nutritionals
Destiny
DeTech, Inc.
Diamond Treasures Network
Diamond Way
Diolink
Diotek India Limited
Discount Home Shopping Club
Discovery Toys, Inc.
DoItAll Travel
DoTerra Earth Essence
Dominator Clothing

Doncaster
Dr. Glass Window Washing
DS-Max
DS-MAX U.S.A. Inc.
Dudley Products, Inc.
Dutch International
DWG International
Dynamic Essentials
Dynamic Freedom, Inc.
Dynasty For Diamonds
E. Excel International
Eagle Express Marketing
Earth Smart
Earth Tribe
EarthCare International
EarthNet
Earth's Elements
Easy Way
EcoQuest International
Elite Health Products
ELIXIR-HEALTH
Elysee Cosmetics
Emerald Coast News
Emerald Passport
Empower Net
Emprise
Enagic
Enchanted Scents Designs
Encoura
Encyclopedia Britannica
Energy Savers Alliance
Eniva Corporation
Enjo
Enliven International
Enrich International
Entech
Envion
E'Ola International
EonDeck.Com, Inc.
Epicurean
Equinox
Equinox
Escape International
Espial
Essante Corporation
Essen USA
Essential Bodywear Essentially
Yours
Etcetera
Euphony Communications
Everest International
EverydayWealth
Eterna Health
Evolution International
Excel Telecom

EXOVAP Ltd.
EZHealthcarebiz.com
Family of Eagles
Fantastic Life Systems
FemOne
FIACom Inc
Fifth Avenue Collection, Ltd.
Financial Destination Inc
Financial Ed, Inc.
Finest Accessories Inc.
FINL
First Fitness International
First Marketing Group
FlashNet Marketing Inc
For*Mor
Forever Living Products
Fortune High Tech Marketing
Fortune Quest
ForYou, Inc.
France Luxe
Fragrant Lemon Peel TFLP
Free Coral Calcium
Free Network
Freedom One Services
FreedomStarr
FreeLife International
Frozen Lease
Fuel Direct
Fuel Legacy Int'l
FuelMedz
FuelZone
Fuller Brush Company
FundAmerica
Future World
FutureNet
Futurewave
Gano Excel
Garden State Nutritionals
GasUpUSA
GEM Lifestyle
GemCap Equity Mngmt, Inc.
Genesis
Geo Worldwide
Get Moving Today
Global Comm. Solutions Inc.
Global Community
Global Daily Pay
Global Domains.(MY.WS)
Global Essence
Global Health
Global Health Trax
Global Information Network
Global Network Marketing
Global Nutrition Network
Global Prosperity

Global Resorts Network
Global Strategic Alliance
Global Travel
Global Wellness Club
Globestar
GMX
GNLD
Golden Neo-Life Diamite
Golden Nutrition
Golden Pride Rawleigh, Inc.
GoldQuest
Golf Connections
Golf Link Int'l
Good Life International
Good to Grow Garden
Gourmet Coffee Club
Great Life Products
Greenway
Greenwood Health Systems
Ground Zero
Gulf Coast / Noah's Ark
H.I.D. International
Happy Gardener, The
HAVVN
Hawaii HerbalTech
Corporation
HB Products
Healing America
Health Club Network
Health Dynamics
Health 4 Wealth
Health Technologies Network
Health Thru Nutrition (HTN)
Health Voyage
Health-Mor (An HMI Industries
Inc. Company)
Healthy America
Healthy Outlook
HealthyPetNet
Heart Warming Creations
Henn Workshops
Herbalife International
Herbatrol
Heritage Health Products
Heritage Makers
Higher Ideals
Highlights - Jigsaw Toy Factory,
LTD.
Holbrook Cottage, Inc.
Home & Garden Party
Home Interiors & Gifts, Inc.
Home Owners Network Club
Homemade Gourmet, Inc.
Homestar Communications
Home Tutoring Opportunities

Hope
Horizons
Howard Whlsl & Promos
Hsin Ten Enterprises
HTEUSA
HUZO
Hy Cite Corporation
iBuzzPro
Icentris
ICR Services Network
I.D.E.A. Concepts
Ideal Health
IHBNO
iLearningGlobal
I-Link
Immunotec Research Ltd
IMN Dot Com Pvt. Ltd.
In Touch
InComm Inc
Infinity In'l Health & Beauty
Infinity2
Initials
InnerLight
Inspire
Integris Global, LP
Intelligent Nutrients
Int'l Consumer Opportunity
Network (ICON)
Int'l Heritage
International Teamworks Inc.
Investor's International
IONYX International
Iron Curtain Labs
Isagenix
isXPERIA
ITV Ventures
It Works Global
iZigg
Jafra Cosmetics International
JangleFish
Janzer Architecture Products
Japan Life
Javita
Jet Set Life Technologies Inc
Jetway
Jeunesse Global
Jeunique Int'l, Inc.
Jewelry at Home
Jewels By Park Lane
Jewel Kade
JewelWay
Jockey Person-To-Person
Joielle LLC
Jordan Essentials
Journey Telecom

Joy Enterprises
JS HomeStyle, LLC
Jurak Corporation World Wide
Just Add Guests
Jusuru
Juvio
K*I*D*S Shield
Kaeser and Blair Inc.
Kadima Inc.
Kaire
Karemore
Kele n Co
KickBrix
Kingsway
Kirby
Kitchen Fair (Regal Ware, Inc.)
Knutek
Kustom Card Int'l. Inc.
Labrada Nutrition Systems
Lady Remington Jewelry
Ladybug Garden Parties, Inc.
Lametco
Lametco Int.
L'aprina
Latasia & Company
Latin Wave Network C.A.
L'Bri Pure N' Natural
Le Gourmet Gift Baskets Inc.
Le Natural Int'l
Le Nautrel
Leaders Club
Legacy For Life
Legacy Health Solutions
Legacy Lifeline
Legacy USA
LegalShield
Lemongrass Spa Products
Lexxus International
Lia Sophia
Liberty
Life Education And Prosperity
Inc
Life Extension
Life Force International
Life Plan Corporation
Life Prints
Life Source
Lifelink
LifeNet Inc.
LifePlus International
LifeScience, Inc.
LifeSciences Technologies
LifeSpan International
Lifes Abundance
Lifestyles 2000

How to Select a Network Marketing Company

Lifestyles International
LifeTek
Lifetime Solutions
LifeTrends
Lifetronix
Lightyear Wireless
Limu
Lindt Chocolate RSVP
Links Worldwide Inc.
Liquid Life
LocalAdPros
Locality.com
Localnet
Logo Express
Longevity Network, Ltd.
LR International
Lunesse
Luxelle International Inc.
LW Publications
Magic Learning Systems
MagNet
Magnus Enterprises, Inc.
Mainstreet Alliance
Mandura
Mannatech, Inc.
MannaValley
Market America, Inc.
Market To Sucess
Marty Wolf Game Co.
Mary Kay, Inc.
Matol Botanical International
Mava D. Enterprises LLC
Max Int'l
MaXeGEN
MAXXIS Group, Inc.
Mayberry
MC2 Global
MegaNet$
Melaleuca Inc.
Metabolife International
Metrin Life USA, Inc.
Million Dollar Body
Millionaire Makers
MILLIONAIRES GROUP
Momentum Worldwide
Monarch
Monavie
MoneyMatters
MOR Vacations
Morganics
Morinda, Inc
MotorMoney.com
MOXXOR
MPAD Tech Group, Inc.
Multi-Pure

MultiWay
Muscle Dynamics Fitness Network, Inc.
Musical Magnets
My CD Inc.
Mycomputerclub.com
My Tax Man, Inc.
My Wireless Rep
My.WS
Nanci Corporation
NATAL
National Companies, Inc.
National Safety Assoc. - NSA
Nationwide
Natural Air Products
Natural Body Lines Inc
Natural Choice Products
Natural Connections
Natural EFX
Natural World
Natural You
NaturaLab
Nature's Sunshine
Nature's Aromatherapy
Nature's Bodycare
Nature's Gold
Nature's of Scandinavia
Nature's Own
Nature's Sunshine Products
Nebullis Network
NEFX
Nest Family
Nettincome.net Limited
NetVision International Inc
Networker2000.com
NeuroGenesis, Inc
New Generations
New Image International
New Resolution
New Vision Int. Inc.
Neways International Inc.
Nexwork
Nexx
Nikken International, Inc.
Ninja Jump
Noevir USA, Inc.
North American Athletic Wear
Northern Lights at Home
Norwex
Nouveau Cosmeceuticals
Nova Chrome
NOVAGENIX
NRG
NTC
Nu Care International

Nu Creations
NU CREATIONS, INC
Nu Directions
Nubotanic Int.
Nu Botanical
Nu-Concepts in Travel
NuEworld
Nugenix
NuLife
Nu-med USA, Inc.
Nu-Med, Inc.
NuSkin International, Inc.
Nutrition For Life
NutraQuest
NutriCare
Nutri-Metics
Nutrimetics North America
Nutrition 4 Life
Nutrition for Life
Nutrition For Life International, Inc.
Nutritional Now Inc
NuVia3
Oasis Life Sciences
Oasis Wellness Network
Oceans
Omnitrition International
OneGroup.com
One Life
OneSource
Open Invitation From House of Lloyd
Optimal Telecom
Oragen International
Orbitalk
Orenda International
Organics Made Easy
OrGano Gold
Oriflame U.S.A.
Original Solutions Inc
Oro Club
Our Own Image
Outback Secrets
Oxyfresh Worldwide, Inc.
Oxygen4Energy
OZMOZIZ
P.M. International
Pampered Chef
Pangea
Panver Corporation
Paradigm
Paramount Technologies
Partners Across America
Partners for Wealth
PartyLite Gifts, Inc.

Passion Parties By Amy
Passport To Adventure
PattyCakes Int'l. Inc.
Performance Plus Nutritionals
Performance Source Inc.
Personal Touch Products
Personal Wealth Systems
Pet Lovers
PetShop.biz
Petra Fashions, Inc.
Pharmanex (NuSkin)
PHD Products
Pinnacle Plus
Pioneerbizz.com
Plexus
Pola U.S.A., Inc.
Polar
Popular Club, Inc.
Portfolio
PortOmega
Premier Designs, Inc.
Premier Health Link
Premier Plus Inc
Pre-Paid Legal Services, Inc.
PrimeQuest
Primerica
Primerica Financial Services
Princess House, Inc.
Private Quarters
Profit Masters
ProJoba International
Pro-Ma Systems
Promise Net Inc
Pro Monde Travel
PRONET INC
Prosperity Unlimited
ProStep
ProWealth Solutions
PS I Love You
Pur3x
Quality Health Products
Qual-Life
Qual-Life Systems
Quantum Leap
Qnanza
Quest For Life, Inc.
Quest Group International
Quest IV Health
QuestNet
Quixtar (Amway)
Quorum
Quorum International Ltd
R.J. Morgan
Rachael
RDAY, Inc.

Regal Ware, Inc.
Reinhardt Enterprises
Reliv International, Inc.
Rena Ware International, Inc.
Renaissance For Life
Renaissance USA
Repspace
Retire Quickly Corporation
Re-Vita
Revolution Road
Rexair, Inc.
Rexall
R-Garden
Richway
RightSize
Rodan and Fields
Rosemarie Collections
Royal BodyCare, Inc.
Saladmaster, Inc. (Regal Ware)
Salu International
Scentsy
Scent-Sations
SciMedica
Scriptures
Seaborne, LLC
Seasilver USA, Inc.
SeaAloe
Secure America
Secure Independence
SeneGence International
Shaklee Corporation
Shape Your Future
Shaperite
Share the Wealth
Shopper's Advantage
Sierra Judgment Recovery
Signature HomeStyles
Silpada Designs
Simplexity
Simply CD
Simtex
Skinny Body Care
SkyBiz.com
SKYCOM Telecom.
Slumber Parties
Soaring Eagle
Soteria Corporation
Southern Heritage, Inc.
Southern Living At HOME
Spectrum Unlimited Inc.
Sportnuts
Sportron International, Inc.
Spring Wellness, Inc.
Springboard
Staff of Life

Stampin' Up!
Stanley Home Products
Starfire International
Starlight
Startouch
Startronics
Sterling Health
Streamline
STS
Success America
Sunnet
Sunset Gourmet Food Co.
Staff Of Life
Sunrider International
SupraLife International
Swiss Colony Occasions
Symmetry Corporation
Syncom
Synergy Worldwide
Syntec Nutraceuticals
Syntek Global
Tahitian Noni
Take Shape for Life
Talisman Marketing Inc
TalkFusion
Tarrah Cosmetics, Inc.
Taste of Gourmet
Tastefully Simple, Inc.
TCN
Tea Connexions
Team Beach Body
Team-Up
Team USA
TEL3 NeTel
Texas D'Lites
That Free Thing
The Art of Better Living Inc
The Balance Company
The Body Shop At Home
The Breakfast Club
The Claudia Jean Collection
The Comforts of Home
The DHS Club
The Fairy Tale Princess
Storyteller
The Free Store Club
The Fuller Brush Company
The Gillette Company
The Golf Club
The Good Nature Company
The Hall Group Inc.
The Homemaker's Idea
The Kirby Company
The Limu Company
The Lonebuster

How to Select a Network Marketing Company

The Longaberger Company
The Masters Miracle
The Pampered Chef, Ltd.
The People's Network
The Regal Gourmet
The Right Solution
The Southwestern Company
The West Bend Company
The Winners Circle
Theta Technologies
Thirty-One
Tianshi
Tomorrow's Treasures
TopLine
Total Body Care
Total Life Changes (TLC)
Total Link
Total Wellness
Totally Tropical Interiors
Touchstone Crystal
TOYS/GAMES
TPN
TradeNet
Traffic Oasis
Transform America
TravelMax
Travelencia
TraVerus Travel
Trek Alliance, Inc.
TrendMark International
Trilogy International (Healthy Pet Net)
TriLokin International, Inc.
Trim International
Tristar Enterprises, LLC
Trivita
Tupperware Corporation
Turning Point
Tutor Trek
U Design Jewelry
U.S. Safety & Engineering Corporation
UCC Total Home

Ultra Corp
Unicity Network, Inc.
Unipay2U
Unique Opportunities Inc
Unique Solutions
United Buyer's Service
United Health Programs of America Inc
United Herbal Sciences
United Plan
United Sovereigns
Universal Consumer Services Inc
Upland
US Career Institute
US Health Advisors
USANA Health Sciences, Inc.
Usborne Books at Home
Vantel Pearls in the Oyster
VAXA
Vemma
Versativa
ViaViente
Vigorlife
Visalus
Vision For Life
Vita Craft Corporation
VitaCorp International
Vitalife2000
VitaMark
Vitamin Power Inc.
Vitality Labs
Viva America
Viva International
Viva Life Science, Inc.
Viviane Woodard
VM Direct
Vorwerk USA Company, LP
Votre Vu
Voyager
Wardson International
Warm Spirit, Inc.
WATCO

Waterwise Inc.
Watkins Incorporated
Wealth International Network
Wealth Masters Int'l
Weekenders USA, Inc.
Wela
Wellness
Wellness Associates
Wellness Premium Plus
WesState Mortgage Inc.
Wicker Plus, Ltd.
Wildtree Herbs
Wine Shop at Home
Woofgangs
World Book, Inc.
World Class Network
World Connect
World Financial Group
Worldnet International Inc
WorldQuest International Inc
Worldwide InterNet Marketing
WorldxChange
WowWe
XanGo
XB-Fit
Y2K
YOR
Young Living Essential Oils
Youngevity
Younique
Your True Colors
YourTravelBiz
Youthflow
Yves Rocher Direct Selling
Zenith
ZeoliteDepot.com
Zija
Zotango
Zowie
Zrii
Zurvita

Have I made my point? Now you might be able to understand the process my research team and I went through to scrutinize these programs. By the time you finish studying and applying the concepts outlined in this book, believe it or not, you'll be able to narrow this list down to a few top companies.

Chapter Three Review

1. Here are the *Six Keys* or criteria for selecting the best company.
    a. Profit Mindset
    b. Product Industry
    c. Timing
    d. Compensation
    e. Company Leadership
    f. Product Integrity

2. Most new distributors simply select a company at random. It's like throwing a dart to choose your destiny.

3. Randomly selecting a business opportunity is a great way to waste time, lose money, lose credibility, and become very discouraged.

4. To narrow down your list of company choices to a handful of top MLM programs, carefully study this book and apply its principles.

Chapter 4

Key #1
Profit Mindset: Think Like a Marketing Pro

Before we get ahead of ourselves by diving into the actual criteria for selecting a company, it's important to understand how your attitude and mindset play into your ability to select a winning opportunity. So important, in fact, that "Mind Set" has become the first of the *Six Keys*. The following chapter is an exercise to see if you can develop the mindset of a marketing professional. Without the proper mindset, your efforts towards selecting the right company will be wasted. You'll be looking for success in all the wrong places and all the wrong faces. We'll see if you're ready to proceed by the time you're finished reading this chapter.

To some, this chapter may seem out of place in this book. If you think this content does not belong here, you need it more than anyone. Like it or not, everyone must develop a certain attitude and mindset to be able to process the kind of information contained in later chapters. Selecting a business vehicle without the proper mindset is like going to a car lot to purchase an automobile without knowing what your budget is, how many people you're usually transporting, and how much cargo space you'll need. You're unprepared to make a very important choice. This chapter is designed to help you gain the knowledge and tools necessary to recognize that perfect vehicle when you see it.

The Money-Making Mindset

Why are you in business? Have you ever asked yourself that question? Have you really thought long and hard about the answer? For many, this is the one concept keeping them from success in network marketing. Pay close attention to the following.

So many of the clients that come to me looking for a company bring so much emotional baggage and prejudice with them, not to mention so many unsubstantiated opinions, that I spend a significant amount of time just trying to get them to the starting line in their minds. Sometimes I wish I could just scrub their hard drives, and then start again with a fresh, reformatted disk. If you can allow this book to act as a program to repair and even replace some of the bad programming that is in your mind now, it will serve you well in truly developing a strategy that will produce long-term prosperity in any home business.

The wrong reasons for starting a business

As the famous millionaire-maker T. Harv Eker states in his best-selling book, *Secrets of the Millionaire Mind*, "Give me five minutes, and I can predict your financial future for the rest of your life!" I do the same thing as it relates to a person's potential for selecting a winning network marketing company, but it only takes one question. All I have to ask is, "Why are you in business?" Most of the time I get answers like, "I want to make the world a better place," or "My widget is so powerful that I'm on a mission to share it with the universe," or "I already had ten years of experience in my field so I decided to become self-employed instead of work for my boss." I've also heard things like, "I was introduced to this distributorship by my Uncle Rico, and I was really impressed with what his sponsor Lafonda had to say at the opportunity meeting." Or I might get, "I was on the product for just two weeks and I noticed a huge reduction in the pain and inflammation in my coccyx (tailbone)." I hear things like, "Well I'm a physical trainer (or registered nurse, or chiropractic assistant, or massage therapist, or kinesiologist, or health store clerk) and I have a lot of interest in nutritional products." None of these are intelligent reasons for starting your own business. Most of the people who answer this way are dead broke and their profits are flat, or they soon will be.

The magic question

"So why are you in business?" It's an important question that demands an intelligent answer. Otherwise, you'll be sacrificing success and profits that you won't even know you're missing. Only on one occasion in my life did I ask that question and the person responded immediately, "Daren, why else would I be in business? To make a profit, of course! I want to acquire as many customers as I can in the shortest period of time possible and keep these customers for life. I want residual profits for myself, my kids, and maybe even my children's great grandchildren!" When I heard this statement, I fell to the earth and began kissing this individual's feet ... at which point I awoke from sleep when my wife nudged me saying, "Why are you kissing my feet"? Alas, it was too good to be true.

Maximum profits!

You and I have a mission. We must teach everyone we meet that there's only one reason for starting and maintaining a successful business and that is to make a profit through the acquisition and retention of customers. If you're not solving people's problems, and if you're not filling a need or satisfying a want or desire, you're not in business. And if you're not giving huge value to others and turning a huge profit in the process, you're not helping people in substantial ways. You might have the noblest of intentions, but if your business can't survive and eventually thrive in time, you're just delaying disaster. You've become part of the problem instead of part of the solution. If you have trouble with this principle, put down this book and seek professional counseling. This book was not written to help you overcome your fear of making a profit. It was written to teach intelligent people how to make maximum profits in network marketing in honest and ethical ways. If you have issues with money, you need to go see T. Harv Eker and get over it. Then come back to this book.

Understand that I'm not trying to offend anyone with an overemphasis on profits. I just want everyone to understand that it's how you make your money and what you do with it that defines your character. The amount of money you make only amplifies your character, intentions, and influence. Bestselling authors Robert Allen (*Multiple Streams of Income*) and Mark Victor Hansen (*Chicken Soup for the Soul*) call this "the enlightened way to wealth." Mark and Bob wrote a book together entitled *One Minute Millionaire,* where they describe in detail the concept of the Enlightened Millionaire. Yes, you can make money while blessing people's lives in incredible ways. As a matter of fact, most of the Enlightened Millionaire master trainers that I know have made more money than they could spend in several lifetimes, and they're still teaching, because that is the way they can touch the largest number of lives. Try helping a lot of people when your business is failing, your cash flow isn't flowing, and your creditors are howling. I know, I've tried it! I couldn't even help myself, let alone anyone else.

> *"The best way to help the poor is not to become one of them."*
> -J. Paul Getty

A successful business is your birthright

Broke people depend on others for assistance. Impoverished people add to the problem or create new problems. Many broke people have the best of intentions, but nothing to show for their time pursuing a career or a business. Don't be afraid of turning a profit. It's your birthright, and your responsibility as an entrepreneur to create abundance. Mark Victor Hansen turned me on to a religious text written around 600 BC in India called the Upanishads. Mark often refers to this quote from the book, "Out of abundance He took abundance and still abundance remained."[2] Have I made my point yet? I'm going to spend just a little more time on this topic to make sure we're crystal clear on these ideas.

An Experiment in Community Involvement

I'd like to share with you an experience I had last year that will illustrate the next critical principle. Over the last few years, I've been trying something new. It's a special new program I like to call *leaving the house*. Yes, when you start to enjoy the advantages of staying home and operating a lucrative home business, you can really get used to it. Imagine getting up on Monday morning with no alarm clock, no staff meetings, and no boss hanging over your shoulder. Instead of rushing out the door so you're not late, you put on your robe and slippers, admire your "bed hair" in the mirror, and enjoy a leisurely breakfast with your family. Showering and getting dressed are discouraged, and turning on the car to defrost the window (or cool it down, as the case may be) is out of the question.

Sorry, I digressed a little. Back to leaving the house. Instead of my typical morning of barefoot, bed-head entrepreneurship, I decided to make a commitment to broadening my horizons. I started getting out at least twice per month to work in my own community and meet my fellow town folk, even if it meant showering, throwing on a sports coat, doing something with my hair, and ultimately leaving the comforts of my home office for the morning. Trust me when I say, twice per month is really pushing it for me. But through this process, I've discovered what most people still believe about home-based business.

Broke-A-Holics Anonymous

One of my adventures involved attending a monthly home-based business club, which consisted of a few dozen network marketers from my town sprinkled with a few self-employed folks who were supposedly looking for more business. To me, the group seemed more like a support club for unsuccessful home-based business owners. I envision this kind of greeting at our meetings.

Daren: "Hi, my name is Daren, and I'm a home business owner."
Everyone: "Hi, Daren."
Daren: "Let's see, I've been losing money in home business for three years now, but I'm really making progress with my new twelve-step plan. I'm hopeful that with the support of this group, I'll be breaking even sometime during the next thirty-six months."
Everyone: (Thunderous applause, many holding back tears.)

Okay, so it wasn't that bad. But the sad part was that I saw at least a dozen people in this group who had the intelligence and ambition to literally earn a minimum of six figures per year, if not much more, in their own home-based business, and they were all settling for peanuts. A few of them could be millionaires. But they simply lacked direction, and they didn't know how to select the right home-based business. They also didn't know any of the best strategies to build their businesses large and fast. Most of the activities planned by this group were focused on supporting each other's promotions and events. It's kind of like, "I'll come to your home party this week and bring a friend if you come to my opportunity meeting next week and bring your mother."

Exiting the pity party

Already having years of experience in selecting and building successful home-based businesses and network marketing distributorships, I found myself feeling sorry for most of these struggling business owners. It seemed so obvious what the problem was, but they weren't seeing it. Some of them were even a bit resentful about the fact that I was doing so well, yet no one asked my advice about anything. I felt like standing on my chair and shouting, "People, wake up! Your lives are passing you by! When are you going to learn the principles of wealth and prosperity? When are you going to see past the end of this month? When are you going to stop working so hard for your money and stop stressing about your finances? When are you going to realize your business is not about you and your product? It's about your customers and their wants and needs! When are you going to begin incorporating some kind of leverage into your businesses so you don't have to be slaves to your businesses for the rest of your lives?"

Of course I bit my tongue and resisted the impulse, because I didn't want to break up the pity party. They seemed to at least be enjoying each other's company. I guess that's what many support groups are all about, helping you feel better about the perpetual miserable state you're in. But trust me when I say this: you may not need a support group ever again for any aspect of your life once you establish your first successful home-based business. There's so much more to this lifestyle than just making money, and if you embark on this adventure with me, you will soon understand what I'm saying.

After a few weeks of being pitched on many great products built around mediocre business models, I just stopped attending the home business support group. I realized that I was not looking to interact with other typical home-based business owners (too depressing). Most of them didn't have any ambition to be financially free. They were just like employees, working and living month-to-month, just to make ends meet. Most of them did not see their home business as a BIG business. They didn't see it as an opportunity to accumulate wealth. They didn't see their business as a means to financial independence. Most of them were pursuing a home business because of some circumstance that prevented them from holding a regular job or because they had some technical expertise that led them to self-employment by default. One of the things you'll learn in this book is the difference between self-employment and business ownership, and knowing the difference makes all the difference.

*"Most people would rather spend the rest of their lives
trying to justify their decisions for business failure rather
than swallow their pride and ask for help and advice
from a successful home-based business owner."*

Would You Rather be Right or Rich?

So are these lost souls worth saving? They all could turn their businesses around if they were willing to let go of their own ideas (the ideas that brought them to this miserable point) and seek the advice of industry experts who have already blazed a successful trail. But it has to happen before they're too far gone. I've discovered that once people are emotionally indoctrinated with erroneous marketing principles or bad business ideas, it's very hard to turn them around. Approach them early or lose them forever. Once they've made up their minds, most people would rather be right than rich. In other words, most people would rather spend the rest of their lives trying to justify their decisions for business failure rather than swallow their pride and ask for help and advice from a successful home-based business owner and earn profits in the process.

Again, writer Josh Billings comes to mind in this situation when he stated, "Most people when they come to you for advice, come to have their own opinions strengthened, not corrected."[3]

Here's My Advice, If It's Worth Anything to You

My job as company selection coach and consultant is not to help you take a network marketing deal you've already started and make it successful. That's also another book, and another course. My job is to give you the criteria for selecting a winning company. If you've already picked a loser and you're unwilling to change companies, I can't help you. If you're in the process of selecting a new company, you're reading the right book. If you're in a winning company, this book should only be a confirmation to you that you made the right choice. Most people come to me trying to rationalize why they selected the company they did. They're not coming to me for my advice or counsel; they're coming to me for my approval of their decision so they can feel better about their choice. When I don't give my blessing, they usually go away incensed.

Seek advice *before*, not after

Others approach me for my advice after they've already selected their company. Even knowing that my services exist, they don't consult me before joining the program because they're too afraid of what I might say about their new deal. Isn't that scary? To be so emotionally attached to a product or business opportunity that you don't even want to know the truth? *Their* truth is more important than *the* truth. They'd rather keep the perfect image of their new company in their minds than have anyone try to poke holes in it. If that's your strategy, and you're not willing to change, this book will not help you. I've found that the best way to convince someone that they're in error is to allow them to have their way. Experience is a powerful, and often painful, teacher. It was for me.

Starting with a clear mind

From my experience in coaching others, choosing a company for emotional reasons will lead to disaster. It's like trying to force a square peg into a round hole. You must clear your mind of all ideas, ventures, or schemes. My job is to help you realize that existing companies, products, and programs you may know nothing about may be very lucrative alternatives to the struggle you're experiencing now. My job is to get you to identify viable markets on your own, and then you can find a premium product to match that market. Then you can find a highly experienced, high integrity company that supplies such a product. Many people try to take a product they like and force it into the marketplace against its will. Instead, start paying attention to the mass marketplace while at the same time identifying powerful market niches. If you pay attention to the principles taught in this book, you'll be on your way to selecting a winning business model every time.

Becoming Aware of Your Marketplace

One of the greatest secrets to becoming a master marketer is to learn how to pay attention to the marketplace. To do this, we need to become aware of our surroundings and pay attention to the subtle clues that others are overlooking. I have a friend who attends my local church who is a Green Beret. He offered to teach my family and a few others in our church a course on home and personal defense. One of the strategies we learned for identifying a threatening individual was not to look at his face or listen to his speech, but to focus on the person's hands. Most perpetrators are con artists. Our coach explained that if a threatening individual wants to lull you into a sense of security, he might make non-threatening gestures with his face, eyes, and voice while reaching for a weapon. Our instructor gave the class the assignment of watching people's hands while out in public. At first I had a hard time remembering to do it, but with a little practice I'm now much more aware of what people are doing with their hands while I'm on an elevator, in a parking garage, or walking in the park. I can detect a dangerous situation seconds before others around me, even when the face of a potential perpetrator may be giving a completely different message. These seconds count when it comes to personal safety, and they also count in the marketplace. Knowing what to look for and what to ignore in the marketplace can make all the difference in identifying rising markets.

Here's another example of awareness that everyone can relate to. Have you ever bought a new car, and before you purchased that car you never really noticed others like it, but afterwards you started seeing them everywhere? It's like this for everyone. It's not that cars identical to yours weren't there before; they were. You just didn't notice them because you were unaware. Learning to be aware of the marketplace around you and learning how to pick up on the wants and needs of people is a skill that you must practice. This new awareness will lead you to make the correct choices in selecting the most lucrative home-based business ideas and products. Start paying attention to all of the messages people are sending out to the marketplace and you'll begin to understand how master marketers think and act.

For starters, you can pay close attention to news, current events, and even commercial advertisements and promotions. Next, you can subscribe to some of the most informative business journals and periodicals such as the Wall Street Journal, Success Magazine, Entrepreneur Magazine, Newsweek, The Economist, USA Today, and other national publications. I also love some of the more progressive information magazines such as Fast Company, Wired, Business 2.0, and Selling Power. I also like to check out Oprah Magazine to see what's happening in her world.

Next, you can read or browse all for the trade journals related to home business and network marketing such as: The Network Marketing Business Journal, Network Marketing Insider, Small Business Opportunities (and related magazines), Upline Magazine, Network

51

Marketing Magazine, Home Business Magazine, Home Business Connection, Home Business Advertiser, and any others related to this field. Don't get me wrong, I don't actually read all of these cover to cover every month, but I do browse many of them on a regular basis. It's also a great idea to search for anything you might have an interest in on www.google.com. Subscribe to the RSS feeds in blogs you find informative. Search by topic or author. Find out about everything and anything. Ask questions and seek answers. Pay attention to the messages and conversations around you and you'll start developing a type of sixth sense. This intuition will start pointing you to opportunities that you didn't see before.

Be sure to attend any seminar, webinar, teleclass, or online chat that will give you information on your industry, on the marketplace, or on marketing on or off the Web. Not only have I gained a substantial amount of information and insights by becoming a seminar junkie, but I've created and cultivated some of my most profitable relationships here.

Finally, you must read, read, read. I try to pound through a book a week. Sometimes I get through two in a week, and sometimes I don't read a single page. But I strive to read for at least 20-60 minutes or more daily. Most of my reading is through audio books (check out www.audible.com). Turn your car into a rolling University as you listen to and re-listen to the most powerful books in the world. If you would like a list of my recommendations, visit me at www.networkmarketingbook.com.

Pour information onto your brain without ceasing. Even if you find that your brain cannot hold any more, trust me when I say, you're getting something, especially when you repeat the same or similar information. If you're going to be gluttonous about anything in your life, make it about feeding your mind. Ideas and inspiration will flow only from a full vessel.

Seeking Mentorship

Don't forget to ask for help. You'll waste a lot of time, energy, and money if you don't. Let's say you're an amateur stock market investor, and you want to make the right choices with your money. Wouldn't you want to hire an investment coach who could teach you how to earn the best returns on your investments? What if the advice your coach gave you was so good that you immediately started earning dividends, interest, or equity on all of your investments? Would this coach be worth keeping? Would you want to listen to an investment coach who did not invest in the same stocks that he or she was advising you to invest in?

What if you had the opportunity to be coached by Warren Buffet, considered by many to be the world's greatest investor? Would you take his advice? Would you trust his counsel? Now, wouldn't it be nice if you could hire a consultant to help you select the best home-based business model? Would you feel more confident if you could have all of your decisions reviewed by someone with over a decade of experience? Well, Warren Buffet does not have the time to consult the masses on how to invest wisely, and most home-based business consultants, like me, also have limited time to counsel aspiring home-based business owners on how to pick a winning opportunity. So I've taken very special care to make sure that I cover everything you will need to know in order to do your own opportunity evaluations and choose your next home business with confidence. You won't need Warren Buffet after all.

Chapter Four Review

1. There's only one reason for starting and maintaining a successful business and that is to make a profit by acquiring and retaining customers. If you're not making a profit, you're not helping anyone. It's your birthright and your responsibility as an entrepreneur to create abundance in your life and in the lives of others.

2. Most home-based business owners are not business people and they don't have any ambition to be financially free. They're simply self-employed worker bees who have created a job for themselves, and they can't afford to quit that job. They generally have little or no control over their time or money, and they will eventually give up and go back to working for someone else.

3. Would you rather be right or rich? Swallow your pride and seek assistance and solutions. Constantly act on advice from people qualified to give it.

4. If you want a lucrative home-based business and it's not network marketing, be prepared to work much harder for less money. Nothing is better for leveraging your time, energy, and money than a home-based network marketing business.

5. Most people come to me trying to rationalize why they selected the company they did. They're not coming to me for my advice or counsel; they're coming to me for my approval. When I don't give it, they usually go away incensed. Others approach me for my advice after they've selected their company, not before. To them, *their* truth is more important than *the* truth. Don't fall into this trap. Get advice from those who know the truth, don't make up your own truth to justify hasty decisions.

6. To make the right company choice, first clear your mind of all existing ideas, ventures, or schemes. Companies you may know nothing about now can be very lucrative alternatives to the struggle you're currently experiencing.

7. One of the greatest secrets to becoming a master marketer is to learn how to pay attention to the marketplace. Start paying attention to all of the messages people are sending out to the marketplace through media, Internet, and word-of-mouth, and you'll begin to understand how master marketers think and act.

8. Don't forget to ask for help. There are thousands of mentors out there who are willing, and even eager, to share their knowledge, wisdom, and experience with the right student. When you persist in asking for help, even if you get a few refusals, you'll eventually find someone willing to advise you. A great mentor will save you years of frustration and tens of thousands of dollars.

PART III
Narrowing the Field

Do you want to take your list of hundreds of choices and eliminate 50 percent of them in twenty minutes? Pay special attention to the next enormous chapter as I detail the process I went through to scrutinize and remove more than half of the competition. This is the beginning of the actual research and study portion of the book. In this section you'll identify the most profitable products and services and learn which ones are worthy of your time and attention. You'll also learn about the dangerous products and services and learn how to avoid them. This section may be the most important section in the book. Take your time with this process. Commit to reading it multiple times.

Chapter 5

Key #2
Product Industry:
What to Sell, and Why

Part One: First, What Not to Sell

A Daunting Task

Imagine looking at a list of thousands of companies and trying to figure out how to narrow the list down to just one excellent program. This thought is enough to discourage anyone, even someone like myself who actually went through this process. I decided that if I could get the initial list down to several hundred companies instead of several thousand, this study would be doable. Here's how I got started.

Who's out of business?

Before I even started to seriously evaluate any single company, I decided to check to see if it was actually still in business. You see, in the time it took me to gather the list of companies printed in Chapter Three, many of these companies had already gone out of business. Why? Because there are no requirements or prerequisites for starting a network marketing company. Oh, I take that back. There is one qualification; you have to be able to fog a mirror. Now do you understand why so many companies don't make it? It's not due to the instability of direct sales. It has more to do with the incompetence or the lack of commitment of these wannabe entrepreneurs.

One of my general rules (which I will elaborate on in later chapters) is that I like to wait at least a couple of years before doing a serious evaluation of a new company. Why waste time on companies that will probably not make it? My first step in narrowing the list was to not consider any company that was no longer viable or was looking like it would soon be defunct. I gathered this information by visiting websites like www.mlm.com, www.npros.com, www.marketwave.net, and www.mlmwatchdog.com, and looked for information on www.google.com. At the time we also used www.aol.com, www.compuserve.com, and www.prodigy.com. Now, of course, I would use www.facebook.com. Back in the day, I also subscribed to trade publications such as Money Maker's Monthly (now Network Marketing Business Journal), Inside Network Marketing Newsletter (no longer in circulation), Network Marketing Today newsletter (no longer in circulation), and other trade journals. Today I use a dozen trade publications that are still circulating such as: Home Business Magazine, Small Business Start-Ups, Cutting Edge Media's Home Business Connection, Opportunity World/Money 'N Profits, Franchise Handbook.

Remember any of these gems?

- AL Williams
- AOL Select
- Consumer's Buyline
- Destiny Telecom
- Dynamic Essentials
- Excel Telecom
- International Heritage
- Jewelway
- Network 2000
- Nutrition For Life
- Quorum
- Seasilver
- Skybiz
- The Tax People

These are just a few of the most famous defunct network marketing companies that tanked many years ago. For every well-known company that goes under, there are hundreds more that slip silently into oblivion without much notice. So why do I even mention the losers? As Brian Tracy, one of my favorite sales mentors says, "Success leaves clues." If that is true, which I know it is, then failure must also leave clues behind, warning those who come after to beware. As I have studied both what causes companies to thrive and what causes them to die, I'm enlightened and empowered to make the right choices and advise others to do the same. Never underestimate the power of failure as a tool for success.

Bad news

They say bad news travels fast. This is even truer in the word-of-mouth world of network marketing, especially now that we have access to the Internet. Accurate and up-to-date information on any subject or topic is readily available to us with the click of a mouse. By cross-referencing just a handful of Websites, blogs, and discussion boards on a regular basis, you can now keep your finger on the pulse of the network marketing industry and know much of what is going on behind the scenes. I further narrowed my list of choices by keeping my ear to the ground and keeping totally up to date on industry news and events. I used sources already sited, plus I maintained contact with the best and brightest network marketing consultants and their work. By being in the know, I can avoid wasting time evaluating companies that will soon see their end.

What's in a name?

This may be difficult to believe, but one of my all time most reliable criteria for eliminating bad companies from my consideration is to simply review the company's choice in corporate names. With nearly 100 percent accuracy, I've been able to predict the demise of hundreds of companies. Some may call it a gift; I simply call it common sense. Take, for instance, the following examples of names that could literally drive a company right out of business. These are just a few of many examples of names that have been used in network marketing.

The first way to commit corporate name suicide is to try to use pieces of the most overused and over-copied names in the business. These names are usually borrowed from some of the more legendary companies. The fact that they were used the first time is not the issue. It's the constant attempt to reapply them that creates the problem. Here are some words to avoid when naming your network marketing company.

(Anything) Way
- Life (Anything)
- Natural (Anything)
- Nu or New (Anything)
- Wealth (Anything) or (Anything) Wealth

To keep the network marketing industry safe from scams and schemes, governmental regulators are always searching for programs that appear to be illegal. Even if a company is totally legitimate, it must have a name that does not draw unnecessary scrutiny from regulators.

Here are some companies that send the wrong message with their company name.

- EasyWay
- Everyday Wealth
- Share the Wealth
- Cruise to Cash Vacations
- Health 4 Wealth

These companies do not focus on traditional products openly accepted by the marketplace; they focus on the concept of making money. When you lead with money-making, you may as well be vigorously waving your red flag in front of the government, taunting them to take aggressive action against you.

Now I don't mean to insult anyone's intelligence, but you might agree with me that these next few names are lacking a certain something. I'll let you draw your own conclusions to these company names.

- 1to1everyone
- Awesome Specialties
- Y2K

Here are a few more names that might raise an eyebrow or two. Now that we're getting better at this game, why don't you tell me what is wrong with these names? I call these the scary names.

- United Sovereigns
- Iron Curtain Labs

Actually, that last one is totally legitimate. In all fairness, Iron Curtain Labs markets body building products. I don't want any of their spokes models coming to my house to crush my spine so I'll let them off the hook. However, at first glance, your thoughts might turn to the Cold War rather than protein powders and energy pills. Remember, first impressions count.

The following three names receive the Bad Acronym Award for obvious reasons. Give these a quick read through and you might get a chuckle.

- Pro Ma Systems
- Staff of Life
- State of Being

Now I'm not saying that giving your company a weak name will put the company out of business. I'm also not saying it won't. But I do stand firm to the belief that if these companies do survive the test of time, they're limiting their potential with names such as these. Branding starts with selecting the right name for your company and products. If you don't have the gift, hire someone who does.

A little nudge

If you're ever involved in the company naming process, here are a few of my best tips for building an excellent brand:

1. Select a name that is easy to say.
2. Select a name that is easy to spell.
3. Select a name that is a made-up word so you're not competing in the search engines. In other words, names like USANA or OxyFresh are better names for the search engines than Nature's Sunshine or Longevity. A search for "oxyfresh" will reveal only sites related to that company. A search for "longevity" will turn up other sites related to the word "longevity". This is not a deal breaker by any stretch of the imagination. However, if you have input, this point is worth considering?
4. Select a name where the domain name is available or you can acquire it. Does someone else own your domain name? Make sure it's a DOT COM and make sure you can acquire it for a reasonable price.

5.   Select a name that is not trademarked by another entity under your given product category. You don't want to represent a company that starts off their existence fighting in a courtroom only to lose their corporate name to a predecessor.
6.   Find a name that has significance and meaning.
7.   Find a name that matches the company's brand, mission, and product category.
8.   Select a name that does not have an offensive meaning when translated into another major world language.

These are the principles I consider when helping with the corporate name game. Be sure to keep this list handy just in case you ever get the opportunity to assist a company in coming up with a winning corporate name.

Industry Breakdown

In my analysis of over four hundred programs over the last thirteen years, I was able to determine which product industries within network marketing are the most viable now and which industries will be the most viable during the next twenty years. First, I will list the industries I studied in alphabetical order. Then, I will run through the criteria used to select the most viable product industry and eliminate the duds.

Fifty Current MLM Industries (alphabetical order):

- Automobiles and Auto-Care Products
- Arts, Crafts, Decorations, Framing
- Baby Products
- Benefits Packages and Insurance
- Books, Publications, Educational Products, and Encyclopedias
- Buying Clubs and Catalog Shopping
- Candles and Accessories
- Collectibles and Gifts
- Cosmetics
- Clothing, Fashions, Shoes, and Lingerie
- Computer Hardware and Software
- Electronics, Audio/Visual
- Financial and Debt-Elimination Programs
- Fitness Equipment
- Gardening, Flowers, and Plants

- Gift Baskets and Other Gift Items
- Gourmet Foods and Specialty Beverages
- Grocery and Coupon Programs
- Home Furnishings/Interior Decoration
- Home and Personal Security Products
- Home Appliances
- Home Improvement Products
- Household Products (consumables)
- Information Services
- Internet Services (tech support, marketing)
- Jewelry, Gold, and Silver
- Kitchen and Cookware, Cutlery
- Lead Generation Programs
- Legal Services
- Movies and Music
- Nutritional Supplements (health products and weight loss)
- Oral Hygiene
- Paper Products
- Party Supplies
- Personal Care Products (skin, hair and body)
- Pet and Animal Care
- Photography, Video, and Other Media
- Pottery and Ceramics
- Real Estate Services and Loans
- Religious Books and Accessories
- Satellites (hardware and service)
- Scrapbooking
- Sporting Goods
- Telecommunications Services
- Toys and Games
- Travel and Vacation Programs
- Utilities (electric, gas and water)
- Vacuum Cleaners
- Water and Air Filters
- Website Design and Hosting, Automation

Wow, there isn't much the direct sales industry doesn't carry! It's time to start eliminating some of these product categories so you can select the best industry.

Products vs. Services

The following is a comparison between services, or intangible product companies, and tangible product companies. Let's start with some definitions. *Tangible products* are products you can see, touch, taste, or essentially hold in your hand (nutritional supplements, skin care products, or pet rocks). *Intangible products* are products you can't see (insurance, long distance service, savings bonds, or legal services). There is an ongoing debate about whether or not it is wise to market intangible products through direct sales/network marketing. It can be easier to distinguish intangible businesses by offering exceptional service. With intangibles, you can quickly establish an excellent brand in your local market. Services can be a great business model to start if you understand your income will be capped on each distributorship based on the number of clients one distributor can service in a given day, week, month, or year. When you reach the maximum number of clients a single distributorship can service, you simply must find another distributorship to produce more sales volume. A handful of great service-based network marketing companies have stood the test of time. Some have even developed models whereby the distributor can keep adding unlimited numbers of clients and the service is automatically provided by the company.

However, in network marketing, few services have survived, and those who have are rare exceptions to the rule. Simply compare the number of product-based companies to service-based companies that are still in business today, and you will discover for yourself the overwhelming demand for tangible products and the limited demand for services and intangibles. Building a business exclusively with telecommunications services, financial services, travel services, legal services, consulting services, cleaning services, or any other service is like walking up a down escalator. It is possible, but much more difficult. Why are intangible product companies or services so difficult to operate? It has to do with profit margins, streamlining, and duplication. Let's explore both tangibles and intangibles to see the pros and cons.

With intangibles, information is passed person-to-person from the service provider to the client through face-to-face contact. You can't drop ship knowledge, experience, or wisdom to your customers. You can't drop ship a service either. It generally has to be performed by someone. The person with the information or the skill, the technician or officer, has to deliver intangibles.

For example, if you are a financial agent selling mutual funds through network marketing, you can only market that intangible product through person-to-person contact. The same goes with selling telecommunications. Marketing long distance service requires some degree of technical expertise, and you usually have to be in front of your customer to sell it. When this kind of face-to-face meeting is required to market a service, your customer base is greatly limited.

Products, on the other hand, have universal marketability. You don't need a degree, expertise, or any kind of special training or certification to drop ship a product directly from the manufacturer to the customer. Customers with very little product information and no training can actually call the company themselves and order products, or information about the products, directly over the phone. One distributorship has the potential to produce unlimited amounts of sales volume by retailing that company's product all over the world. Services limit the sales volume per distributor to the number of clients they can service in the time they've allotted to run their business every month.

Duplicating the distributorship

In analyzing the distributorship side of the coin, there is a fair amount of training associated with just learning how to market an intangible product or service. The training required to become an effective distributor consumes time and energy and can greatly disrupt the process of duplicating your business with your downline distributors. For example, let's say Bob is a new agent in a financial office marketing financial services. In order to become a distributor of financial services (life insurance, investments, etc.), Bob must go through training and certification. This takes Bob's time, energy, and, in many cases, money. These requirements discourage Bob from seeking distributors because many of his prospects are not capable or willing to duplicate his activities.

Here's another important factor. Due to the fact that tangibles can be seen and felt, these products always do better in the network marketing arena. People are more impulsive about purchasing something they can see or touch. Tangibles generally have better profit margins because of their exclusivity to one company. Service companies generally have similarities to other services and price becomes more of a factor. Most importantly, tangible products are more suited for duplication. No special technical knowledge is required to hand a bottle of nutritional supplements to someone and say, "Try this." No special skills are required to drop ship a set of scented candles to your customer. Over $1,000 worth of cosmetics can be drop shipped anywhere in the world in a small box. In direct sales, most products are high-end, and they're usually described as being so appealing that they sell themselves.

Final thoughts about intangibles

Profitability in services will change in the future, but it hasn't yet. Most services are characterized by quick growth for two to three years before they go out of business or experience a major dip in sales. Your first step in choosing the most profitable network marketing program is to eliminate services from your list of considerations ... for now.

So what are services good for in direct sales? In some cases, services can create an opportunity for instant commissions. For instance, some intangibles, like pre-paid legal services, offer agents the opportunity to earn an entire year of commissions in advance. An agent might collect only $20 to $30 in revenue and be paid hundreds of dollars in commission per sale based on the fact that the agent is being paid on not one month's commission, but on commission for what that account will collect over an entire year. Unfortunately, pre-paid commission plans, like most direct sales programs, do not offer any substantial residual or passive income opportunity for months or even years in the future. Furthermore, any pre-paid commissions are subject to charge-backs. You could end up paying back most of your earned commissions if your customer cancels their service before the end of the minimum term.

If you're a great salesperson and would rather earn 100 percent of the commission based on your own efforts, then a service-based direct marketing program or a direct sales tangible program may be for you. But then again, if you're interested in making big commissions instantly, you can always get hired on at the local car lot or start a career in real estate.

True network marketing implies building a marketing force of other distributors along with a strong retail business. As your sales team grows, you will ultimately earn royalties on many generations of referrals, creating true long-term residual income. Residual incomes are best achieved with tangible products.

I don't want to frustrate anyone who is associated with a service-based network marketing company. If you chose a service because it is the love of your life and you would rather do nothing but offer that service to clients, then enjoy your career to the fullest and don't let anyone tell you to take another path. But remember, this conflicts with the purpose of starting a business. If you chose a service program because you thought it was the most profitable choice, I challenge you to study this book and think about these concepts. Remember, the first step in creating a duplicable and profitable system is to find products that appeal to the masses ... not in niche marketing or selling to specific market segments. The second step is to create a system (for marketing products) that is easy to duplicate. Ask yourself, "Does everyone have a need for the product?" and "Can everyone do the distributorship without any special certifications?" If you answered yes to both questions, you're on the right track.

Examining Direct Sales/Home Party Plan Companies

Let me start by saying, I love party plan companies, which are any network marketing or direct sales companies that promote their products and services almost exclusively through home parties and home demonstrations.

I've learned some extremely valuable lessons from the home party plan industry. Here are some of my findings:

1. More than 99 percent of the home party plan industry is made up of women.
2. Retail is the lifeblood of any direct marketing company; party planners know this better than anyone.
3. There's no better place to create a buying environment than in the living room of one of your friend's homes.
4. Recognition can be a more powerful performance incentive than money.
5. Many people join direct sales for reasons other than making money. They can enjoy the relationships and camaraderie, they might thrive on the challenge, they may crave the recognition they receive as they advance, and they might have a passion for the products.
6. Party plan marketing is a retail sales and distributor duplication machine.
7. Party plan companies generally weight their compensation plans toward the front end so participants can earn commissions sooner. The reward is directly tied to the party itself (more on this in Chapter Eight).
8. Home party plans incorporate fun, education, and social interaction into the sales and marketing process.
9. Experienced party plan distributors can produce incredible personal sales volumes that would put most network marketers to shame.

As thrilled as I am about the virtues of the party plan model, I did not write this book to promote this particular business model. I don't want to pick on home party plan companies. I'm just letting the reader know that this book was intended to outline the criteria and strategies for selecting a standard network marketing model. Party plan companies, although they are mostly all multilevel marketing programs, are a completely different animal. Maybe another book is in order – *How to Select a Party Plan Company*. I encourage your feedback.

Network Marketing vs. Home Party Plans

In general, network marketing companies that do not use the home party plan model tend to weight their compensation plans toward the middle or the back end of the pay structure. Although we'll explain this in more detail in Chapter Eight, understand that these plans are more suited for the six-figure incomes that professional network marketers and even serious part-timers are attempting to generate. Most career-oriented network marketers won't even consider a compensation plan that does not have seven-figure annual income potential for distributors at the very top of the compensation plan. Many party plan companies, on the other hand, emphasize commission payout on the first several levels, allowing a greater number of people to earn smaller checks. Incentives are tied to the actual party itself, and there's not as much emphasis on building a downline of hundreds or even thousands of distributors.

Since my research, consulting, and writing are geared towards teaching people how to make network marketing their career, I tend to steer most of my clients away from the extremely part-time, lower paying compensation plans and into a more career-centered model. Some of the people I interviewed for this book who were making full-time income in a party plan company made the transition to a more network marketing oriented plan and are now earning many times their previous monthly checks. Although the home party plan is a viable home business option, I don't recommend it to my network marketing clients unless it's one of the rare exceptions that behave more like a traditional network marketing plan. As I mentioned, the standard party plan company gives tremendous advantage to the part-timer who wants to stay exclusive to the home party model, while creating tremendous disadvantage for the more career-oriented network marketer.

If you're already involved with a home party plan company, don't transition out of this company unless you're totally dissatisfied with your results. Simply start incorporating the leadership and duplication strategies utilized by successful network marketing companies, and watch your organization explode. If you're running into challenges with your company that resemble the problems I've described, do some research on the more standard network marketing model to see if it's a better fit for you.

MLM Support Companies

Network marketing support companies are companies that offer products and services (mostly services) that are designed to support other network marketing companies. The most common support companies are lead generation companies, which are designed to produce qualified network marketing leads for distributors who want to build their primary network marketing company. In addition to leads companies, there are also companies that offer replicating websites, web based-contact management, social media marketing systems, and auto-responder services designed to help you promote your primary network marketing company on the Internet. We're also starting to see a lot of web marketing services popping up, like search engine placement services, social media marketing systems, and internet advertising systems. I've only named a few, but you get the picture. Any company providing services designed to help you promote your primary company is considered an MLM support company.

There are many concerns associated with MLM support companies:

1. Most MLM support companies never survive. They take your money to perform a service, and the service is never performed before the company goes out of business. These companies generally are not trying to scam distributors; they're just operating a very poor, undercapitalized business model that doesn't stand a very good chance of survival.
2. The compensation plan conflicts with your primary company. If these companies didn't have a multilevel compensation plan attached to them, they would not be rejected by other network marketing companies like they are. Actually, I use all of these services in my business, as long as they deliver on their promise and don't offer a multilevel payout. But when you start offering a service to your downline that has yet another compensation plan tied to it, all of a sudden your distributors are spending

more time trying to earn commissions promoting the support company than they are building their primary company. These programs can become distracting and they can create enormous problems in your downline.

3. Most MLM companies do not smile on the idea of promoting two companies simultaneously. Sure, you're an independent contractor and you can do what you want, but only with your own contacts. If you were to refer someone to a support MLM who you met through another distributor in your primary company, you could violate your distributor agreement with your primary company and be put on probation or even terminated. It's not worth the risk.

4. Most support companies offer very little value in their product or service. The opportunity only perpetuates based on the fact that distributors make money when they promote the product or service, which makes it an easy target for regulatory scrutiny. Companies that survive based on sign-ups rather than on the value of their product or service are doomed (more on this later in the book).

5. Attaching a multi-tier compensation plan to a leads program or other service can drive up the price of the service. Most distributors are better off purchasing these kinds of services from a company that does not have financial incentives to affiliates tied into the leads.

During my years of MLM experience, I've had several top leaders lured off the sure and steady path to success and into the dark and dangerous waters of support MLM hype, only to permanently lose their way. Their primary distributorship never recovered, and all of them eventually lost both incomes. In all of my years of network marketing and in all of my interviews, I've never met a single person who attributed their long-term success to working a primary program in tandem with a support company. I've also never met anyone who retired working a support company alone.

Based on these concerns, I'm eliminating MLM support companies from my list of considerations. MLM support companies include, but are not limited to, the following industries:

- MLM Leads Generation Services
- Search Engine Services

- Replicating Website Systems (designed to promote your primary MLM)
- Phone Auto-Dialer Systems
- Some Telecom MLMs (particularly pre-paid phone cards and flat-rate long distance)
- Advertising Services (including Website traffic builders)
- Social Media Sites and Services

Loser Industries

While I'm in the mood to slash low-credibility industries from my list of considerations, I'll show you how to quickly get rid of a few more. The following product industries are certainly viable through other forms of marketing, such as retail and wholesale outlets, home-shopping channels, even door-to-door direct sales. We all need these products or know someone who needs them. However, history tells us that these industries are guaranteed losers in network marketing. They won't make it. I will be elaborate on why later in the book.

Here are some of the industries that have never made it in network marketing and will most likely never make it (at least on their own). Even if there is some ember of hope still smoldering, at the very least these are all extremely high-risk, low-return industries (historically speaking).

- *Satellite TV*
- *Gold Coins*
- *DVDs/CDs*
- *Sporting Goods*
- *Gasoline/Gas Additives*
- *Vacuum Cleaners*
- *Home Appliances*
- *Stereos* (Home Electronics)
- *Search Engines*
- *Gas, Water, and Sewer*
- *Cigarettes/Cigars*
- *Fruitcake* (Just seeing if you're paying attention.)

Any industry that has never been successful in network marketing, or is likely not to have success in network marketing, probably will never have success in network marketing. Ultimately, it's still your call, so be smart and make the right choice. The only exception to this rule may be a company that sells everything through a catalog or online store type process. And even then, the primary focus better not be on any of the previously mentioned industries. Some of these could be tag-along products, but don't expect much product volume from them.

Commodities and Utilities

For the sake of being crystal clear, let's define the word *commodity* so we are speaking the same language. A commodity in the world of business is basically a product in massive production whose value is in its sales price rather than its usefulness to a consumer. It's a product that has a value that is somewhat standardized worldwide, no matter who produces the item. When produced by many different manufacturers, these items are considered equivalents. In other words, if a commodity were a food item, it could be an ingredient in a recipe, and that ingredient could be substituted for the same ingredient made by another manufacturer. Examples of commodities might be oil, electricity, grains like wheat and barley, metals, even pork bellies and orange juice. In the modern age, things like computer chips and even bandwidth can be considered commodities.

Commodities such as these are not good network marketing products because they are not unique in the marketplace. The whole point of producing a commodity product is to be standardized in the market. Products marketed through MLM must be unique and exclusive to one company. MLM products must create enough appeal to be competitive and enough profit margin to reward independent distributors for their hard work. Good MLM products should never compete on price, but on exclusivity and quality.

Utilities like electricity, water, gas, sewer, and even phone service can all be considered commodity type products and services. They're controlled largely by supply and demand, and they tend to be somewhat fixed. With utilities, one service is generally not any different than another. A network marketing company really couldn't come into town and start offering better electricity or new and improved natural gas. Companies have tried to offer utilities and have failed miserably time and time again.

My advice is to avoid anything that reeks of commodity. It's much too hard to compete on price, and you already know how I feel about service MLMs. At the same time, avoid companies that market products that other network marketing companies or other stores already sell. Imagine how difficult it would be to try to convince your customer to purchase a name-brand TV or a case of name-brand soft drinks when these identical brands are available through other companies and other outlets. I humbly advise you to eliminate all commodities and utilities from the list of industries before proceeding.

Gold and Silver

Not only do gold and silver coins fit into the commodities model, there are a few other reasons to avoid these guaranteed losers.

Reasons to avoid gold and silver coin MLMs:

1. I fall back on my standard evaluation and conclusion for any industry like this: no matter how many times it has been tried (in this case dozens of times) no gold coin program has ever survived as a network marketing product. This should be reason enough.
2. The price of gold and silver is standardized and fixed by the market, just like the other commodities I just described. It fluctuates up and down from time to time, but there is not a lot of room for profit margins with any kind of commodity. Fluctuations in gold prices can cause the company to fold overnight.
3. Gold and silver is regulated by the SEC (Securities and Exchange Commission) and requires a securities license. Because of this, the SEC keeps a close watch on this industry to make sure buyers and sellers are playing by the rules. Inevitably, distributors will hype the idea that customers and distributors will see an increase in the value of their gold investment even when the market forecasts say otherwise. The SEC will not tolerate this and will immediately shut down any company that violates these laws.
4. Since the gold or silver coin is the MLM product, some companies allow their distributors and customers to make payments on the coins until they pay it off and receive delivery (even a single ounce of gold can be very expensive). This kind of layaway plan could be fine in another setting, but in MLM, these companies actually pay commissions on these payments before the product is totally paid off and delivered to the customer. Regulators frown upon this lag time, and it violates anti-pyramid laws in many states.

MLM Buy Clubs

Now we're going to cover some commonly held myths associated with network marketing buying clubs. I hear these myths so often, that I decided to actually present each myth first, and then provide you with each fact so you can see the contrast and understand the truth as it relates to one of the oldest, most traditional products/services in network marketing.

Wholesale buying clubs

Myth: Wholesale buying clubs are a powerful way to develop a large international marketing business while at the same time enjoying the benefits of wholesale prices on thousands of consumer products.

Fact: Wholesale buying clubs are a fantastic way to save money. However, MLM's version of the wholesale buying club is not exactly wholesale. You can save as a consumer by skipping the middle-man retailers and going directly to the wholesale warehouse, but generally there is not enough profit margin left to run a true wholesale buying club MLM. What you get instead is simply "a buying club."

Here are some definitions of a wholesale buying club vs. a buying club:

Wholesale Buying Club: A group of consumers who band together to form a large purchasing organization to take advantage of volume discount prices. These clubs are exclusive to those who officially become members. Typically, wholesale buying club members will pay a monthly or annual fee for the exclusive right to purchase at factory-direct, wholesale prices. Traditional buying club members only shop at stores, but in today's modern age, it is usually done through catalogs, 1-800 lines, and now, the Internet.

Buying Club: A group of consumers who band together to form a purchasing organization. The organization offers the same items you might find in the retail and wholesale store at similar prices, or possibly a bit higher. The organization retains the profits that would otherwise have been savings to the consumer. These profits fund the organization.

Most buying clubs are designed as fund-raising organizations for churches or other non-profit organizations. You may buy a ticket to an upcoming country western concert, and some of the proceeds go to the local fire department. Your church or school might sell chocolates similar to confections you might find at a local store for about the same price or even much less; however, the church or school retains a percentage of the profits. Also, buying clubs are common among profit-producing organizations, such as direct sales or network marketing companies. A company offers items in a catalog that you can find for about the same price in the stores—the catalog prices could even be a bit higher. The company passes a percentage of its profits to independent distributors who are actively promoting the products and program.

Myth: Amway/Quixtar is a wholesale buying club.

Fact: Amway/Quixtar is a buying club, not a wholesale buying club. When Amway was founded back in the fifties, they offered a variety of household cleaning and maintenance products. These were high-quality products sold at reasonable prices—a good deal. As the company grew, Amway began diversifying. They brought on personal care products, nutritionals, and more household products, and eventually grew into one of the world's largest network marketing companies.

During the last twenty years, Amway (temporarily referred to as Quixtar in North America) has taken a new direction. Amway decided to become a product broker in addition to marketing their own products. A broker is essentially a middleman who regulates the buying and selling of existing name-brand products and services. For example, thirty years ago, you could only buy products exclusively produced by Amway through Amway distributors. These products included Amway soap, Amway cleaners, Amway air fresheners, etc. Amway now offers a large variety of non-exclusive products through its existing network of distributors (name-brand stereos, name-brand automobiles, name-brand food items, etc.). But at what advantage does Amway offer these products? If the same product can be purchased from another source for less, there is no reason for the customer to purchase the product from Amway or any other buying club.

Today you must ask yourself, "Is this company a wholesale buying club or is it just a buying club?" Amway offers nearly every product imaginable through catalogs, and the company claims to be a wholesale buying club when, in actuality, Amway is a classic example of a buying club. Are you saving money? Sometimes you are, and sometimes you're not. Remember that you are still paying the middleman. The middleman has simply become several levels of distributors and the company itself. In other words, when you purchase a Sony TV from Amway, you will typically pay more for that TV than you will at today's popular retail and wholesale stores. Why? Because when Amway purchases that TV from the wholesale warehouse, they take their cut. Then they place more mark-ups on the TV to pay out several generations of commissions to distributors. Since Sony is the manufacturer, they take a large cut, leaving very little room for discount pricing. Even distributors usually pay more for the product with the rationalization that they are buying from their own store and they are supporting the cause of Amway. This distributor loyalty to the cause of Amway is largely what keeps Amway viable. People are in it for the cause, not the discount. They're in to support Quixtar and the American dream, not to save money on toilet paper.

Myth: A true wholesale buying club would be the perfect MLM vehicle since you have all industries under one roof.

Fact: No true wholesale buying club has ever endured the test of time. Let's look at a company that was a true wholesale buying club, Consumers Buyline Inc., or CBI. CBI had the same idea of offering every product known to humanity, but with a completely different concept. CBI charged a monthly fee of around $20 to be a member. This fee allowed you to join millions of other consumers in a gigantic purchasing club. Everyone was allowed access to factory-direct shopping. No mark-ups were placed on the products in order to pay out commissions to the distributors in CBI. The only mark-ups were made by the product manufacturers in order to make a modest profit. This allowed CBI to keep prices so low that they were literally unbeatable. CBI only made money on the start-up fee, annual renewals, and the $20 per month that was used to pay distributor commissions. This was a true wholesale buying club concept. Unfortunately, profit margins were not healthy enough to keep this program afloat, and CBI failed with a little help from an inexperienced management team and a lousy compensation plan. Would CBI have had a better chance of staying in business had it marked up its products? Maybe, but then it would have been a buying club, not a wholesale buying club. The opportunity would have no true value. And don't think other companies haven't tried this model.

Len Clements includes a laundry list of defunct wholesale buying clubs in his book Inside Network Marketing. Here are some of the more famous (or infamous) programs: Fund America, Life Plan, Mainstreet Alliance, Passport To Adventure, Personal Wealth Systems, Success America, Team USA, United Buyer's Service, and the previously mentioned CBI.

Myth: As a buying club distributor, I can make money representing name-brand products, like Ford, Sony, and AT&T.

Fact: It's not name-brand products but exclusive products that drive *all* network marketing opportunities. When you're a product broker, you're forced to limit payout to your distributors since you have to pay the middleman for the product. It is also more difficult to competitively price your brokered products. When a company is able to establish an exclusive on a product or service, the distributorship then takes on greater value. After all, customers can only get that core product through an independent distributor. They can't simply go down to Walmart and pick up that product. Experts agree that it's better to avoid brokering products altogether. If a company can't afford to research and develop their own products, they can't afford to start a network marketing business.

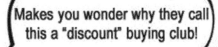

Part Two: What to Sell, and Why

Testing Your Marketing Mind

To become a successful network marketer, you *must* learn how to pick a successful product. So far we have learned some of the reasons people make bad choices, and we have learned some of the initial concepts for making correct choices. This next section will explore several thoughts and ideas designed to get you thinking like a marketing millionaire.

When people are trying to decide on a product, they typically will choose a product based on the wrong reasons. I would like to take you through the following exercise, which will allow you to discover these right and wrong reasons for yourself.

Now pretend that you are selecting a product today by answering the following questions as if your financial future depended on it. Be sure to choose well, because if you make the wrong choice, your chances for success in network marketing will be virtually eliminated. By the way, there is only one correct choice.

Question: In choosing a product to market through your home-based business vehicle, your #1 concern should be what?

A. Marketing products and services that are high tech.
B. Marketing products and services that are luxurious.
C. Marketing products and services that interest me.
D. Marketing products and services that benefit me.
E. Marketing products and services that benefit as many people as possible.
F. All of the above.

If you chose letter E on your own, you're on the right track. I've heard motivational speaker and millionaire Zig Ziglar say, "If you help enough other people get what they want, you'll get what you want." It may be fun and exciting to work with choices A–D, but there just isn't any profit in marketing products that do not appeal to the masses (or at least an enormous niche). Network marketing is mass marketing, not niche marketing. Now don't get me wrong; if you have some of the factors in the A–D list working for you, they could be beneficial in some way. However, when choosing a product or service, keep the following cautions in mind.

Common Mistakes People Make

While in the business evaluation process, most people tend to choose a product or service for some of the following reasons. Understanding these reasons will help you avoid the most common mistakes that people make in choosing a home business product.

High tech is high risk

Don't choose to market stereos, computers, MP3 players, GPS devices, or other gadgets because you want to market products that are high-tech. You should only consider marketing high-tech products if you have done the research and know it is extremely profitable. Emotional and personal choices are for people who aren't concerned about profit. Millions of people have expensive hobbies. Network marketing shouldn't be yours.

For example, there once was a man who had a little boy. He enjoyed nothing better than building elaborate electronic models and devices with his son, especially model trains. He saw an opportunity to get involved in network marketing, which would not only afford him the extra money to purchase the expensive materials for building the tracks, but it would give him the time and freedom he so desperately needed to spend more time at home with his son. After investigating many opportunities, the man narrowed his choices to two programs. By good fortune, one of these programs happened to be an electronics company. They had everything from home and car alarms to home entertainment systems to electronic games. Considering the man's interest in electronics, it might have seemed that the choice would be a no-brainer. However, the man decided to choose the other company. This other company manufactured and distributed nutritional supplements and personal care products (pills, potions, and lotions). Although his personal interests revolved around the electronics company, he saw more mass market potential in the second company. The result? After five years of diligent part-time effort, the man is now semi-retired with a six-figure residual income. He has one of the largest collections of electronic toys and gadgets of anyone in town, but more important, he has the time freedom to enjoy building the most elaborate electric train tracks you have ever seen. As for the electronics company, they went to over 800,000 distributors in five years and then declared bankruptcy. No major direct sales/network marketing company has attempted the high-tech angle ever since. Would you say this man made the right choice? High-risk industries might sound fun at first, but I can guarantee you that no business is fun when it's going out of business.

Serve the classes, live with the masses

Don't sacrifice profit to market products that are luxurious. After all, which company is the larger, more successful company, Coca-Cola or BMW? Which product costs more? Would it be more profitable to market lots of inexpensive consumables or a few high-ticket, non-consumable luxury items?

I just met a woman who recently ended a fairly successful career as a real estate agent to the rich and famous. Her days consisted of showing million dollar homes to high-net-worth clients. Quite glamorous, right? Well, not really. She just quit her job and is now in the process of reading my book in an attempt to learn the steps to selecting the right network marketing company. This high-ticket, high-commission, high-pressure lifestyle was finally catching up with her. Just like J. Paul Getty, she would now rather have one percent of a hundred people's efforts rather than one hundred percent of her own. Or better yet, five percent of five thousand people's efforts! Someone once said, "If you serve the classes, you'll live with the masses, but if you serve the masses, you'll live with the classes."

Don't limit your profit potential by marketing products that interest only you and a few others. I have a personal interest in bagpipes, but I don't know too many others who are in the market for one. Find out what most people are in the market for and market that.

Personal preferences can cripple your marketing strategy

Although it is important to have a firm testimony of your product or service, don't choose to market a product or service simply because you experienced personal benefit from it. Just because you had a favorable reaction doesn't mean others will. Likewise, just because you don't have personal benefit from a specific product or service doesn't mean others won't. In my career, I have run into countless individuals who have chosen their networking vehicle based on their own personal interests, without giving a thought to what the masses want and need; they end up failing miserably.

I met a woman several years ago who really got me thinking about focusing on other people's wants and needs instead of my own. She was a top distributor in a nutritional network marketing program. She proudly pointed out one day that she was earning a high six-figure income by promoting an effective nutritional supplement that she herself did not personally use on a daily basis. You see, this woman was about five and a half feet tall and weighed about 105 pounds. If she got any slimmer, she would be able to walk through doors without opening them. The product that took her to fame and fortune was an herbal weight management product. Almost everyone she introduced to the product was having results. However, she could not afford to lose any more weight so she stayed away from the stuff. The result? Over ten thousand distributors in her downline in three years, and she still does not use her flagship product. It's important not to get hung up on what works for you personally and what doesn't. Find out how many others the product will work for— that's the real test!

Remember that this is marketing, or delivering what your customer already wants, not sales, or trying to convince someone to buy something that may or may not be what they want. You'll want to offer products that people want and need, not what you think would be fun and interesting to sell. Demand in the marketplace is everything. Find an excellent, well priced product with mass appeal and you'll never want for customers.

A fish story

How do you know what the market is demanding today? Ask the bait shop clerk, and then take his advice! Here's a short story to illustrate my point.

Once upon a time there was a man who decided to go fishing out on a lake. While sitting in his rowboat, the man was eating potato chips and casting his line in the water. He was having an okay day. After all, he had just started fishing and he already had a few bites. After finishing his second large bag of potato chips, the man remarked to himself, "Self, you know something, I just love potato chips. I wonder how them fishies would like these things? I can't imagine that they would prefer them slimy worms over these tasty potato chips." So he substituted the night crawlers on his hook for a few ruffled chips. He stuck the chips to his hook using some chewing gum and then he cast his line in the water. After several hours went by with not so much as a nibble, the man decided to hoist anchor and paddle on over to the local bait shop for some advice from the local expert.

The bait shop clerk referred the man to a florescent colored jar with the words Super Bait™ *on the label. The man had been reading about this new fangled stuff in his fishing magazines but hadn't tried it. The shop clerk assured him that it was the most effective bait he'd ever used on this lake. So the man took the shop owner's advice and bought the Super Bait™. The man immediately rowed back out to the middle of the lake, got his hook ready, and proceeded to open the new bait. That's when the smell hit him. "This stuff is disgusting," he remarked. "I can't imagine why any living creature would want with this stuff." However, he decided that it was getting late and he had nothing to lose. So he cast his line in the water, and to his surprise, within five minutes he had caught two fish! That day, the man caught his limit faster than he ever had in his life. The man was glad he consulted the expert. He was able to discard his own limited reasoning and take advice from a qualified expert. He wondered why he hadn't asked for expert advice sooner.*

I'm sure you can draw your own analogies from this story. However, for the sake of those who are still catching up ... the local shop owner represents the many network marketing experts whose advice I have learned from and referenced for this book. These experts have been figuratively working the bait shop and fishing in the local lake for many more years than the rest of us. They know what the fish are biting on and what they aren't. These experts are pointing us to the most profitable trends in network marketing. The Super Bait™ represents viable network marketing products and services. The worms and the chips represent low-demand product industries with limited appeal. The man represents a new distributor, and the fish represents new customers and distributors. The fish are tired of being fed potato chips. How long will it take you and me to forsake our own reasoning, take the advice of the experts, and get some Super Bait™? The fish are waiting!

Success leaves clues

Finally, another great way to find a successful business model is to study successful businesses and business people. Why not learn from the masters? As expert sales trainer Brian Tracy says, "Success leaves clues." Before writing this book, I searched for every clue I could find. I made a list of the top twenty most successful companies of all time, and I found out which primary products or services they were marketing. Then I made a list of the top twenty active (not retired) income earners in network marketing and found out in which industries they were earning their millions. I studied these industries. I also did the same for the bad examples. I took the most prominent companies that went out of business based on lack of sales, and I found out which primary industry they represented. Through this research I've been able to determine what the marketplace is demanding today and what it is not.

Part Three: Daren's Seven Secrets

To this point, we've taken a lot of time to understand why we're in business and how we can stay in business. We've learned how to think like a successful marketing professional and to look at the marketplace with new eyes. We've also studied the importance of finding a high-demand product in a high-demand industry. We've also established that tangible products are the most profitable and stable foundation for a network marketing business. Let's now look at some additional criteria for selecting the best product industry.

Don't take my word for it

Remember what we discussed in the first chapter? We talked about the importance of making your own educated decisions. Here are some steps that will help you make the right choice for you. First, approach the information in an objective, rational manner. Second, do your own due diligence or research the research. And third, with the right information and enough time to review it, make your own intelligent business decision. After all, you're the only one who doesn't have a hidden agenda.

Given the length and detail associated with this chapter, it is obvious that I feel that selecting the right product industry is absolutely critical. This truly is one of the most important decisions of your career, and it should not be taken lightly. Spend a lot of time with this one and it will pay off down the road. Don't settle for a company that does not match the criteria for "best product industry." Your ability to produce wealth through network marketing will be determined in large measure by the choices you make on which product industry you will represent. Don't be hasty; review this chapter again carefully, and then make the right choice. The formula works. Give it a try.

Selecting a Wealth Building Product

Pay close attention to these next few paragraphs. This could be the most important part of this study. When looking for a hot product industry, many distributors feel that any legitimate product will do, as long as it's in high demand. However, in today's competitive market, in order for your company to stay on top, you must have more than just a high-demand product. Through years of documented research, I've discovered seven fundamental characteristics that must be considered when choosing a long-term wealth-generating product or service. I call these seven characteristics *Daren's Seven Secrets*. I've never found a top marketing authority that disagreed on these points.

I've created a statement that will help you remember the acronym for these seven criteria. It goes like this: "Each Criterion Unlocks the Vault to Success!" Now examine the first letter in each of these words and you get the first letter of each of the seven steps.

E C U T V T S

Emotional
Consumable
Unique
Traditional
Valuable
Timely
Stable

Experts agree that the product or service must have the following characteristics:

1.   Emotional: The product must induce a positive mental or physical change that results in an emotional attachment to that brand. Products that help people look and feel better can create an emotional bond between the customer and a specific name-brand product, which may never be broken. This bond can be passed on to others through the sharing of personal experiences.

2.   Consumable: The product must be used up and replaced on a monthly, weekly, or even daily basis. This is one of the most important criterions on the list! Without monthly consumption, it is nearly impossible to establish ongoing monthly income. Distributors offering non-consumables are constantly looking for new customers every month instead of enjoying the residual income that only comes through continual product consumption.

3.   Unique: The product must have a unique twist, something that the competition doesn't have or can't get. A special formulator or scientist, an exclusive ingredient, a twist in the formulation,

creative processing, or an endorsement can make a product unique. Maybe it has a unique color, texture, scent, taste, delivery system, container, or logo. The product must also be exclusive to one company. Your brand shouldn't be available for purchase in chain stores or through other companies, suppliers, or independent distributors.

4. Traditional: Although the product must be unique in some way, it cannot be too uncommon. It must be similar to other products on the market that have been sold for years and years. The product or service category must have a good track record in the marketplace. Traditional products have mass appeal over a substantial period of time.

5. Valuable: The product must be worth its price ... and maybe more! Prices must not be set too high or too low for the perceived value of the product. Customers, distributors, and governmental regulators determine its value. If all three parties pass off on the value test, and if the product could sell unaided in a retail store at the price a distributor sells it at, you have a winner.

6. Timely: The product must be in high demand *right now*. The product must appeal to the masses, especially the Baby Boomer generation, which consists of 76 million Americans born between 1946 and 1964. They are the largest buying force in the history of North America and are accustomed to getting what they ask for. If you can cater to the needs of the Baby Boomers, it's hard to go wrong.

7. Stable: The product must be in high demand *later*. Take a look twenty years into the future. Will the product or service still be in high demand? If the answer is yes, you have a winner. If demand on the product increases with time, that's even better. You may know about the Baby Boomers, but you may be unaware that the 76 million baby boomers have had 74 million babies. Having Baby Boomer children consuming the same products their parents are consuming will not hurt product demand now, nor will it affect demand over the next twenty to thirty years.

Ok, now let's break down each of Daren's Seven Secrets in specific detail.

Emotional

Think about products that create an emotional reaction. How about a skin care product that reduces the appearance of age spots, crow's feet, and other signs of aging? What about a high protein chocolate bar that gives you energy, provides antioxidants, and isn't fattening? How about a nutritional supplement that helps reduce the inflammation and pain of arthritis? Have we mentioned lingerie? How about swimwear that helps you look slimmer? And while we're on the subject, what price can you place on a girdle?

What about a pair of shoes that look just like the ones your favorite movie star wore in your favorite movie? How about a perfume that reminds you of the scent your spouse wore on your wedding day or honeymoon? What about a product that tastes great, and helps you lose weight? And don't forget one of the ultimate emotional products ... jewelry! If your heart stirs when you think of the benefit of the product, you're now emotionally attached to the brand at any price.

Now think about some products that have limited emotional attachment. When I think of low emotional appeal, I think of telecommunications services. People generally shop price on long distance service and couldn't care less if they're on one network or another as long as the call goes through (which it generally always does). Cell phone service is also limited in emotional branding since it really comes down to coverage and price. I also think about household cleaners and consumables. Companies marketing products like gasoline, grain, eggs, pork bellies, lumber, and other commodity products can find it difficult to establish long-term customer attachment. Price becomes a major factor with non-emotional brands.

Emotion Question: Does your product possess benefits that result in immediate emotional attachment?

Consumable

If you were to establish a successful home-based business over the next few years, how often would you like to receive a paycheck? Annually? Quarterly? Monthly? I know what your answer will be, but unless you select the right product line, you'll be bound by how consumable your product is. If you want to be paid once or twice annually, sell a product that consumes annually, like antifreeze, beach towels, family portraits, tires, or spark plugs. Or in the case of services, you might offer pressure washing, vacation packages, or bikini waxes. If you want to make consistent, recurring income, selecting these kinds of products is a very bad idea.

So why not give yourself a 400 percent raise. If annually consumable products are not working out, try selling products that consume on a quarterly basis like cosmetics, candles, motor oil, and dish soap. If you can settle for quarterly profits, one of these might not be a bad choice.

However, I don't like to settle on anything, and you shouldn't either. You should demand maximum profits from the time and effort you put into your business. You should be paid monthly, weekly, or even daily for your marketing efforts. Some of the most consumable products in the world include personal care items, household products, utilities, and especially nutritional products and food items. The more product consumption that happens in your average customer's household, the more income you'll make. Remember, you only have a certain amount of hours to put in every day. You might as well leverage your time with a product that will truly reward you with residual income for life.

A few years ago I did a seminar for a group of ladies in the home party plan business. They all represented one of the largest and most popular cosmetics product lines in direct sales. Without explaining my intentions and without planting anyone in my audience to enforce the point I wanted to make, I conducted an experiment. I had everyone in the room stand up. Then I announced that anyone with monthly sales of $100 or greater could remain standing; everyone else was to be seated. Then I increased the volume amount to $200. More women sat down but many remained standing. Then I continued to increase the amount by $100 again and again until I only had two representatives still standing. We applauded these ladies and their accomplishment of moving thousands of dollars in product over the last calendar month. I then began inquiring into their business, trying to learn their secrets to success. My suspicions proved correct when I realized that both of these ladies had been selling one product more than any other in the line in order to produce these kinds of numbers consistently from month to month. They were selling and reselling a new body wash that had been released the year prior, and this was now their number one seller. Then I asked everyone in the room *why* they thought these representatives were having better results than everyone else. I was shocked when not a single hand went up. None of these people understood what I was getting at.

After I spelled out my points on consumable products and encouraged everyone to start selling more soap and less eyeliner, I saw a few of the ladies had gotten it. I could tell they were getting excited. They were starting to work out sales volumes with their paper and pen. Still, most of them didn't have a clue what I was getting at. At the end of my presentation, I felt like saying, "If you're all going to start concentrating on selling soap instead of cosmetics, why don't you quit your cosmetics business and go look for the best soap company? You'll make a lot more money." I bit my tongue and waited for that urge to pass. I realized that some people are in business to acquire and keep customers in order to turn a profit, and some are in business for other reasons. I decided from that day on that I only wanted to address my comments to those who are interested in getting better results for their time, energy, and money. I'm glad you're still reading. This is a good sign. If you're getting this stuff, your fortune is waiting; there are just a few more things you need to know to boost your potential earnings.

> *"I realized that some people are in business to acquire and keep customers in order to turn a profit, and some are in business for other reasons. I decided from that day on that I only wanted to address my comments to those who are interested in getting better results for their time, energy, and money."*

Non-consumables do have their place. Surprisingly, many non-consumables have withstood the test of time. Products like water and air filters, non-consumable car care products, electronics, home entertainment products, and others continue to supplement the consumables market. *Supplement*, however, is the operative word. Companies that try to build a dynasty on non-consumables alone usually end in disaster. Through the history of network marketing, no non-consumable product company has ever been able to keep from diversifying into a high-demand consumable in order to stay competitive. In some cases, the non-consumable nature of the product acted as a catalyst to drive company sales and growth for a few years until the company could afford to diversify into a solid base of consumables. But don't think for a moment that non-consumables do not have a place in network marketing. They can be a good compliment to a consumable product base.

Trust me, you'll want to select a highly consumable product for your business. The more consumable, the better. You need to have people calling you every month and even weekly to order more of your product. This could be the most important of the seven steps.

Consumable Question: Is your product consumed on a monthly or even weekly basis and then reordered? Do you have strong month-to-month customer retention?

Unique

What are some of the factors that can make a product unique? First of all, it is very important to understand that your name-brand product must be sold *only* through one company: your company. If your product can be found in major department stores or through the distributors of other companies, you're sunk.

Next, a product must have a unique formulation or formulator. I love the stories I hear about the origins of some of the popular herbal products on the market. You might pop in a company DVD and hear a tale of how some explorer in the Amazon basin found a tribe of indigenous peoples whose average lifespan was 120 years.

Furthermore, the chief was 135, had all of his original teeth, and was still fathering children. Of course, credit was given to a special natural spring of miracle water that could only be found in this one location in the world. Yes, the *Fountain of Youth*. And it is the exclusive property of XYZ Corporation, a new network marketing company that is now paying you on seven generations of referrals to sell the stuff. Now that's unique!

I'm not trying to make fun of anybody; I tease because I love. And I don't mean to make light of some of the amazing "exclusive" discoveries that are available through network marketing today. Almost every great product has a great story behind it that makes that product unique to the marketplace. If you can believe wholeheartedly in that story enough to represent that product as an independent distributor, you may have a very powerful product on your hands. A word of caution: make sure the story checks out. You don't want to be associated with a company that makes things up. You also want to avoid companies who tie a lot of sensationalism into their story. Make sure the product story is believable and not too over-the-top. More on illegal product claims later.

Here are just a few of the things that can make a product unique:

1. Unique formulation that cannot be found in any other product
2. Unique formulator (someone with a great reputation and an exclusive agreement with your company)
3. Unique, exclusive ingredient or formulation process
4. Patent or trademark
5. A first-to-market product (everyone else is second in line)
6. Unique and exclusive branding, logos, trademarks, colors, textures, or packaging
7. Celebrity endorsement
8. Unique affiliation with a prominent company, organization, or individual

Unique Question: Is your product unique and exclusive in the marketplace?

Traditional

Although a product should be unique, it must not be so unique that people cannot identify with it. Otherwise, you'll have to become a salesperson and this can kill duplication in your business. Traditional product categories are those that have been sold through direct sales/network marketing over the last forty years. It should also be a product that has been commonly used in daily life over the last forty years.

Some of the most traditional products in direct sales today are:

- Personal Care Products
- Water and Air Filtration Units
- Nutritional Supplements
- Vacuum Cleaners
- Cookware

Non-traditional products might include:

- Compact MP3 Players
- Web-Based Photo Albums
- DVD/CD Clubs
- Yoga Training Videos
- Video E-mail
- Anything Related to the Internet
- Anything never tried previously in MLM

Some might criticize the more traditional product lines for being "me too" products or products that are very similar or even identical to other products now on the market. However, like top personal development coach Anthony Robbins says, "If you want to have extraordinary results, find out what successful people are doing and *model* their behavior." Why do we have "me too" products? Because "we too" want to make a profit. Certainly every product line needs to be unique. And granted, some product lines are so "me too" that they don't have any unique qualities whatsoever. But if you want a 99% chance of failure, try marketing a totally unique product industry that has never been successfully marketed through MLM. This is almost a guaranteed failure.

Look at all of the programs that have tried marketing satellite dishes, jewelry, gasoline, and grocery coupons. Although people try to blame these failures on other factors (like compensation plans), I assure you that product industry is the relevant issue. Don't try to pioneer a new product industry through network marketing, and don't try to copy an industry that has tried and failed over and over again. Find a traditional product industry that is proven, and then find a product within that industry that has a unique story, an exclusive formulation, and a special branding strategy.

Remember, it has to be a traditional product sold consistently through direct sales over the last forty years, and used in common life from day to day. If the product is considered uncommon or rare among common people, it does not qualify as traditional. When you're required to convince the marketplace of the usefulness and importance of your new gadget or gizmo, you're selling instead of marketing. This is a sure-fire duplication killer. Find a product that is rooted in tradition, but also carries a unique, exclusive benefit that separates it from the competition.

Tradition Question: Has your specific product been sold successfully through network marketing over the past forty years or more? Do the masses consider it a commonly purchased product?

Valuable

One of the biggest mistakes that amateurs make when selecting a product is trying to compete on price. Price wars are vicious and bloody, and there are no winners. You may win a few battles, but everyone ultimately loses the war. When you focus on competing with price, you fail to build product loyalty. Customers don't understand the true value of your product or service. You may win temporarily when you undercut the competition, but as soon as another competitor undercuts your price, all of your customers will leave.

Products with value allow you to build brand loyalty and lifetime customer retention. When customers understand the true value of your product, they will continue to purchase your product even when competitors try to offer knockoff products at discounted rates. The value of your product should be in its unique and exclusive qualities, and it's emotional appeal. Don't get caught up in the price wars. Brand value means quality comes first. Having a low price is not as important as whether or not the product fulfills a valuable consumer want or need. In fact, the direct sales industry has always operated better on a model of higher quality, higher priced products. In the best-selling book *The 22 Immutable Laws of Branding*, authors Al and Laura Ries talk about the importance of creating brand value instead of lowering prices. "To build a quality brand, you need to narrow the focus and combine that narrow focus with a better name and a higher price."[4] It's often said in market circles, "If you live by price, you'll die by price," meaning if you gain business by undercutting your competition on price, soon someone will undercut you and you'll lose customers in the same way.

However, prices must be realistic and they must be set within the bounds that the marketplace deems reasonable. If your products had all the same benefits that they do now, and they were sold in a retail store at the current retail price, would consumers purchase this product right off the shelf? If you had one hundred customers currently taking your product and they were not distributors and had no financial incentive to sell the product or recommend it to others, how many of these customers would stay on the product month-to-month over the course of one year? All of these factors determine the value of your product.

Value Question: Is your product worth its price and maybe more? Based on its benefits, would it sell at full retail price in the store?

Timely

Don't be fooled by the lure of future profits. I'm approached on a monthly basis by people who want to sell me on some incredible new product or service that is going to be the next big thing. Unfortunately, the popularity and demand on this product is purely speculative. I simply tell them, "I can't feed my children, give money to my church, and build my future dreams on speculation." If they tell me this will be *huge* within twenty-four months, I say, "Call me in about five years. By that time, you should have all the kinks worked out and it will be time to make some great money with that idea. Until then, give me a product that is in demand in the marketplace *right now*! Not next week, next month, or next year. I'm building my empire today." Needless to say, I've never received a single call. Not because the person was insulted by my comments (ok, maybe a few were), but because the new opportunity never materialized. If you want to earn large profits, you must select an industry with substantial sales and significant momentum *right now*. Do current events, news, word-of-mouth opinion, business trade journals and books, and popular culture indicate an explosion in sales right now?

Timing Question: Is your product in extremely high demand in the marketplace right now?

Stable

Just as important as selecting a product that is in huge demand right now, is selecting a product that will still have an enormous demand in the future. Where will your products be five, ten, even twenty years into the future? It doesn't take a crystal ball to understand what products will be exploding tomorrow. Just focus on the Baby-Boomers and try to think about what Baby Boomers need now and what they will need fifteen years from now. If there is any doubt in your mind as to which product industries the millionaires of the twenty-first century will be coming from, just go to your local book store and start reading what top economists are saying on the subject. It's all there in black and white. You can go read about it, or you can stick your head in the ground and make your decisions about your business and future based on hearsay, personal prejudice, and old news.

The best way to find out if your product or service will be doing well in the future is to take a look at the economy in the state of Florida. Per capita, Florida has the largest population of retirees in the world. What Florida is demanding now is what North America will be demanding over the next twenty to thirty years.

Here's another point to think about. It's true that the baby boomers are still driving our economy in North America. As mentioned before, the 76 million Baby Boomers had 74 million babies. These Boomer children are purchasing the products their parents have taught them to purchase. Do current events, news, word-of-mouth opinion, business trade journals and books, and popular culture indicate a long-term increase in sales? This is a very important question to answer.

Stability Question: Will your product be in high demand over the next twenty years?

Applying the Seven Steps

Okay, now we know the seven steps for selecting a wealth-generating product. Now let's look at some examples of products that match, or don't match, each product criterion.

In the following section, we'll take specific product industries and put them to the test to determine how they do against the seven steps.

Home security industry

Let's say you were interested in marketing electronic burglar alarm systems for the home. How does this product industry check out with the Daren's Seven Secrets?

- *Is it emotional?* People have strong feelings about keeping their families safe? There is no question as to whether or not parents would invest in the safety and security of their children, as well as their valuable property and belongings. Personal and family security is a very emotionally charged topic.
- *Is it consumable?* No. Buy one and you don't need another for a *long* time. It is extremely difficult to build a residual customer base with this type of non-consumable. It may be argued that the monthly security monitoring service is residual; however, I've never seen a plan yet that paid the distributor residuals on the monthly service. Show me one that does and I'll rewrite this section.
- *Is it unique?* It may or may not be unique, depending upon the features. Generally there systems are fairly similar in design and function.
- *Is it traditional?* Traditional, yes. Successful track record, no.
- *Is it valuable?* The value of the system depends on the price. It is hard to put a price on your personal safety and the lives of your family. However, high-ticket items usually do not do as well as lower-priced consumable products. A system with easy features priced at a reasonable amount could be quite valuable, especially since it could be a one-time purchase.
- *Is it timely?* Absolutely! Baby Boomers are more concerned about personal security than ever before.
- *Is it stable?* Should be. Although the product would have to continue to evolve, demand should only increase as the Baby Boomers get older. It's not a bad industry to diversify into as the Baby Boomers mature.

As you can see, the home security industry does have some redeeming qualities; however, there are a few concerns in terms of value, tradition, and uniqueness, and a major concern in the area of consumption. In my opinion, the consumable criterion is at least twice as important as the other six steps, and it is critical to industry success. Let's try another industry.

Long-distance telephone service

Now let's take another example and put it to the test. Let's say you decided that you wanted to market business or residential long-distance service.

- *Is it emotional?* No. You might argue that talking to your favorite Aunt Betsy in Maine is a very emotional experience. However, your emotional attachment is to Aunt Betsy, not to AT&T or Sprint (unless Aunt Betsy works for one of these companies). Most consumers are more concerned about other features, like saving money on those frequent calls to relatives. They are not concerned about which brand they use.
- *Is it consumable?* Yes. Everyone uses long distance every month. Utilities are the ultimate consumable.
- *Is it unique?* No. Although every plan has different features, when you pick up the phone to call on any of the thousands of services available, you should get the same result - a long-distance call. A few very creative traditional telecom companies have tried to incorporate some unique calling plans, like free evenings and weekends, but these promotions are easily copied.
- *Is it traditional?* Sure. Since the deregulation of telecommunications, long distance has been common among network marketing products/services on the market.
- *Is it valuable?* Most telecom programs offer very competitive rates. Therefore, today more than ever, telecom is an excellent value. However, profit margins are poor so distributors need to make up their lack of commission payout by producing massive calling volume. Since most people rarely change their calling volume from month to month, finding more customers produces more volume.
- *Is it timely?* When I first wrote this book, timing for telecom was still excellent. The industry was still highly competitive and young companies were battling it out with the big carriers. Today, the telecom landscape is littered with battered and bloody companies, and some of the largest companies of the twenty-first century have now gone bankrupt. Those that remain are diversifying into other technology services and even

consumer products in an attempt to survive. Several companies have even considered offering electric power, cell phone service, and other utilities.

- *Is it stable?* The long-distance market is in a constant state of change based upon increasing competition and new technology. No one can be certain about the future of long-distance service, especially with cellular calling plans costing less and less. We have also seen the introduction of flat-rate long-distance plans coming through cutting-edge Internet technology. Could you imagine having unlimited long distance for less than you pay for your phone? How about free long distance through the Internet with VOIP (Voice Over Internet Protocol)? This already makes our traditional long-distance plans obsolete. In addition, satellite phones will be affordable to the masses in just a few more years, and many people have them now.

So telecom has some serious issues. Although phone service could be considered the ultimate consumable, this industry falls down in emotional appeal, uniqueness, and stability, as well as no profit margins left for distributor commissions. That's three strikes against anyone considering this industry for a future business. Let's try again.

Personal care products

Now let's consider another great product industry. You might hear people say that no one is interested in potions and lotions. No one, of course, except the Baby Boomers, 76 million Americans with an obsession for staying young and the disposable income to purchase products and services that will help them do just that. Most of the potions and lotions ballyhoo is the result of aggressive attacks from companies that don't promote consumer goods, like telecommunications programs. Go to any opportunity meeting for a telecom MLM and you'll see what I mean. Go to any other opportunity meeting and you'll know the real story. Personal care is one of the leading product industries in network marketing and continues to be a major contender year after year. Personal care products traditionally include skin, hair, and body care products.

- *Is it emotional?* Absolutely. Some of the better personal care products cannot only help people to feel younger, but can even enhance their appearance. What can be more emotional than looking and feeling younger?

- *Is it consumable?* Personal care products are consumable at an average or medium range. Sure, these products are used up and replaced. However, most skin care products are usually replaced every two to four months rather than every two to four weeks. This makes a huge difference when it is multiplied by hundreds of thousands of consumers. If you lump cosmetics into personal care, now you're looking at six to twelve months to consume an eyebrow pencil, a bottle of mascara, or one lipstick.
- *Is it unique?* With so many herbal extracts, exotic fragrances, and all-natural ingredients now available, it is very easy to customize personal care products and come up with a one-of-a-kind product. And it's difficult to copy these complex formulas.
- *Is it traditional?* Very! As a matter of fact, personal care products are one of the most traditional product lines on the market. One popular cosmetics and personal care company that is still popular today established its direct selling roots over one hundred years ago.
- *Is it valuable?* Because of outrageous advertising and marketing expenses, traditional cosmetic lines don't have any budget left over for the actual product ingredients. Most non-MLM cosmetic lines spend more on the lids of the skin care containers than they do on the actual contents of the product. Network marketing companies do not spend money on advertising and marketing. They budget more for product development in order to provide a superior product. Are these products worth the price? You bet!
- *Is it timely?* The Baby Boomers will spend *any* amount of money to look and feel younger. Statistics show that even the male Baby Boomers are beginning to purchase more and more top quality personal care products every year.
- *Is it stable?* As these Baby Boomers move through the age wave, they will continue to demand high quality anti-aging products. This trend is expected to last for the next thirty years or more.

It may be of interest to know that personal care products designed exclusively for men are now hot sellers and one of the fastest growing trends in the world. With thousands of Baby Boomer men turning fifty every day, it may not surprise you to be standing in line at the supermarket and see men purchasing exotic lotions, expensive shampoo, hair treatment, and even skin care products. Twenty years ago, men's personal care products consisted of a bottle of dandruff shampoo and soap on a rope. Try taking a look into the showers and bathroom cabinets of men today, and you might be surprised how many products you'll find.

It's clear to see that the personal care industry is a major contender and it shines in nearly every category. The only concern is in product consumption. As mentioned previously, the consumable criterion should count for two to three times more points than the others, so this is a major issue to consider. Most people consider personal care a great secondary industry and a compliment to an already existing line of popular products.

Household consumables

Let's examine household consumables, like soaps, detergent, toilet paper, and light bulbs.

- *Is it emotional?* Not really. There are ways to make some of these products a bit more emotional with an environmental focus. I would highly recommend pushing the green play for those looking to get involved in this industry.
- *Is it consumable?* Yes, highly!
- *Is it unique?* Not so much. Some will have different scents, shapes, and textures, but they're usually quite similar.
- *Is it traditional?* Absolutely. One of the most traditional industries around.
- *Is it valuable?* Could be, it just depends on pricing. Sometimes household consumables can be outrageously overpriced, and even if they're superior products, this can affect the overall value to the consumer.
- *Is it timely?* This is a bit hard to measure. You might call household consumables a commodity type industry, although great efforts are given to make each product a little different than the competition. These products will simply increase in demand as population increases, but there is no current trend towards home products that would imply any kind industry explosion.
- *Is it stable?* This industry is steady and stable. Not exciting, but very consistent.

Consumers are getting more and more particular about household brands, based upon an increase in awareness. The Internet is not only giving people access to more knowledge and information, but it is helping the consumer to make informed decisions. For the first time ever, we are considering the emotional, ethical, and environmental implications of how we spend our money. I know of thousands of individuals and families who are purchasing detergents that are two to three times more expensive than average, based on the fact that these detergents don't harm the environment. I know other individuals who understand that their money is going to a corporation that supports their favorite cause or even political belief. Still others are simply using the brand their mother used, and they have an emotional attachment to the brand because of that connection.

Another reason consumers purchase brands regardless of price is based upon what trend expert Faith Popcorn calls "small indulgences." As financial pressures press down on consumers, they are compelled to indulge in smaller, less expensive luxuries (expensive sheets, soft toilet paper, high-quality ice cream, etc.) since they are forced to abandon the greater luxuries (cars, homes, vacations). This trend, driven by the Baby Boomers and multiplied by our current economy, is forcing manufacturers to consider quality along with affordability. Price is not the only issue anymore.

Overall, household consumables have great potential, but currently there are several strikes against this industry. Emotional appeal is the only criterion that scored really low, but there are issues in four of the other criteria that can affect the overall demand on this industry. Household consumables are a great compliment to other high-demand industries.

Nutritional supplements

Now let's consider one last product industry, and then I'll have you do the rest on your own. Some distributors have expressed a concern that they feel the nutritional industry is saturated and there is no room for new companies. Nothing could be further from the truth. After in-depth research into product industries, I found the nutritional supplements industry to not only be alive and well within network marketing, but it is also thriving outside of the industry. Anything dealing with health, nutrition, or weight management is on the rise. It is the opinion of many top network marketing professionals that there are still not enough top nutritional companies on the market to take advantage of this phenomenal growth. Economist Paul Zane Pilzer, author of *The Next Trillion*, claims that the next trillion-dollar industry will be the wellness industry, and much of the growth in this market segment will be driven by the direct sales/network marketing industry.

- *Is it emotional?* Consider a product that helps you with your health and wellness. Nothing could be more emotional. Anyone who has a significant result from using the product will be attached for life, and they'll shout their praise from the rooftops.
- *Is it consumable?* Nutritional products are probably one of the most consumable products in network marketing. Nutritional supplements are used up and replaced on a monthly, weekly, and sometimes even daily basis.
- *Is it unique?* Nutritional supplements are made unique through exclusive ingredients, exclusive formulators, a unique story, one-of-a-kind packaging, and special features. The degree of uniqueness varies from brand to brand.
- *Is it traditional?* It is one of the most traditional products sold through direct marketing.
- *Is it valuable?* What price tag can you put on your health? Nutrition comes in at number one in value to consumer.
- *Is it timely?* The Baby Boomers will spend any amount of money to feel more energy, avoid or relieve pain, or prevent aging and disease. Baby Boomers want supplements big time.
- *Is it stable?* As these Baby Boomers move through the age wave, they will continue to demand high-quality health and anti-aging products. This trend is expected to last for the next thirty years or more.

You may now be able to understand why it is important to put every product industry to the test before investing your time, energy, and money. You need to be able to predict whether or not a product industry has good potential or bad. Make sure you put all industries to the big seven test. The more frequently you can answer yes to the seven questions, the better chances you have for success with a given industry. The number one rated industry got a big fat yes in every single category.

Top One Hundred Companies Snapshot

Before I updated my study, I took a bird's eye view snapshot of the industry. I generated a list of the top one hundred most successful and popular network marketing companies in existence today. These companies represent over 90 percent of the product volume and profits flowing through network marketing. Companies qualified to be on the list through annual sales volume, longevity, total number of distributors, good press, and solid marketing. For fun, I broke these companies down by industry. The results are very interesting.

I found that seventy-five out of these one hundred companies were primarily marketing nutritional supplements, although about one third of these companies also had personal care products in their line as a secondary focus. Only nine of these companies lead with personal care product and/or cosmetics, while three focused on household consumables, two were telecom companies, and two focused on financial services. Not only is nutrition still the king of the hill, but compared to previous editions of this book, nutrition is actually gaining ground in overall sales and retention while all of the rest of these industries have fallen back substantially.

Top One Hundred Companies Snapshot Study—Primary or Core Product Line

- 75% Nutritional Supplements (34% of these companies also have personal care as a secondary focus)
- 9% Personal Care/Cosmetics (43% of all companies reviewed had nutritional products as a complimentary line)
- 3% Household Products (as a flagship)
- 2% Telecomm/Cell Phone/VOIP
- 2% Financial Services
- 9% Other

The Final Score

Based on a review of the above criteria, here is a list of industries ranked in order of profitability, stability, and long-term growth potential.

The A List: Top network marketing product industries
- Nutritional Supplements and Health Products

- Personal Care Products (Skin Care, Hair Care, Body Care)

The B List: Other popular, less profitable, less stable industries
- Household Products (if products are very unique and environmentally friendly)

The C List: Alternative MLM industries with some exposure and appeal, but not yet proven over the long term in more than one company.
- Telecommunications (residential and commercial long distance, cell phones, VOIP)
- Financial Programs (financial planning, debt elimination, investments, asset protection)
- Travel and Vacation Programs
- Legal Services (identity protection, pre-paid legal services, wills)
- Buying Clubs and Catalog Shopping
- Greeting Cards/Gifts
- Video Email/Online Video Advertising
- Internet Advertising

The D List: Industries with extremely limited exposure in network marketing
- Computer Hardware and Software*
- Internet Access and Services (hosting, broadband, websites)*
- Books, Reports, Newsletters, and Publications
- Water and Air Filters
- Buying Clubs and Catalog Shopping*
- Lead Generation Programs
- Jewelry, Gold, Silver, and Collectibles
- Satellites (Hardware and Service)
- Automobile and Auto-Care Products
- Home and Personal Security Products
- Electronics and Appliances
- Grocery and Coupon Programs
- Information Services*
- Clothing, Fashions, and Lingerie

*Up-and-coming industries with future potential, yet absolutely not proven in today's market

Conclusion

In his book *The Ideal Business*, network marketing researcher and author Rod Nichols makes it crystal clear. "Historically, the best products have been nutritional supplements and skin care. They are the most highly consumable and also fit the growing needs of the Baby Boom generation."[5] All of our research points to the health and wellness industry as the top profit industry of this century, literally dominating the direct sales/network marketing landscape. Personal care products are usually a secondary line of products within companies that primarily distribute nutritional products.

No one is following the health trend closer than economist and best-selling author Paul Zane Pilzer, author of *The Wellness Revolution*. In Pilzer's book, he states, "If Baby Boomers are spending all this money on things that simply remind them of when they were young, think of how much these boomers will soon spend on wellness products and services that actually make them young or slow the effects of aging. It's easy to see why boomers are about to add an additional $1 trillion to our economy as they seek to preserve what they hold dearest ... Over the next ten years alone, boomers will increase their spending on existing wellness-based services from approximately $200 billion to $1 trillion or more."[6]

Faith Popcorn, trend analyst and best-selling author, has an interesting comment on this topic. She states, "Watch the entire food industry change. Food, prescribed in doses, will be preventive medicine. 'Foodaceuticals' will blur the edges between drug therapy and nutrition; daily-dose soups or drinks will give you prescribed doses of anti-oxidant beta-carotenes, or therapeutic doses of anti-disease nutritives, or even mood-enhancers." [7]

I've included the previous quotes as to not appear bias on this subject. But if you're not convinced, there's no need to take my word on this. Simply seek out the economic experts' opinions on this subject as you make your final choice and I'm convinced that you'll come to the same conclusion.

Chapter Five Review

1. Virtually any product or service can be offered through network marketing. The possibilities are endless. However, most of these industries are not viable and will leave you with disappointing results.

2. Profitability in services will change in the future, but it hasn't yet. Most services and intangible product businesses are characterized by quick growth for two to three years before they go out of business or experience a major dip in sales. Your first step in choosing the most profitable network marketing program is to eliminate services from your list of considerations.

3. Although the home party plan is a viable home business option, I don't recommend it to my network marketing clients unless it's one of the very small number of companies that behave more like a traditional network marketing compensation plan.

4. Network marketing support companies consist of companies who offer products and services designed to support other network marketing companies, like lead generation programs, website systems, social media marketing and advertising, and phone support programs. These programs are highly volatile and should be avoided.

5. Avoid any product industry involving gasoline, satellite TV, gold coins, CD/DVDs movies or music, sporting goods, vacuum cleaners, home appliances, electronics, search engines, gas, water and sewer, cigarettes, or any other industry that has never been successful in network marketing. Focus on proven industries only.

6. Products marketed through MLM must be unique and exclusive to one company. Commodities are too common and uniform to be considered viable MLM products. Examples of commodities might be oil, electricity, grains (like wheat and barley), metals, pork bellies, orange juice, computer chips, and even bandwidth. Also avoid utilities like electricity, water, gas, sewer, and phone service.

7. Avoid gold and silver programs. No gold coin program has ever survived as a network marketing product. Not only do gold and silver have all the problems of other commodities, but the SEC regulates them. Distributors can easily violate the laws of the

SEC while promoting these products, without even knowing the violations.

8. To become a successful network marketer, you must learn how to pick a successful product. There are many reasons for selecting one product over another. However, you must take the focus off of you and your needs, and learn how to select products and services that benefit as many other people as possible. Market to the masses.

9. Success leaves clues! Learn how to study successful business models and take notes on how they do business. Through this process, you will be able to determine what the marketplace is demanding today and what it is not.

10. There are seven fundamental characteristics that must be considered when choosing a long-term wealth-generating product or service. I call them *Daren's Seven Secrets*. A product must be:
    a. Emotional: The product or service must induce a positive mental or physical change that results in an emotional attachment to that brand.
    b. Consumable: The product or service must be regularly used up and replaced on a monthly, weekly, or even daily basis.
    c. Unique: The product or service you're marketing must have a unique twist, something that the competition doesn't have or can't get.
    d. Traditional: Although the product must be unique in some way, it cannot be too uncommon. It must be similar to other products on the market that have been sold for years and years.
    e. Valuable: The product or service must be worth its price ... and maybe more!
    f. Timely: The product or service must be in high demand *right now*.
    g. Stable: The product or service *must* be in high demand *later*. Take a look twenty years into the future. Will the product or service still be in high demand? If the answer is yes, you have a winner.

11. The product industry A List includes nutritional supplements and health products as well as personal care products, such as skin care, hair care, and body care products.

12. Selecting the right product industry is absolutely critical. This is one of the most important decisions of your career and it should not be taken lightly. Don't settle for a company that does not match the criteria for "best product industry." Don't be hasty; review this chapter again carefully, and then make the right choice.

PART IV

Looking at the Numbers

I don't offer any apologies for spending a lot of time and energy on choosing a product industry. These initial chapters are essential to your success. But now we're getting into the meat and potatoes. In the next two chapters, we'll be looking at historical statistics and trends, to make predictions about the present and future of network marketing. The focus will be on deciding when in a company's lifecycle to jump onboard, and we'll look at the different ways to get compensated in network marketing. This information was drawn from the experiences of top network marketing leaders and consultants over the past fifty years, and it was collected and compiled over the last twelve years. Don't rush through the information. Read it over and over until it sinks in. Remember, even if you take a few days or a few weeks to absorb this material, you'll still save critical time, energy, and money that you would have spent doing this on your own.

Chapter 6

Key #3
Timing: When to
Join a Company

*"To everything there is a season,
and a time for every purpose under the heaven."*
-Ecclesiastes 3:1[8]

It's clear that the prophets of the Old Testament understood the power of proper timing, as did the Greeks. In ancient Greece, time was differentiated in terms of *chronos* and *kairos*. Chronos relates to the progression of time, while kairos refers to the opportune moment or correct time for something to happen.

In this chapter I'll be encouraging you to discover the chronos in each MLM company so you can learn how to identify the kairos and join a company at the right moment in time to maximize your distributorship opportunity. We'll learn about network marketing company lifecycles and the seasons of these lifecycles. I'll discuss the best strategy for deciding when to join, and I'll also warn distributors when not to join.

Catchin' the Big Kahuna

First, allow me to share a personal story that will illustrate the importance of waiting for the right time to join any top company. Several years ago, my wife Sandy and I earned a free vacation to the island of Maui, in Hawaii, through our network marketing company. On our shuttle ride to the hotel, we made friends with Tom and Kristen, a very pleasant couple from Colorado on their way to the same hotel. After a few days of company activities and sightseeing, we got together with our new friends. Tom and I decided we wanted to explore the surf, so we left the women to their shopping. We grabbed our sun block and towels and headed for the beach to enjoy a few hours of body boarding in the warm, turbulent surf near our hotel on Maui's west coast.

While checking out our body boards, a hotel representative informed us that we would be swimming at our own risk as the waves had increased overnight to ten-foot swells. "Kowabunga," I shouted (I still don't know what it means but it seemed appropriate at the time) with elation as we scurried out into the surf and literally exhausted ourselves playing in God's natural water park. These were some large waves! Not enough to kill us (we thought), but definitely enough to maim. "Bring it on," rang our battle cry.

After about twenty minutes of frolicking, we finally got the hang of it. You see, if we waited for the perfect wave, and hit that wave at the perfect time with the right technique, the wave would lift us off our feet, launch us toward the beach, and thrust us forward and downward in a series of three powerful cascading rushes of water, much like a rollercoaster ride. Then the wave would push us up the shore and park us gently at the top of the beach, where we would relax in the sand for a moment, enjoying the nice warm sun. Then we'd suddenly hop up, run back out into the surf, and start the process all over again.

Missing the wave

That, of course, was a description of the ideal experience. You see, it didn't always work out that way. Sometimes things would not go according to our plans. Sometimes we picked the wrong wave to catch, and then, even if we timed it perfectly, our time and efforts really didn't amount to much. If we caught a great wave too late, we simply missed out on the thrill ride and were forced to watch as fellow boarders pulled away from us to enjoy the ride.

But, the worst case was picking the right wave too early. My first experience of catching the big kahuna too early started off pleasant enough. First, I simply felt my feet pull out from under me, and I enjoyed the dreamy sense of weightlessness. Of course, I could tell I was no longer facing up; I could feel myself rolling with the wave, and the sun's rays kept passing by, over and over again, as if I were tumbling in a washing machine. Then it happened, that rude awakening of being smashed headfirst into the beach, the force of the wave driving my ear and the right side of my face into the sand. Then the powerful momentum of the wave flopped my body around like a rag doll, and then rolled me sideways up the beach. I gasped for air only to get a mouthful of salt water.

As my world came slowly to a halt, I found myself thinking, *That was fun. I wonder if there's a chiropractor on the beach today.* After what seemed like a few minutes, I started to get my bearings and decided to try to see if I could move my extremities. I wanted to see if I'd be in a wheelchair for the rest of my life, or just for today. Just then the second wave smashed into me with enough force to roll me a few feet further up the beach. But then, something really unexpected happened. I got caught in the undertow of that wave and it rolled me back down into the surf only to be thrashed by a third wave which rolled me up ... and then back down ... and then wave number four hit. I was like a surf yo-yo. I was actually laughing out loud at this point, because there was nothing else to do, all the while taking in more seawater with every chuckle. I must have looked totally ridiculous. I finally managed to crawl up the beach on all fours, far enough away from the undertow that I could rest and thank the Lord for his tender mercies, sparing my life yet again.

Will we ever learn?

Now I don't want you to think me unwise, but no more than three minutes had passed before I was back in the surf, waiting for the next perfect wave. We spent hours out there, risking paralysis, sunburn, shark attack—hey, it's just part of the game. After a while, Tom and I actually got really good at catching the right waves almost every time, and we even learned how to avoid the beatings. I can't wait to go back and play some more. Sure, we finished the day with some bumps and bruises, but all we remembered and talked about later were those perfect rides.

I live for catching the wave! To me, it's not about becoming a millionaire, it's not about the recognition, and it's not about the lifestyle; it's simply about the ride! Who wants to play in the kiddy pool when you have the opportunity to swim in the ocean and ride the big one?

I live for catching the wave! To me, it's not about becoming a millionaire, it's not about the recognition, and it's not about the lifestyle; it's simply about the ride!"

The New Real Estate?

For decades the commercial real estate market has been cycling up and down throughout the country and throughout the world. Financial experts are often asked, "What is the most important factor in selecting a valuable commercial real estate deal?" Many experts still agree that the three most important keys to real estate success are *location, location, location.* Acquire a high-traffic, convenient, and functional location for a business, and it's tough to lose.

Today, as we enter the twenty-first century, financial experts are realizing trends have changed. Real estate is cycling again, the stock market is unpredictable, and big companies are downsizing. Network marketing is being called the real estate of the twenty-first century by many top MLM earners who've make money in both industries. In fact, two of my current business partners who have made tens of millions of dollars in real estate, have walked away from their full-time focus on real estate and are now involved in network marketing full-time. Since they're now focused on network marketing, they're no longer preoccupied with location. In fact, the key to exponential profits in network marketing is not location, but "timing, timing, and timing!"

When to Join

Although timing could not be better for network marketing as an industry, especially in an unpredictable economy, every network marketing company in existence has its own time line, or its own wave. In other words, although it may be an excellent time to become associated with the network marketing industry, it may or may not be a good time to join a particular company. So if timing is so critical, when is the best time to get involved? Should you join a company immediately after it launches, or should you wait? If you wait, how long should you wait? How late is too late? I will attempt to answer these questions in this chapter.

SUCCESS Magazine *on Timing*

I was first exposed to the concept of selecting the right time to enter a network marketing venture when I read an article that appeared in the June 1993 issue of *SUCCESS Magazine* (yes, I've been around the industry for a while). This article, written by Richard Poe, author of *Wave 3: The New Era in Network Marketing*, was entitled "The Curve of

116

Prosperity" and quickly became one of the most popular references among serious network marketers. I remember practicing blatant plagiarism by making hundreds of copies of this article and passing them out to people I came into contact with to get their opinions.

In the article, Mr. Poe interviewed Charles King, a Harvard Business School PhD and professor of business and marketing at the University of Illinois at Chicago. Dr. King diagramed the growth stages of successful network marketing companies. According to Dr. King, a company goes through several major growth phases as it matures into a stable, long-term opportunity. The first growth stage is known as *the formulation stage.* This is the start-up phase when companies are most vulnerable and over 90 percent go out of business within twelve to twenty-four months. The second phase of growth is referred to as the concentration phase. During concentration, the company is getting its ducks in a row and working out the bugs. This usually lasts a couple of years, but can be much longer or much shorter. Similar to the formulation phase, the concentration phase is still considered a start-up phase, and it is a risky time to get involved. Most network marketing experts refer to a company's start-up phase as the pioneering phase.

Burke Hedges, the well-known network marketing author and trainer, comments about the pioneering phase in his best-selling book, *Who Stole The American Dream?* Hedges says: "You could call the foundation phase the pioneering years. The business is just getting started and the general public doesn't understand what you're doing because it's 'new' and 'unproven.' The pioneering years are tough. Lots of rejection … lots of ups and downs while the foundation is being laid. These are the high-risk years. It's like the pioneers who settled the West. Because they were the first ones to open up the frontier, they had the first shot at the best land. But they were also the ones who got the arrows in their backs!"[9]

As I mentioned before, start-up companies are very risky. Most MLM experts agree that the risk-to-reward ratio is still too large to consider getting involved during this phase. Corey Augenstein, owner of mlminsider.com, counsels network marketing distributors to avoid start-up companies, reasoning that distributors should never have to pay for a new company's learning curve. On the upside, getting involved in the pioneering phase can be very profitable if the company is able to overcome the over-90-percent failure rate and go on to become a top company. Being a founding distributor has its merits if the company can survive. By understanding what it takes to build a long term MLM company, experienced distributors are better able to choose a company earlier and thus take advantage of being a "founding distributor" or at least be in early. Most distributors do not have the knowledge and experience to make this choice and I advise them to wait.

Ground floor opportunity hype

The term *ground floor opportunity* is possibly the most overused and misunderstood business start-up analogy in the world. So what does it mean? Picture the birth of a huge skyscraper, the kind of building that literally touches the clouds. It could be as high as eighty, ninety, even one hundred stories or more. Have you ever driven by a construction project where the construction crews are just breaking ground on a new skyscraper? I have. I've driven by the site for weeks and weeks, peering down into a massive hole in the ground. It seemed as if the builders would never emerge from the abyss. Then, all of a sudden, the crew reaches the ground floor. Everything above ground zero is what we see, and everything else is below ground. Have you ever noticed how fast a building goes up once it reaches ground zero? That's why it seems like these enormous buildings are created overnight. But this mega-growth would not have been possible without all of the planning, preparation, and massive effort that go into building a solid foundation below ground. Everything depends on this solid foundation.

This is why the term *ground floor* is so commonly used in business. It perfectly illustrates the most opportunistic time to get involved with a major venture. If you join a business opportunity after the foundational work is complete, just as the business is swinging into its momentum phase, you can enjoy all the benefits of growth without the hassles, delays, and complications of the pioneering phase. The reason the term has become an industry joke, is that it is used by every company to promote their business as a momentum company, even if that company doesn't have  anything that resembles momentum growth. So here's a very important principle you must memorize and recite from time to time in order to save you years of grief and potentially tens of thousands of dollars. The principle states, "Most ground floor opportunities will leave you for dead in the basement." This theory has been proven time and time again.

Don't be lured into the dark crevasse of ground floor hype. Carefully study this book to determine when to move on a new opportunity. Rather than lose you in the cold and dreary basement of regret, I'd prefer to shake your hand in the penthouse, atop the tower of financial freedom. This book will help you avoid the hazards that may otherwise prevent you from reaching the summit.

Momentum phase

> *"There is a tide in the affairs of men,*
> *Which, taken at the flood, leads on to fortune;*
> *Omitted, all the voyage of their life*
> *Is bound in shallows and in miseries.*
> *On such a full sea are we now afloat;*
> *And we must take the current when it serves,*
> *Or lose our ventures."*[10]
> -William Shakespeare

If and when a company surpasses around $10-20 million in annual sales and sales seem to be escalating upward, the company often experiences a phenomenon known as *critical mass*. *Critical mass* means the products have gained popular acceptance, and they become market driven.

Critical mass is a real phenomenon, and it will occur with only the best companies. This critical mass marks the beginning of the company's momentum growth phase. During this momentum growth, if the foundation work has been good, a company can go from obscurity to becoming a household name within five to twenty years.

Burke Hedges shares this analogy in *Who Stole The American Dream?*: "It's like someone pushes a cultural button, and 'voila'... everybody wants what you've got. When critical mass hits, growth goes into overdrive ... and sales begin to explode!"[11]

444

Stability phase

The last stage of a company's growth is the stability or maturity phase. This is a great time to have a large downline (or sales force), but a tough time to build one. The company is so well-known that distributors must be more skilled at handing the objections that prospects might have to joining the business or using the company's products, and many prospects will have already been approached several times. Growth in the stability phase is significant, but slower. However, based on recent studies, it is clear that many companies have learned how to maintain healthy growth during the stability phase.

There are several ways companies have managed to stay viable in the stability phase. They can continue to diversify the product line, introduce new marketing programs, and develop educational clinics, seminars, and trainings that focus on the product or service offered by that company. Sometimes companies will go through second, third, and fourth momentum cycles as a result of this type of innovative marketing. NuSkin is an excellent example of a company that has continued to diversify and spark new momentum growth with exciting new product launches and new divisions. Also, entering new international markets every year can keep a company profitable for decades. When a mature company expands into a new country, this creates a true ground floor opportunity, without the risk associated with start-up programs.

Daren's Timing Strategy

So how can we spot a momentum company? How can we discover the best time to join? I've developed a strategy that seems to work, is most cases, to help identify the best time to get involved in a company's growth cycle. Again, I'm trying to help distributors avoid the risky and painful years of pioneering, and join a company during the momentum phase. There's so much more to gain by joining during momentum, yet you're really not giving up much by getting involved earlier. There are a lot of MLM junkies out there that would disagree with me, but their track records speak for themselves.

Again, as a consultant to career oriented network marketers, I'm compelled to share with you the mathematical formula that I use when selecting network marketing companies. This is a formula designed to identify what I call the *major league* companies of network marketing. You see, if you want to experience a much larger momentum cycle that

lasts much longer than most companies, you must seek out a major
league company. There aren't even two dozen major league companies
in existence today in network marketing. Major league companies have
billion dollar potential. I only recommend major league companies to
my clients, or companies that have the potential to become major
league companies. Professional network marketers should keep in mind
that they can be among the top 200 distributorship in a major league
company and earn a larger check than a top 20 distributors in a minor
league company.

Here's a breakdown of the different phases of growth in a company's
momentum lifecycle.

Major League Company Momentum Cycle

Phase of Growth	Annual Sales	Good Time to Start?
1. Pioneering	$0–5 million	Almost Certain Failure
2. Concentration	$5–10 million	Proving Grounds-Scrutiny Required
3. Pre-Momentum	$10–20 million	Still Risky/High Opportunity
4. Momentum	$20–100 million	Great Time to Join/Build
5. Advanced Mo.	$100 - $500 million	Take Massive Action
6. Stability	$500 mil –2 bil	Continue to Build
7. Maturity	$2 billion +	Maintain and Enjoy For Life

Now the difference between the major leagues and the minor leagues in
network marketing can be similar to the differences between the
majors and the minors in baseball. There is a huge contrast. Everything
from earnings potential, to recognition, to perks and benefits. On the
other hand, there can be less pressure, and not as much expectation
required of minor leaguers and the federal regulators tend to leave
them alone. There is opportunity for you, but at an entirely different
level. If you're willing to settle for much less, you might be happy
playing in the minors.

Minor league companies are characterized by an early growth
plateau. They usually don't make it past $100-$200 million in annual
sales before they start flattening out. They'll start peaking when major
league companies are still ramping up for momentum. If you'd prefer to
be the big fish in a smaller pond, and stay under the regulator radar, a
minor league company may be the right fit.

Minor League Company Momentum Cycle

Phase of Growth	Annual Sales	Good Time to Start?
1. Pioneering	$0–2 million	Almost Certain Failure
2. Concentration	$2–5 million	Slim Chance of success
3. Pre-Momentum	$5–10 million	Serious Scrutiny Required
4. Momentum	$10–20 million	Great Time to Join/Build
4. Advanced Momentum	$20–50 million	Take Massive Action
5. Advanced Momentum	$50 million +	Continue to Build

*Minor League Companies Generally Don't Exceed $200 Million in Annual Sales

Little League Companies

Another kind of company that I won't spend much time on in this book is the little league companies. These are companies that manage to survive in network marketing, and continue to plug along for years, but never seem to establish any kind of major momentum growth. They're usually doing less than $10-$20 million per year, and they tend to remain flat, or they grow by a few million dollars per year at the most. The industry is full of such companies and many of them are fantastic. They're usually family run companies with smaller, but very loyal distributors.

The $200 million wall

There's a trend that I have identified in network marketing that is very common among new companies that are aspiring to be major players. I call it the $200 million wall. If a company shows promising results by bursting into pre-momentum with substantial sales and growth, it can be very tempting to join the opportunity. However, most companies I have studied that made it to the Pre-Momentum phase experienced a plateau in sales somewhere slightly before or after the $100-200 million mark. What is causing this phenomenon? Is it lack of financing? Is it changes to the compensation plan? Could it have something to do with the product line? All of these criteria, in part or in whole, can be causes for this stall. However, I've found in most situations that the root cause of this lull can be attributed to the leadership of the company. A $200 million company is a large and substantial operation. There are so many decisions to make when a company reaches this level of success. Corporate leaders are spinning a lot of plates and juggling many responsibilities, which are critical to future growth. Just one bad choice can stall the company indefinitely. Companies with experienced management that think and act like they're running a billion-dollar operation tend to have the resources and leadership skills to hop over the $200 million wall and keep growing against all odds.

Some companies will eventually learn how to climb over the $200 million dollar wall and keep growing. Others get stuck and plateau at or around this level for years. Many companies will hit a certain level of sales, plateau, and start spiraling downward. This is just something to keep in mind as you're building your distributorship.

In some rare cases, based on the knowledge gained about a company through hours of advanced scrutiny, you may decide to get involved earlier or later than these recommended phases of growth. I admit that I have chosen an opportunity during the stability phase, and it was a good choice at the time. I also took a chance on a pre-momentum company that survived and thrived in later years. However, for every time I've taken a big risk and had success, I've also failed two to three times in each phase of growth. Here's the key principle to always keep in mind: if a company is good today, it should be *great* tomorrow. Selecting a pre-launch or start-up company can be risky. If you find yourself in a cycle where you keep selecting start-up companies and you continue to have difficulties with these companies, it's time to break this cycle by learning how to wait and watch before getting involved. Use the lifecycle chart to help you decide the ideal time to get started.

I've met a few professional MLM distributors in my life who had the ability to pick winning vehicles from the start every single time. This is an amazing gift and can be very profitable. If you know someone with a solid track record of selecting winning companies, it might be profitable for you to keep an eye on their every move. But don't assume that you have all the pieces to the puzzle. It's generally always better to miss out on a little of the early momentum growth than to run the risk of going out of business. It can also be frustrating to be a distributor during the start-up phase because there can be hiccups in the system, delays in products or in checks, computer glitches, shipping glitches, and many other complications. Don't be frustrated if you chose a company early and are now forced to put up with inconveniences during the first two years.

Don't Be Fooled By These!

Here are three of the most common statements you'll hear from people regarding the timing of their opportunity.

Statement: We're just entering the momentum phase!

Truth: Every company claims to be entering the momentum phase, no matter if they're brand-new or forty years old. They're either lying about their momentum, stretching the truth, or don't really know what the momentum phase is. Don't take anyone's word for it. If you want to review the true nature of momentum, go back to the beginning of this chapter and study it carefully.

Statement: Our company is ground floor.

Truth: This statement is so overused, and so often misused, that it no longer has any meaning. Just keep in mind that most companies that claim to be ground floor will leave you for dead in the basement. I advise my clients to wait at least two to four years before joining a company, if not longer. If a company is a great company this year, it will still be a great company next year. Sometimes it takes longer to determine if they'll be successful long-term. Joining a start-up is usually the kiss of death.

Statement: Our company is in pre-launch ... better than ground floor!

Truth: Sometimes a company will do what is called a *pre-launch* and start signing on distributors and sending out product. One purpose for doing this is to test the company's systems with real-time activity (good idea). However, there are other reasons for pre-launch that can be major red flags. Sometimes companies can't afford to launch officially with their own financing, so they get assistance from their own distributors. They'll use money from sign-up fees or initial investments in large quantities of product to finance the start-up of the company (bad idea). And finally, many companies use this as a gimmick to make their numbers look better. They stay in pre-launch for their first two years of business. Then, when they officially launch, they say, "We generated one million dollars in revenue in our first month of business," when in fact they had already been in business for twenty-four months. It's a classic example of the smoke and mirrors tactics that low-integrity people use to try to compete with the larger companies. My advice is to never, never, never join a pre-launch company. Having read this book, if you join a pre-launch company and your company goes out of business, you'll have no one to blame but yourself.

Now a "pre-enrollment" phase is different. Pre-enrollment is simply a period of a few weeks where you can place people into the system in a pre-signup situation. No credit cards are drafted and no commission checks are cut. It's just a time to fill the matrix with a few hundred or a few thousands eager beavers. If a company opens up a pre-enrollment phase, they must be capable of dealing with the potential explosion of product sales, or the potential lack thereof.

Conclusion

Experts agree that selecting a company in any start-up phase is risky. Although there are some terrific rewards associated with being one of the founding distributors in a network marketing company, the risks seem to outweigh the rewards. Leave the start-up phase to professional network marketers, risk taking entrepreneurs, and those who have nothing to lose. Selecting a company in the momentum phase can bring the same exciting growth, but at this point the risk is significantly reduced. Regardless of when you join, an entrepreneur's primary concern is selecting a company that has long-term stability, not short-term flash-in-the-pan profits.

Selecting a company in the stability phase is a much more inviting option than it once was as we proceed further into the twenty-first century. More companies and distributors understand the principles of dynamic marketing and can generally maintain healthy growth for decades. Once a company has been established in a country for twenty years or more, it may be more difficult to recruit new distributors in that country based on everyone's familiarity with the program, but it's still a viable opportunity. I've seen many distributors become top leaders in a mature company within twenty-four months. If you choose the right program, building during the stability phase can be effective, but there is still no better time to build a network marketing business than during the hyper-growth momentum phase.

And finally, the most important momentum in your company is the momentum you make. I've known hundreds of people whose companies experienced incredible momentum growth, yet these individuals didn't take advantage of that growth and missed out on the opportunity of a lifetime. I've also known people who have joined companies in the advanced stages of stability or maturity that have created their own momentum within their company and have launched themselves to the top of their pay plan. Ultimately, the most important momentum is the momentum that you create yourself as an independent distributor. To achieve this, all you need is a stable company, and the heart of a lion, and you're on your way to the top.

Special note on timing

Please remember the only timing factors I have discussed in this chapter relate to timing in selecting a company during a specific growth phase. I also briefly mentioned industry timing and indicated that the MLM industry is currently entering its momentum phase. Another important consideration includes the timing of the product industry with which you are associated. This topic was thoroughly covered in the previous chapter and should not be overlooked. Is your product industry on an upswing? Do current events, news, word-of-mouth opinion, and current market conditions indicate a long-term increase in sales? Is the industry you are marketing in its momentum phase? How about timing in your own life? You may be convinced that network marketing is your destiny. However, if the timing in your life is wrong, you may be setting yourself up for a struggle that has nothing to do with the viability of the MLM industry or the company you choose. There are many timing issues to think about. Consider them all before making your ultimate choice.

Chapter Six Review

1. The key to exponential profits in network marketing is not location, but timing, timing, and timing! Although timing could not be better for network marketing as an industry, every network marketing company in existence has its own time line, or its own wave. Although it may be an excellent time to associate with the network marketing industry, it may or may not be a good time to join a particular company.

2. Most companies that claim to be ground floor will leave you for dead in the basement. I advise my clients to wait at least two to four years before joining a company if not longer. If a company is a great company this year, it will still be a great company next year, and the year after. Joining a start-up is a high risk option and I only advise doing so if you're a professional network marketer with advanced experience.

3. If and when a company reaches around $20-100 million in annual sales, the company usually experiences a phenomenon known as *critical mass*. This critical mass marks the beginning of the company's momentum growth phase. During momentum growth, if the company's foundation is built to last, a company can go from obscurity to renown in five to twenty years.

4. The last stage of a company's growth is the stability or maturity phase. This is a great time to have a large downline but a more challenging time to build one. The company is so well-known, distributors must be more skilled at handing objections, and many prospects will have already been approached several times. Growth in the stability phase is significant, and your business in more stable.

5. Nearly all company spokespersons claim their company is entering the momentum phase whether they're brand-new or even forty years old. These people are either lying about their momentum, stretching the truth to the extreme, or they don't really know what *momentum phase* means. Don't take anyone's word for it. Do your own research or ask an objective, reliable authority.

6. There are many reasons why a company will do a pre-launch, and they're all bad. This is the worst time to join a company. If the company is great, they'll still be great for years to come. Avoid the pre-launch phase unless you're a professional network marketer and you've done advance scrutiny on the company and its founders.

7. As a consultant, I recommend only major league companies to clients looking for the best network marketing companies. These are companies that have billion dollar potential.

8. Some modern companies with experienced management, solid financing, and an undying focus on branding have literally skipped the start-up phase and gone straight into momentum. These companies are rare and worth investigating with diligence.

Chapter 7

Key #4
Compensation: How to
Scrutinize a Pay Plan

What is a MLM Compensation Plan?

As I write content for the network marketing industry, I often forget that a large percentage of my readers do not have any experience with or knowledge of the network marketing model. For clarification, I first want to review the basics of network marketing compensation plans and how they work. Network marketing incorporates a system of paying independent distributors not as employees of a company, but as independent sales agents. All MLM distributors are paid commissions on the products they personally sell, and on the products their sales force (or downline) sells. The formula for paying distributors is commonly referred to as a network marketing compensation plan or pay plan.

  Distributors earn commissions when they purchase product wholesale and sell it retail. They also earn commissions on any products purchased by or sold by distributors they "sponsor" into the business. These are called bonuses. To sponsor a new distributor simply means that you're the one responsible for introducing that person to the distributorship. There are usually special bonuses and recognition associated with the sponsorship of new distributors. As you accumulate more distributors, generally you will produce a larger "group sales volume" and with that comes a larger commission check. Ultimately you are paid not just on your own personally sponsored distributors, but on the distributors they sponsor, and on the distributors they sponsor, and so on for multiple generations. The number of generations paid and the percentages paid on each of those generations are determined by the company's compensation plan.

The word upline refers to distributors positioned in the compensation above you including your sponsor, and their sponsor, and so on. The word downline refers to everyone below you - your sales force. Retailing simply refers to the process of selling the company's products or services at a retail price.

As I progress through this chapter, I'll be getting into some deeper concepts that may confuse those new to network marketing. I apologize for this in advance. I wanted to cater some of this chapter to veteran network marketers who are trying to sort out the different nuances of MLM compensation plans. I'm happy to provide training on these ideas to my readers.

Compensation Plans: the Good, the Bad, and the Ugly

When I began investigating networking companies, I found more hype associated with a company's compensation plans than with any other criterion, including product hype (and we all know how out-of-hand product hype can get). The purpose of Chapter Eight is to first identify the various compensation plans used in network marketing today and then share with you the pros and cons of each plan. Now, many of my readers may not agree with everything I have to say in this chapter, especially if they're already involved with a network marketing company with a compensation plan that has some of the unsavory characteristics. But I can assure you that most network marketing consultants and trainers do agree with what I'm reporting. My comments and conclusions are based on years of careful and objective research, not on which companies I'm earning money from at the time of my review.

Which Compensation Plan is the Best?

The four most commonly used pay plans in the network marketing industry are the breakaway, the unilevel, the matrix, and the binary. You may also hear about a hybrid plan from time to time, which is basically a combination of any two or more of the most common plans.

We'll also touch briefly on a few of the gimmick plans such as the two-up plan and the single-line downline plan.

Your job here is to review the following plans and choose the one you feel is the best. But remember, when someone is introducing their pay plan to you, they will say anything to make their plan look better. Many distributors feel their compensation plan is the *best,* regardless of whether or not they have compared it to other plans. Picking the right compensation plan can make the difference between success and failure in network marketing. Learn to look past the hype and the rumors, and concentrate on the facts. I decided to look at all of the plans on the market and then choose the best compensation plan. Here's your opportunity to do the same.

In his masterpiece, *Understanding Multilevel Commission*, Mark Rawlins, a twenty-six-year veteran of the MLM compensation-plan-building business and proprietor of MLM.com, explains that a compensation plan must meet the following three goals: it must generate enthusiasm among distributors, it must encourage distributors to sell product and recruit distributors, and it must retain distributors. Let's take a close look at the most common network marketing compensation structures and we'll find out how we're doing.

The Matrix

The matrix compensation plan started in the 1980s as an answer to some of the traditional compensation plans that were being used at that time. The matrix is everything its name implies. You start with a prearranged numerical matrix similar to an organizational chart for a large corporation. Most compensation plans are designed to allow you to sponsor unlimited numbers of distributors on your first level. With the matrix plan, you can only sponsor a certain number of people on your front line. Also, your front line distributors can only sponsor that same designated number of distributors on their front line. Distributors generally cannot sponsor outside the matrix, and there is a limit to depth. For example, in a 2 x 9 matrix, you sponsor two on your first level, four on your second, eight on your third, sixteen on your fourth, thirty-two on your fifth, sixty-four on your sixth, 128 on your seventh, 256 on your eighth, and 512 on the ninth level (or last level).

Common matrix configurations include:

2 wide x 12 deep
3 wide x 9 deep
4 wide x 7 deep
5 wide x 7 deep
7 wide x 2 deep

In most matrix plans, distributors do not earn commissions past the last pay level in the plan. Most matrix plans pay monthly, with commission checks being deposited around the twentieth of the month following the month in which they earned the commission check. The matrix sometimes incorporates fast-start bonuses, which are special bonuses paid to distributors to give incentive for them to immediately sponsor distributors and retail product. The matrix plan is used by about 4 percent of the companies I reviewed.

Let's take a look at some of the good features of the matrix. In theory, distributors can receive spillover, which means they can have

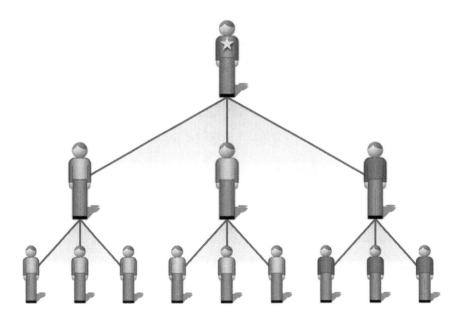

distributors who are sponsored by their upline fall into their downline. This benefits both the sponsor and the respective downline. Because of this spillover theory, the matrix plan looks great on paper and can be exciting to present to prospects. Also, the matrix plan is easier to learn and teach to others.

7x2 MATRIX

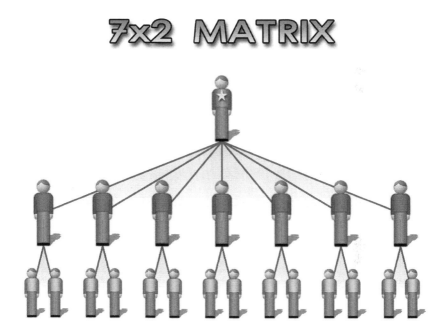

Matrix plans tend to be suited to buying clubs, service companies, Internet affiliate programs, and subscription sales companies that have predetermined monthly costs for the product or service because these programs are generally designed to pay out part-time commissions on fewer levels.

In a matrix plan, distributors typically know how many active distributors they will have to recruit in order to make "x" amount of monthly income. It is also easier to predict income potential on each level with the matrix. For example, a particular matrix plan may claim to pay $5 per person, per level. If you add up all of the possible positions that can be filled in the matrix, you will know exactly how much you can make. For example, in a 2 x 12 matrix, there are exactly 8,190 positions that can be filled. If each position is worth a $5 commission to the distributor, the plan can pay a maximum potential of $40,950 per month.

Now let's look at the bad aspects of the matrix. On paper, compensation plans can look glorious. However, upon reviewing matrix plans in great detail, I discovered that most matrix organizations pay on about 15–20 percent of their "hypothetical" potential at best because not all of the positions in the matrix fill up in real life. Once a matrix is about 20% full, almost all of the new sponsoring activity occurs beyond the distributor's pay levels. Even though his/her organization is growing by leaps and bounds, the distributor receives no compensation on distributors below the maximum pay level.

The forced matrix is a concept that seems to answer the above problem. In a forced matrix, each position on every level must be filled before distributors spill down to the next level. Theoretically, this would allow the distributor to eventually fill every position in the matrix. Unfortunately, due to the nature of the forced matrix plan, the distributor is left to sponsor most of their downline by themselves. In other plans, building a downline is more of a group effort and more emphasis is placed on creating synergy and teamwork. The forced matrix is one of the only plans that reward lazy distributors if they sign up under a dedicated distributor. Since all of the downline positions must be filled, a lazy distributor can essentially sit back and watch his or her downline fill up. If the distributors can succeed without doing anything ... they won't do anything. As resentment and animosity build in the downline, the organization eventually breaks down and everyone ends up losing.

If you establish a successful business and fill up much of your matrix, you will inevitably sponsor a *hot* distributor on your fifteenth, twentieth, or even fiftieth level and beyond. In the matrix, you can miss out on commissions that should be yours but aren't since this hot distributor is beyond your payout levels, making someone else money.

People who promote matrix plans will always try to lure you in with the enticement of spillover. They'll tell you, "If you get in now, you will have hundreds of people spilling into your downline, people you were not responsible for prospecting or recruiting." However, the only time spillover will actually occur is when a dud signs up under a superstar distributor, remains active, but doesn't recruit any distributors. The dud gets all the spillover while the superstar distributor, who works hard, is only rewarded for his or her personal efforts. Don't be fooled by the spillover myth. With limitations on payout levels, it is mathematically impossible to create spillover for more than just a few people among your entire distributor force.

In some non-forced matrix plans, the payout levels are radically different from level to level. For example, a matrix plan might have a heavy payout level (like 30–40 percent) on the third level but a 5 percent payout level on every other level. Distributors might stack other distributors on the first and second level in order to get to this large third level payout sooner than it would naturally occur. This pushes volume and downline past the heavy payout levels and beyond the last payout levels so quickly that potential compensation is jeopardized. Matrix programs with level limitations that encourage any form of stacking should be avoided.

Matrix: Overall evaluation

The matrix plan can be a good plan for certain types of products and services. As a whole, it has not been accepted as a mainstream plan and is commonly utilized by smaller service and support MLMs, like sales lead generation programs and other support MLMs. Also, matrix plans are often being utilized for a new breed of MLM programs, called *affiliate programs*, which can be found frequently on the Internet. Affiliate programs are simply direct sales programs that pay one or two generations of commissions, not several generations like in network marketing. For some affiliate programs, a shallow matrix plan (two to three levels deep) seems to be an appropriate alternative to a more traditional MLM plan.

There is one matrix plan that has a better track record than the traditional matrix plans. This is the 5 x 7 matrix. This matrix plan and others like it behave more like a unilevel compensation plan because of adequate width and depth. If you are considering a matrix compensation plan for your main MLM program, make sure the compensation structure has a width of five to eight people and a depth of at least seven levels. The other plans, especially the 2x, 3x, and 4x plans, have proven to lack stability.

The Breakaway

The breakaway plan is historically the most widely used plan in network marketing. It offers the new distributor many options and carries with it some distinctive characteristics. The breakaway plan pays monthly and is characterized by high quotas and high commissions. The breakaway has been called the *full-timer's plan*. In a breakaway, sales volume is accumulated through the end of the month, and checks arrive in the distributor's mailbox around the third week of the following month. The breakaway plan makes up over 39 percent of the companies I reviewed, but most of these programs are fifteen years old or older. There were no other choices in former years.

Breakaway: The good

Unlike the matrix, the breakaway plan allows distributors to sponsor an unlimited number of people on their front line. This fosters a sense of unlimited, quick growth potential.

The Stairstep

In most breakaway plans, there is a preliminary compensation structure tacked onto the front of the plan, called the *stairstep*. As you and your new distributors purchase product volume, you systematically progress to higher and higher commission levels. If you're doing a significant amount of retailing and are sponsoring people who retail the product, you have a chance to make substantial part-time income in the stairstep right from the start.

STAIRSTEP BREAKAWAY PLAN

				PLATINUM 25%
			GOLD 20%	5%
		SILVER 15%	5%	10%
	BRONZE 10%	5%	10%	15%
NEW REP	5%	10%	15%	20%

MANAGER
(STAIR-STEP)

RUBY	EMERALD	DIAMOND	DOUBLE DIAMOND	Level
5%	5%	5%	5%	1
5%	5%	5%	5%	2
	5%	5%	5%	3
	5%	5%	5%	4
		5%	5%	5
		5%	5%	6
			5%	7
			2%	INFINITY

DIRECTOR
(BREAK-AWAY)

When you get to the top of the stairstep, you can't progress any further on your own. Your incentive is to promote those below you to your level. As the distributors below you progress up the stairstep, those distributors will progressively make more commissions from their group product volume, and you make less until you're making a typical 3–8 percent, with 5 percent being the most common. The purpose in paying more in the front of the stairstep and less in the back is giving incentive for distributors to constantly sponsor new distributors every month. As your commissions decrease in the stairstep, the product volume you're being paid on drastically increases making up for the lost percentages.

Once these distributors reach your level, they go through a process known as *breaking away*, where they become independent from you, their sponsor. You can still earn commissions on your breakaways, but in order to earn significant commissions you must have a significant number of breakaway distributors on your first level. The more first generation breakaways you have, the deeper your payout.

Some of the more traditional pay plans, and some party plan companies, have a unilevel (we'll explain this soon) type structure in place of the stairstep, but it behaves similar to the stairstep in purpose and in function.

Breakaway: The bad

Here's the sticky part! In order to earn a percentage on your breakaway's group volume (GV), you must fulfill a group volume requirement or GVR (a fancy name for a group sales-volume quota). This quota is made up of the product volume that you personally purchase and all of the product volume that your distributors purchase. However, once an individual in your downline breaks away from your organization, his or her entire downline volume no longer helps you qualify for your group volume quota. If you do not fulfill this quota each and every month with your non-breakaway legs, you don't get a check on your breakaway legs (which incidentally makes up most of your income at higher levels). Some companies have even greater penalties associated with not making the numbers, like losing all of your breakaway legs to your upline! Watching your distributor breakaway is a mixed blessing. You're excited for their success, but at the same time you are disappointed since the compensation plan instantly penalizes you. It's kind of like watching your mother-in-law drive over a cliff in your new Mercedes (easy now, just a little fun).

GVRs range anywhere from $300 per month to over $7,500 per month, depending on the company. My research has shown that companies with group volume requirements of $500–1,500 or more per month can develop a significant attrition problem (or distributor fall-out). Companies with volume requirements of $2,000–5,000 or more per month encourage front-end loading, stock piling or garage qualification, and other unethical and unnecessary practices. Front-end loading refers to the action of loading brand new distributors up with more product inventory than they can generally sell within a month's time. When someone becomes "garage qualified" this means they purchased inventory they did not need or could not reasonably retail in one month so they could reach a certain qualification level for increased commissions and recognition. Usually this inventory collects in the garage. Imagine the number of distributors who join a program expecting to gradually build a tremendous group of thousands of distributors, only to be beaten and discouraged by constantly missing their qualifications for their paycheck.

Rod Nichols, author of *Successful Network Marketing for the 21*[st] *Century,* states, "I know dozens of people who have gone deeply into debt buying products they don't need, just to fulfill their group volume requirements to get a commission check. This is one reason you find people who have garages full of products. In the industry, we call this 'garage qualified.' The end of the month arrives and you are $2000 short on your group volume requirement. You call around to all your active distributors begging them to place an order, but they've already placed their end of the month orders. So, you break the credit card out and place the order yourself —another $2000 worth of products you don't need."[12]

Because of these characteristics, the breakaway plan has become known as *the sponsor monster plan*. Distributors must constantly bring on new distributors or risk losing their downline. Salesmanship and an aggressive sponsoring and duplication strategy are essential in a breakaway. Using the shotgun approach to recruiting in a breakaway is considered unethical by many network marketing authorities. In other words, many would not be as opposed to this plan if the recruiters using the breakaway plan were more selective in who they approached. Distributors using the breakaway plan should be up-front by letting potential distributors know what to expect. This plan is not for the part-timer, and it is not for anyone with a meek or mild personality. It is designed for the affluent, the highly connected, the extremely ambitious, the charismatic, and the sponsor monsters. These folks can make a bundle!

To be fair, many companies have realized the difficulties associated with breakaway plans and have acted accordingly to make the group volume requirements and other rules easier to deal with. Many plans have changed to become more user friendly, behaving similar to a unilevel plan.

Home Party Plan Compensation

Nearly every direct sales/network marketing company that promotes their product and opportunity through home party plans utilizes the breakaway compensation plan. However, party plan companies reward distributors with different payout percentages. Where a traditional network marketing company will generally pay out half of its commissions to those making the retail sales and the other half to the distributor leaders in the form of bonuses, party plan companies will pay out as much as 60–75 percent to the retailers while only retaining 25–40 percent for the leadership teams. This type of plan seems to work best for the party plan model, though it really comes down to the actual rules and quotas associated with each plan. Not all breakaway plans are created equal, so you must check out the rules, quotas, and penalties associated with each plan.

Breakaway: Overall Evaluation

The breakaway is still the most widely used plan in network marketing, because twenty years ago there really were no other choices. The breakaway is considered the old-school plan. It's a full-timer's plan, designed for well-connected, charismatic, heavy recruiters. For this type of person, the breakaway can be the most lucrative plan in network marketing. Many of the traditional breakaway companies are still recruiting new distributors heavily, especially in foreign markets where there are few other choices. However, the breakaway is more difficult for part-timers and newcomers. Over the last ten years, virtually no top performing programs have selected the breakaway plan. The breakaway plan is a dinosaur, and if it does survive over the next twenty years, it will be to serve the home party plan industry almost exclusively.

The Unilevel

The unilevel was developed as the answer to the breakaway plan. In fact, at first glance, the unilevel structure looks similar to the breakaway, but it is actually very different. The unilevel is one of the simplest forms of network marketing compensation structures, and one of the best. Unlimited width, limited depth, and monthly payouts characterize this pay plan. Traditional unilevel plans pay out about 30–50 percent of the company's net profits. Most unilevels pay five to seven levels, with seven being the most common depth. Most have roll-ups, compression, and/or infinity bonuses (all of these terms refer to the process of product volume rolling to the next qualified distributor when distributors don't qualify to earn it), allowing top distributors to be paid temporarily on deeper levels until downline distributors catch up. Volume accumulates through the end of the month, and checks arrive in the distributor's mailbox around the twentieth of the following month. Over 35 percent of the plans I reviewed were unilevel plans, but over 70 percent of the companies started in the last ten years are now using the unilevel. This percentage is growing.

Unilevel: The good

The unilevel plan allows unlimited sponsoring on the first level. This creates unlimited income potential. Unilevel plans are fair to everyone, based on generally low group volume quotas and no breakaways. Unilevels are also characterized by lower personal volume requirements than breakaway plans. This makes it easy for most distributors to stay active. The unilevel doesn't give as much incentive to front-end load or stockpile product.

UNILEVEL PLAN

FAST START BONUS 25% On 1st Order

REP	BRONZE	SILVER	GOLD	RUBY	EMERALD	DIAMOND	Level
5%	5%	5%	5%	5%	5%	5%	1
5%	5%	5%	5%	5%	5%	5%	2
	5%	5%	5%	5%	5%	5%	3
		5%	5%	5%	5%	5%	4
			5%	5%	5%	5%	5
				5%	5%	5%	6
					5%	5%	7
						2%	INFINITY

Unilevel: The bad

In the 1990s, the unilevel was called the *part-timer's plan* because of easy volume requirements and no breakaways. It has also been called the *vanilla plan* because it's a plain-Jane structure. In the 1990s, part-time distributors found it more appealing because they could increase their chances for success by surviving in the plan for a longer period of time without being forced out by heavy volume requirements, like those associated with breakaways. However, this part-time philosophy did not go over well with the breakaway crowd. For this reason, the unilevel usually repelled the big guns. They simply couldn't make money as fast as they could in the breakaway, nor could they make as much. However, in recent years, due to improved rules and enhancements to the basic unilevel structure, these weaknesses no longer apply.

To overcome this part-time stigma, some top unilevel plans now offer lucrative infinity bonuses and other forms of compression to bring the big money into the plan. These bonuses are designed to allow top producers to draw upon commissions generated from deeper in the compensation plan. It's working. Now some of the largest checks are being generated with unilevel plans. The unilevel plan is considered by many to be the most stable and lucrative plan in network marketing today.

Overcoming the average

To get rid of the plain vanilla stigma, pay plan innovators have enhanced the unilevel in recent years by offering several powerful incentives. First of all, distributors complained about not being able to earn money quickly, so now nearly every unilevel plan has a front end fast-start bonus, paying a special bonus on the first orders of new customers and distributors. Top MLM leaders complained that they could not earn the same kind of checks that the breakaway distributors earned. So the pay plan developers went to the drawing board and developed a couple of tools to help.

One of the most powerful enhancements to some unilevel plans is a structural rule called dynamic compression. Compression allows you to earn commission beyond the last level of your pay plan if that leg is still in the process of moving up the ladder of success. Commissions not earned by downline members roll up to distributor leaders instead of becoming breakage (profits by default) to the company. Dynamic compression is only present in a handful of companies. Where dynamic compression is not present, it's common to find some kind of infinity bonus. The infinity bonus is a misnomer, since no company could really afford to pay a bonus to infinity. However, it does help distributors temporarily dip down to deeper levels to capture profits.

Whatever you call it, dynamic compression is one of the most important features in a network marketing plan. It overcomes many of the compensation plan functions and features that can discourage distributors. It pulls volume produced by leaders in depth up to those leaders who deserve to be paid on it. For example, a distributor who recruits ten leaders and produces $20,000 in monthly sales volume may be paid on generations deeper than someone who recruits two distributors and produces $2,000 in monthly sales volume.

In addition to these enhancements, top leaders expect some kind of powerful leadership bonus designed to reward top leaders. Leadership bonuses generally consist of taking a very small percentage (usually 1–3 percent) of the company's overall monthly sales and dividing it equitably between the leaders. These bonuses can eventually pay out more than the standard monthly unilevel plan.

Front-end heavy or compressed plans

Even if you haven't seen one of these, you're likely to run into what we call front-end heavy plans, or compressed unilevel compensation plans. These plans cycle in popularity; they come and go, and then they're back again. Compressed unilevels look excellent on paper and typically pay 15–45 percent on the first few levels of the plan, but leave very little for the backend. Developers of this plan contend that distributors can't make money fast enough to feel encouraged to stay in the business. So they pay a lot of commissions up front. However, when you pay up front, you leave nothing for the full-time or professional distributors who want to make the big bucks.

Compressed plans are easy to spot since 70–90 percent of the promotion is focused strictly on the compensation plan. I've been in sales presentations where the products were treated like some technicality that had to be thrown in to make the plan legal. These programs resemble direct sales organizations that only pay on one to several generations of commission and have not been proven to be contenders among today's compensation plans as of yet. Programs that encourage all width and no depth can sometimes unintentionally alienate distributors too soon. When distributors are taught to go wide, they can forget about the needs of their downline distributors, who are several generations removed. Also, the heavy-hitters can become discouraged by how long it takes to reach the big money that almost every good pay plan offers to those with extraordinary abilities.

Unilevel: Overall evaluation

The unilevel is a fantastic alternative to traditional breakaway plans. The unilevel does not have the fast income potential of some of the front-heavy plans and plans that encourage front-end loading (buying lots of inventory up front), but it also does not have the high attrition rate (distributor fall-out rate). You're not going to hear any of the horror stories that are sometimes associated with other plans. Although there are many variations, the basic unilevel plan can be a very fair and lucrative plan.

Avoid unilevel plans that are plain vanilla, and look for the enhancements I described. Try to avoid any unilevel gimmicks like two level (front-heavy) plans and plans that pay different percentages on every level. Compressed plans are ideal for affiliate programs but are not yet proven as mainstream compensation plans. In time we will see if the compressed plans will ever remain popular instead of continuing to come and go.

The unilevel is one network marketing payout structure that is here to stay. I rarely hear complaints about the unilevel. Governmental regulators in North America generally prefer the unilevel plan to other plans. Dedicated distributors who follow a proven system for a two-to-four-year period of time can have substantial results with this plan. Top distributors can earn incomes that can definitely contend with the breakaway plans. The unilevel is a great choice.

The Binary

The binary was developed in the 1980s as an exciting alternative to traditional network marketing pay plans. The binary plan is based on a structure of two legs, a right leg and a left leg. One-leg downlines are considered illegal by many government regulators since they all seem to give too much advantage to the first distributors who get into the company. Therefore, two legs are the industry minimum. Distributors can only sponsor two on their first level, and everyone else spills down below those two distributors, similar to a 2x matrix, except the binary counts volume, not levels. Maximum commissions are earned by balancing the left and right side of the binary. Over 23 percent of the programs I studied were binary plans. The number of companies using the binary plan is slowly increasing every year.

Binary: The good

In a binary, all you need are two strong legs and you are on your way to a full-time income; most plans require many more. Add a third solid leg to most binary plans and you are on your way to a six-figure income. Sure, you may have to sponsor more than just two or three distributors to achieve financial independence. When you sponsor your third distributor, that person must go down under one of your initial two distributors, creating excitement and synergy. By placing more distributors into a binary plan, leaders can create pockets of synergy. The matrix is the only other plan that gives the upline incentive to place people under other distributors in their downline.

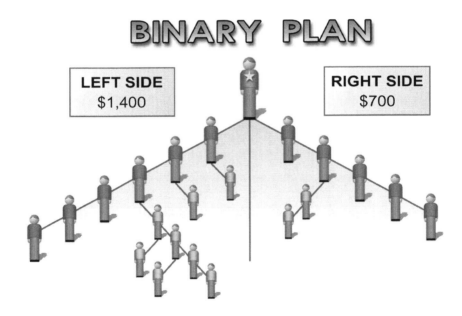

BINARY PLAN

LEFT SIDE	RIGHT SIDE
$1,400	$700

Most binaries pay weekly. In addition, new distributors can earn their first check during their first week and receive that check in the mail within ten days. This helps with distributor motivation and retention. In most compensation plans, the reward is so far removed from the work that the distributors get discouraged and quit. Also, the binary plan is designed without levels; only volume counts. Levels can restrict distributors from earning commissions on their entire downline. There are no group volume requirements or group quotas in most binary plans. With a modest personal product volume requirement each month, you remain active to receive commissions on unlimited levels.

Payout Percentage

Traditional plans pay around 5 percent on breakaway or unilevel volume. The binary plan averages 5–10 percent payout on unlimited depth. You must be balanced to earn maximum commissions. This balancing act is designed to create "breakage" to the company or commissions that flow up to the company based on some distributors not qualifying for them. When distributors don't balance their legs, they don't earn the full payout that is possible in a given week. The balance rolls up to the company. All pay plans have some form of breakage strategy employed in the plan.

Those who like games of strategy generally enjoy this type of plan. Where you place new distributors in your downline can affect your payout. Also, most binaries reward top distributors with re-entry certificates that allow distributors to reenter their own downline and place another distributorship position in a place where it is needed the most. Placement of these new business centers requires careful placement strategy.

Attitude Check

Now there are two types of distributors in network marketing: those with good attitudes and those with bad attitudes. The binary plan is the ultimate attitude check. The binary structure is the only pay plan besides the matrix that actually gives the upline incentive to place people into the downlines of distributors below them. The distributor with the good attitude is going to be appreciative of any sponsoring of new distributors in his/her downline, even if the new recruits are placed on the stronger side. The distributor with the bad attitude may object to these downline placements since these new distributors may not necessarily be placed on the side that they want them on. With the binary, you can find out right away if your distributor has a "glass half empty" or a "glass half full" attitude. Negative people will not survive the binary, while positive people feel the plan tends to be more synergistic than other pay plans.

Strength of Most Binaries

Most binary plans, especially the most recent plans developed over the last five years, are quite fair and can generate fairly substantial checks. In most cases, binaries favor the middle of the compensation plan. A distributor who is generating between $2,000 and about $40,000 in monthly sales volume can earn an excellent percentage in payout if this volume is distributed evenly according to the plan's balancing standards. Once gross sales volumes exceed $40-50,000 per month, the unilevels and breakaways tend to kick into high gear. However, you will generally earn a better percentage with a binary in the midrange volumes.

Binary: The Bad

The binary plan is a very exciting and synergistic plan, but it can also carry some baggage. No pay plan is perfect and the binary has its own set of issues. Some deal with the way the binary plan can be manipulated by leaders, other issues deal with the basic structure. Here are some things to be aware of when evaluating a binary plan.

Overemphasis on Pay Plan/Recruiting

Trust me when I say that I'm just as much a recruiting machine as the next full-time network marketer, so in no way am I discouraging this activity. However, many of the binary plans put far too much emphasis on their compensation plan, leaving little room for anything else, including product promotion. It's tempting to do this when you have a compensation plan that is so much fun to demonstrate on paper. But distributors who learn how to balance their presentation between product, company, and compensation plan will ultimately build a more stable, long-term business. Governmental regulators are constantly dropping into distributor opportunity meetings to make sure the product is still emphasized over the compensation plan.

Does binary mean two or four?

Even though the name *binary* implies two, meaning it is a two-legged plan, most binary plans allow and even encourage distributors to sign up with three business centers (more on this later). This allows distributors to launch their business with four legs. In order to optimize the pay plan and make maximum commission percentages from your work, you not only have to find leaders to populate all four legs, but you must balance these legs. If it's difficult to create balance in two legs, think about how much more difficult it is in four legs. In almost every binary pay plan I've researched, serious networkers are building four legs from the beginning of their business, not two legs as most pay plan demonstrations describe. However, there is generally no requirement to build four legs.

Balance is the key

Balance is the key to maximizing payout in the binary plan. If you have only one leg take off, you cannot benefit from the volume on the larger leg until you have balanced the same amount of product sales volume on the opposite leg. In other words, if you sign up a distributor who takes off and signs up ten distributors in one month on your right side, obviously you will have more product volume being purchased on that right side. Before you earn commissions on the product volume on the strong leg, you must start working on the left side to balance the same amount of volume on the weak leg. If you do not balance, you get paid on the amount you can balance and the rest sits in that strong leg like a bank account, waiting for you week after week.

Some plans have tried to deal with this issue by offering a 1/3–2/3 balance rule that allows distributors to get full payout if they are not quite balanced. The 1/3–2/3 allows distributors to cash out on all of their product volume during a given week if their volume in their weaker leg is at least one-third of the volume represented in the strong leg. So if distributors had 5,000 volume in the left leg and 30,000 in the right leg, they would be paid on 5,000 volume on the left, and 10,000 on the right for a total of 15,000 in volume for the week. The remaining 20,000 volume that is not paid on the right leg generally carries over in most plans so you can have a chance to balance out the next week to earn the rest of this commission. Even with the 1/3–2/3 incentive, most distributors develop one huge leg and the other legs are much smaller. A 1/3–2/3 option can help a little but it will not correct this problem.

Since the binary allows and even encourages spillover, many people may have distributors signing up underneath them that they did not personally prospect and recruit. However, almost always, these bonus distributors are placed on only one side of that distributor's organization. In order for the distributor to take advantage of the new volume in their group, they must place an equal number of distributors or customers (product volume) on the weaker side. Unlike the matrix plan, distributors have to earn the right to receive commissions from spillover. In other words, there is no free lunch. Distributors must prove themselves worthy of receiving commissions from upline volume placed under them. Add the dynamics of building four legs instead of two, and you can see how complicated the balancing act can become.

Some non-binary distributors will criticize the binary because it seems to give the wrong incentives. Instead of encouraging you to work hard with your workers, it actually penalizes you for working with your best legs and rewards you for bailing out the less dedicated distributors. Binary proponents believe that the binary is unselfish because it forces you to lift the weaker person and try to strengthen them. It's really all in the way you look at it.

Runaway legs

Odds say that one of your legs will take off before the other in the binary plan. When one leg takes off like a rocket, this is called *a runaway leg*. These runaway legs are the best and the worst thing that can happen to a distributor. Before this leg takes off, you are carefully balancing each new distributor on the left and right. Essentially, your efforts are divided between building two legs. As soon as one of those legs takes off on its own, you can then begin focusing most of your attention on your weak leg. When distributors focus on building one leg only, the chances of it becoming another runaway leg are twice as high as before. It's just a matter of time before this leg becomes a strong leg, and soon both legs will be maximizing weekly.

Generally speaking, when two legs are maximizing in a binary plan, distributors will produce an above-average full-time income. Three maxed legs will produce a six-figure income. (These payout figures are hypothetical examples of the typical binary structure. Commission payout can vary from plan to plan.)

Sometimes distributors can become frustrated at how long it takes to balance out a strong leg. This can be a problem for some distributors. However, keep in mind that you may never have a leg take off in any other plan like you do with the binary. That's why you may only hear the term *runaway leg* in reference to the binary plan.

Runaway legs can be discouraging. Distributors who do not have a strong, long-term commitment to building their binary downline may become discouraged when they see the money they are leaving on the table. Some distributors even quit and curse the binary plan forever. This is ridiculous, of course, since building a runaway leg is one of the greatest things that can happen to you in any pay plan. In the binary, pray for a runaway leg. Then, once you have one, pray for another one.

Volume caps: the momentum killer

Instead of limiting levels, the binary plan limits volume. In other words, once you reach the maximum level of downline sales volume in a particular leg during one week, you must then reenter into your own downline and start a new leg in order to increase income. As distributors persist in building any network marketing downline, eventually they should experience a phenomenon known as momentum growth. This is a very exciting period in most pay plans, and this momentum growth could continue for years. However, in the binary plan, since volume can be capped, and no more commissions can be generated after this cap without reentering the downline and starting over with a new position, momentum growth can be squelched. When distributors have existing legs that are maxing out in volume every week, they have no more incentive to place new distributors downline in these strong legs, and they lose incentive to work with distributors in stronger legs. They turn their attention to starting new momentum growth in their new legs. It's almost like starting over again from scratch. This cap on volume can also be discouraging to some distributors.

Powerleg hype

The worst part about being associated with the binary plan is the powerleg hype that you hear about in almost every company that uses the binary. Since only two legs are required to start making good income, many aggressive MLMers will stack all of their new distributors, one after the other, into two large powerlegs so everyone can receive the advantage of spillover.

These powerlegs are very helpful and encouraging for active, productive distributors who happen to fall in the powerleg. But many unfortunate souls miss out on the powerleg because they come in under someone who is in a powerleg and needs to build the weak side of their group. Their sponsors place them at the top of the weak leg, and now instead of hundreds of people building this massive powerleg on one side for them, they have to build both legs themselves and generate their own momentum. This can be extremely dispiriting for the nonpowerleg distributors who are aware of the powerleg concept and hear of all the success stories but were not invited to the party. Anytime there is a lack of fairness in a pay plan, it can breed contempt.

The best way to avoid this problem is to avoid distributor organizations and companies that stress the powerleg or powerline concept. It shouldn't be something that is openly and publicly promoted. Yes, it can be a benefit to those who are involved, but it can be a bone of contention for everyone else. Also, keep in mind that even though the powerleg may or may not help every distributor, other plans like the breakaway and the unilevel don't have any powerleg stacking incentives, and it can be a disadvantage to do a substantial amount of stacking in these plans.

Binary Variations

The binary plan does have significant variations from plan to plan. As mentioned earlier, some binary plans are split with a balancing requirement of 50/50, meaning that volume needs to balance on each side to receive commissions that week. The 50/50 plan is the safest and the most traditional binary. We also previously mentioned the 1/3–2/3 split binary, meaning you can have up to 66 percent of your volume on the strong side and still match with 33 percent on the weak leg. In theory, this plan can help distributors more easily balance their legs, but distributors I've interviewed who have worked both plans are convinced that it really doesn't make that much of a difference.

Be aware of binary plans that allow the purchase of more than three business centers at start-up. Business centers are like separated distributorship positions stacked on top of each other. Each center must be activated with approximately $100-$200 in product purchase. Some binaries allow a seven-pack or even a fifteen-pack. This generally can increase the cost of start-up to $700-$3,000. These plans usually do not last long, and in many states they're illegal. Many states now have a law that prohibits companies from offering business start-up expenses that exceed $500. Purchasing 7-15 business centers is the binary's equivalent to the front-end load in the breakaway.

Can binary plans pay out too much? The answer is a resounding... *YES*! Some companies using variations on the binary plan have actually gone out of business because they paid out too much. One such binary variation is called a *cycling binary*. The cycling binary plans accumulate volume just like other compensation plans. But instead of paying distributors once each week, the pay plan cashes out and distributors receive their check immediately when a certain volume is reached in the weak leg. This cycling process can occur several times per month, several times per week, or even several times per day in extremely fast-growing organizations. Since the cycling binary cashes out so often, very little breakage is left for the company to pay for operating expenses and employees. This breakage is absolutely necessary for a company's survival. Some cycling binaries have even been known to pay over 100 percent! As a result, many companies using cycling binaries have gone out of business. Even with a poor track record, you can expect to see this plan again. There's always some hotshot out there who thinks he is going to revolutionize the industry with a new plan, but hasn't done his homework. It's a good thing you've done yours.

To prevent cycling binaries, and other binary plans with limited breakage, from bankrupting the company, some plans have developed rules that act as a safety net to catch runaway plans. If the commission payout percentage becomes too high, the plan will start limiting the commission payout to each distributor so the plan doesn't pay out too much. This can discourage some distributors, but most intelligent networkers understand that this practice is absolutely necessary for the survival of a company.

Experience Can Break the Binary

In a few cases, experienced network marketing pros have joined a binary plan and have started recruiting at a massive rate. Having experience with compensation plans, these pro networkers know how to place all of their recruits into the plan to maximize profits for themselves. However, many company owners who implement the binary plan assume that enough distributors will not be able to balance their organizations perfectly, so enough breakage will flow upline to the company to pay for corporate operational expenses. A network marketer who launches a massive recruiting campaign and manipulates all of the volume to his or her advantage can sometimes "break the bank," so to speak. These savvy network marketers perfectly balance their organization to exactly match the 50/50 or 2/3–1/3 requirements and maximize their commissions.

When companies create pay plans that pay too much, they're still obligated to pay earned commissions, even if they have to pay more than they took in on the sales. Most companies now have safety clauses that restrict distributors from earning too much from their balancing act. Make sure the binary you're investigating has a safety clause to protect your company from paying too much.

Controversy

The binary has been the target of some bad media and rumors in recent years. Some of these negative reports are based on the fact that many of the most visible or popular binaries have run into snags. In reviewing the case histories, it seems that in every case these programs were investigated, fined, or shut down based on criteria other than the compensation plan. Explosive growth, illegal income or product claims, unethical conduct, and unproven or ineffective products have had more influence on company shutdowns than the compensation plan. Some of the rumors about the disadvantages of binary plans have been started and perpetuated by distributors in other programs who consider the binary to be competition to their plan. The breakaway plan still has the record for number of shutdowns but it is also more widely used than any other plan as of this year.

Even though most of these shutdowns have little to do with the compensation plan, the perception is that binary plans will attract more heat from regulators, thus putting the company at more risk. This controversy can be difficult to deal with. If distributors do not believe in their compensation structure, they will have a hard time promoting it to others. If you have hang-ups with the binary or any other type of compensation plan, either get over it or get out of it. So many people hold psychological blocks because they think their compensation plan is repressive, when in fact it is their lack of productivity that is keeping them from making progress.

Binary: Overall Evaluation

Although the modern binary is constantly evolving, I found it to be a revolutionary plan and a top contender among today's innovative plans. The binary is fair, lucrative, and has an element of synergy and teamwork not found in other plans. Avoid binary plans that market the compensation plan over the product line. If the main focus of every presentation is the dynamics of the compensation plan, the company will probably not make it. This can lead to trouble, even shutdown. Avoid companies that put a cap on their distributor's volumes too early and force you to reenter your downline for additional streams of income. Try not to join companies that stress joining the powerline.

Remember, many distributors will never have the advantage of being in a powerline and this can lead to major resentment and massive distributor attrition. Also, avoid binary plans that market non-consumable products or one-time-purchase product lines. History teaches us that these two elements don't mix.

Mark Rawlins has been working with network marketing pay plans for over two decades. Mark commented on the binary plan, saying, "One thing is sure: the binary has been around long enough and has had enough success and has enough supporters that its place in the network marketing industry is assured. I think the controversy surrounding the binary will continue to subside. As the plan has become more mature, companies, distributors, and software vendors all know how to make the most of the strengths and deal with the weaknesses. There is no reason for the 'surprises' that plagued binaries in the early days to continue."[13]

The New Binary Hybrid – Best of Both Worlds?

A hybrid plan is simply a combination of two or more of the above plans. The most popular combination plan today is the binary/unilevel. At the moment, some might say that compensation plan designers have *cracked the code* on modern day compensation plans with the invention of the "new binary" with a unilevel matching or leadership bonus. This plan seems to offer the best of both worlds – all the benefits of the binary and unilevel plans without the drawbacks. Some feel the new binary is a radical plan and the math does not add up. Or in other words, what you see on paper and what you're actually getting are two different animals. Let's take an objective look at the new binary to see what we can learn.

How does the new binary work?

First of all, let's break down the new binary to see how it works. Though it might seem more complicated than the binary or unilevel by themselves, most people can get the basic concept with a basic whiteboard demonstration. If you want to view the binary diagram and the unilevel diagram from the previous section, this might be helpful to visualize this plan.

Like other plans, the new binary generally has retail commission incentives, one or more fast start bonuses, and leadership bonuses which sometimes include car incentives (bonuses that pay for the lease on your car) and the like. The structures that make this plan unique are what I call the enrollment bonus or the binary, and the matching bonus or the unilevel. In the enrollment bonus, new recruits are placed into a binary. Generally this binary is not the three business center stack that you see in most of the classic binaries, but you usually start out with one business center and you're responsible for a left and right leg. Although some of the new binaries do a 1/3–2/3 split, most of the new plans do a 50/50 split meaning you earn commission on the match of the right and left legs. To simplify this process, trainers now refer to the two legs as the greater and lesser legs and they explain that you earn around 10% commission on the lesser leg. Before, we would say you earned 5% on the balance of the left and right leg. Both mean the same thing.

Unlike the classic binary, new binary compensation plans explain on paper that their plan can pay up to $10,000 per center per week. Some plans claim much higher payouts such as $12,500 per center per week, and sometimes even $25,000 and $50,000. We'll comment on this claim in a moment, but first I'll finish explaining the structure of the plan. Distributors build a right leg and a left leg and try to keep their volume in each leg as even as possible. When one leg takes off, we call this the "runaway leg" and all efforts are put into attempting to build the lesser leg to match the runaway leg.

In the binary side of the pay plan, everyone you sponsor and everyone your team sponsors are stacked vertically in long rows, distributor after distributor. If you want to understand how the unilevel portion of the plan pays, simply disregard the binary for a moment and take all of the distributors you personally sponsored and place them on your front line in a unilevel structure. If you personally sponsored two, place two on your front line. If you personally sponsored fifty, place these all on your front line. This is your matching bonus structure. Any distributors sponsored by your front line distributors are placed on your second level and so on. Based on sophisticated software technology, the computer can first calculate your bonuses based on how you placed people in the binary, then it will recalculate bonus commission based on the number of people you actually sponsored yourself. Those who recruit the most still earn the most, but they're able to assist downline members by initially stacking that volume under newcomers.

Unilevel commissions are generally paid in a matching bonus meaning that you earn a percentage match on the commissions generated by distributors you personally sponsor, and a bonus on the distributors that your distributors sponsor up to several generations.

The matching bonus is generally paid on 4-8 generations. If you take all the volume designated to be paid in the matching bonus portion of the plan, generally payouts can range from 8-25% per level with the average being about 12-14% of the entire pool paid on 7 generations. Remember, it can't add up to more than 100% of the matching pool. Or you could say the average payout per level is about 4-8% on the entire payplan if you're not calculating based on 100% of the pool. If you would like a great breakdown of how these plans work, you can generally find examples at www.youtube.com or other video sites online. However, I'll caution you. Some of the trainers who are explaining these plans don't understand them so you might get some top distributor leader misrepresenting their own compensation plan.

New Binary: The good

First of all, you can't argue with results. As you can tell, I'm a very results oriented coach. If I see a system, strategy, or structure that is getting results with another company or leader, I like to jump on the idea and break it down to see why it is so effective. The new binary is such a beast. It's hard to be critical of a compensation plan that newer companies have used to break all time industry growth records. One young company has accomplished approximately one billion dollars in gross sales over just one year of business after only four years in business. Is this kind of growth healthy? Time will tell. We could see a major leveling off and a struggle for survival, or we could see the company go on to break more records as they move into the "big boys club". Other companies have achieved $100-$400 million in annual sales using a form of the new binary over the last several years. Why the success? I've spent that last year breaking it down in detail and here are my findings.

At first glance, the new binary plan seems to compensate for the weaknesses of both the binary and the unilevel. For instance, the new binary solves the volume capping issues of the old binary by allowing distributors to earn matching bonuses or leadership bonus to continue building their income even while they're hitting the wall with their earning in the binary portion of the plan. Most companies have set up check matching bonuses or some sort of sponsorship bonuses in the unilevel portion of the plan, thus giving distributors more incentive to continue to sponsor and recruit. This follows along the generally accepted philosophy among compensation plan designers of "reward the activities you want to see in your distributors."

Although it is still debatable whether these numbers even work long term, it does seem that these compensation structures allow new distributors to get into profit faster than other plans. This phenomenon is not generated by a higher payout which some new binary endorses tout. In fact, new binary commission recipients may actually be earning less per distributor than the more classic binary plans. However, with the excitement of the matching bonus to motivate them, and with the inherent benefit of stacking distributors in long vertical lines to create synergy, this plan tends to attract new distributors faster than other plans.

New Binary Hybrid: The Bad

I have yet to see a binary hybrid breakdown on paper/internet that did not have major discrepancies, faulty mathematics, and outright deceptions. In most cases I feel the companies promoting these plans are simply not aware of these problems. At the very least, they were unaware of the discrepancies when they launched their pay plan, and now they're adjusting commissions, cutting payout percentages and volumes, and capping paychecks more and more every month as they begin to realize their mistakes.

I've literally attended company conventions where corporate representatives are touting the virtues of their amazing and unique comp plan that pays more than any comp plan. The next week I'm on the phone with the same corporate officers who are in a panic because the CFO told them they have to cut volumes on the leaders checks because they're earning too much while at the same time new distributors are complaining about not earning enough. It's a constant battle to try to balance these plans without paying out too much or too little. When developing a plan, companies need professionals experienced in compensation plan development, mathematics and accounting, and you also need input from top leaders who are experienced field distributors so you can make good choices in developing the plan.

Most new binary hybrids that are less than 4 years old have adjusted volumes, commission percentages, and qualifications in significant ways as many as five to twenty five times. Distributors may never find out about these adjustments. Many of my friends in new binary hybrids only know the changes, limitations, and volume caps based on their commission check reports.

In many of the new binary hybrid plans, the numbers flat out don't work. One company can say they pay out $1,000 per business center per week and the company pays 38% of their revenue to the field. Another company pays as much as 48% to the field, yet they claim a $10,000 cap per business center per week. Some plans boast $25,000 to $50,000 in potential commissions per center per week. It becomes blatantly obvious that, although companies have different qualification rules, there's a fair amount of smoke and mirrors being perpetuated in the MLM industry.

New Hybrid Binary: Overall Evaluation

The reason compensation plan designers combine the binary and the unilevel into one plan is to take advantage of the strengths of both. The binary is a great plan for rapid recruiting and creating massive team synergy while the unilevel works better for rewarding distributors on their personal recruiting, duplicating, and leadership skills. Overall it's a great plan.

Some might argue that it is more complicated to explain a hybrid plan, and it certainly can be. Others might say the written plans are inaccurate at best, openly deceptive at worse. Unlike some of the classic binaries of the '90s, the hybrids have safety valves designed to cut of leader's commissions so they can't earn too much for fear of bankrupting the plan.

Time will tell if the new hybrid binary will become the new compensation plan of choice, however, I believe you will start to see companies being more conservative in their compensation plan diagrams once they understand how the real world math plays out in these plans long term.

Other Hybrids

Another popular hybrid is the unilevel/breakaway. Very traditional and proven companies like NuSkin, Herbalife, Shaklee, and other top programs use a form of unilevel bonus on the front of their breakaway plans. I usually don't classify these as hybrid plans. Rather, I simply refer to them as a standard breakaway, or a breakaway with a fast start unilevel bonus, similar to the stairstep bonus we described earlier.

Some hybrid plans are far from proven and generally cause tremendous confusion among the distributors who are using them. The unilevel/matrix, for instance, is a completely unproven plan. My advice it to avoid any hybrid that does not have a track record.

Many hybrids are so complicated that they confuse the distributors who attempt to explain them to others. If you can't understand the compensation plan your own company is using, you won't be able to effectively explain it. I remember being a spectator in a network marketing meeting back in the late '90s. The person giving the compensation plan demonstration became flustered as he began to explain the complicated compensation structure of his hybrid plan. I asked if I could assist and proceeded to diagram the plan for the audience. I could tell even some of the leaders had not understood their own compensation plan until that moment. Compensation plans can sometimes be too complicated to explain. If you can't explain it, you can't duplicate your knowledge of the plan to your downline and to prospects. And if you can't duplicate, you're dead. Be sure to compare any hybrid plan you're investigating to other plans in current use that are proven in the marketplace.

The Australian 2-Up

The poor Australians are taking a beating for this when, in fact, it was us darn Yanks who introduced the 2-up plan in the United States in the mid-1980s. The 2-up, like the matrix, looks fantastic on paper, but when you put it into practice, it's a disaster. The Australian 2-up is considered a gimmick compensation plan for reasons that are quite obvious to intelligent network marketers; no company has ever survived this plan. For this reason, we will not spend any time on this plan other than to describe what it looks like so you can avoid it. Only 2 percent of the companies I researched use the 2-up plan. The most common form of this plan is the 2-up, but there are also variations called the 1-up and the 3-up. All of these basically behave in a similar manor.

The 2-up works like this: you sacrifice your first two recruits to your upline sponsor. Then you start earning commissions on anyone sponsored after the first two. Since your first two recruits go to your sponsor, it stands to reason that the first two distributors sponsored your first two distributors go to you. The Australian 2-up is famous for looking great on paper. It lures thousands of suckers every year. However, even Australian network marketers can tell you that no one in their right mind would join a 2-up today.

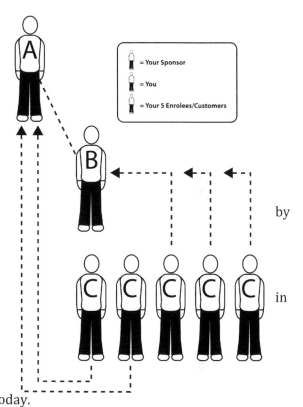

by

in

Some consultants claim that the 2-ups go out of business because they pay too much up front instead of rewarding distributors in the long run. Others claim it's because you have to give away your first two sales to your sponsor and most distributors will never recruit their third distributor, thus, they never get paid. Still other consultants argue that it's not the plan itself but the type of products that are usually associated with 2-ups. Travel companies, financial training programs, tax reduction and avoidance training programs, and seminar MLM companies all with steep start-up expenses (usually $1000 and up) are famous for using the 2-up. They're also famous for being here today and gone tomorrow. One of the most common models that has tried and failed at least a dozen times involves the purchase of a $1,200 audio series that teaches you how to avoid debt and invest your money offshore to avoid taxes. More and more travel companies are popping up every year utilizing the 2-up. If you encounter these programs, flee with your family to safety.

Guidelines for Compensation Plans

Finally, I wanted to create a list of some of the most important things to look for in a compensation plan. No matter which company you're examining, look for the following characteristics:

1. A company should have moderate start-up costs ($150–1500). If the total start-up is less than $100 and more than $2,000, proceed with caution. If start up is less than $50, including product and distributor kit, or more than $3,000, consult an objective network marketing consultant before proceeding. I repeat, do not proceed without consulting an expert. In fact, I'd rather have you email me and wait for a reply before proceeding (daren@networkmarketingbook.com). More on this in Chapter Nine.

2. Most companies require the purchase of a distributor kit. The price of a distributor kit should be around $50, but can range from $20 to $100. Low priced kits make it easy to join, but high priced kits can offer needed tools and create a barrier of entry to attract better leaders. Commission cannot be paid on distributor kits or sales materials. If your start-up kit alone is more than $100, proceed with caution.

3. A compensation plan should have some kind of fast-start bonus, like a one-time fast-start commission or a stair-step or front-end unilevel bonus.

4. Legitimate plans have monthly personal qualification requirements of $50–200 in product purchases to qualify as an active distributor. Any more or less can be a red flag.

5. The company must have a monthly auto-ordering program. Every company I've researched that did not have an optional auto-order program did not survive.

6. Compensation plans should be performance based and should reward those who reach the top of the plan with leadership bonuses.

7. Distributors should be able to keep their earned pin levels or titles once earned, but they should be paid based on their qualification or re-qualification at that level each month.

8. Plans should never reward distributors who do nothing or who are not actively participating in the plan. Lazy or inactive distributors should be disadvantaged.

9. Pay plans should never allow downline organizations to roll past you under any circumstance. If you're inactive in purchasing product, then volume should roll past you by default, but you should never lose your distributor organization without your own signature, unless you violate your company's policies and procedures.

10. Levels where distributors are inactive in purchasing their monthly required volume should compress up to the next active distributor. Unearned leadership commissions should compress up to the next qualified leader and not be paid as breakage to the company.

11. Distributor commission plans should pay out an actual 33–50 percent on revenue taken in by the company (not just on paper, but in actual payout). Paying more could put the company in financial jeopardy. Paying less is simply unfair to hardworking distributors. Most companies claim to pay certain percentages to their distributor force. This is almost never accurate due to faulty math. Ultimately, private MLM companies are not required to disclose these numbers so you its best so choose a company you trust. Public companies are forced to disclose their numbers in their annual report.

12. Compensation plans may have minor adjustments, but the inherent structure should never, ever change. And I mean never, never, never, ever. This is critical. Nothing I've seen in my research will put a company into a tailspin faster than a drastic change to their compensation plan. Bonuses can be changed and adjusted, new incentives can be added, no problem. But you cannot go from a binary, to a unilevel, to a breakaway, changing from one structure to another.

13. As a company expands internationally, the compensation plans should pay commissions seamlessly from country to country. Some plans require you to have a different organization in every country. This can become burdensome to independent distributors.

14. The payout of a commission plan is controlled as much by the rules as it is by the commission percentages. Each compensation plan has its own set of rules. These rules provide structure for the sponsoring of new distributors and the placement of product volume. The rules of a plan also dictate how distributors advance from level to level and qualify to receive commissions. Rules can have just as much, if not more, influence

on a compensation plan as the type of structure used (breakaway, binary, or unilevel).

15. If the corporate leaders are inexperienced, or if they don't understand compensation structures, the initial structure of a company's compensation plan at the time of start-up will tell this tale like a crystal ball. It's critical to show your new or unique compensation plan to an experienced and knowledgeable network marketing consultant. It could save you a lot of grief.

16. Each compensation plan is generally weighted in the front of the plan, in the middle of the plan, or in the back of the plan. The best kind of plan is one that is balanced in all three areas. Even a balanced plan may have emphasis on the front, middle, or back. The important thing is to understand your goal in network marketing. If you want to start churning out supplemental income quickly, choose a front-weighted plan. If you want to replace your job and make network marketing your career, a middle-weighted plan is great. If you want to become wealthy, a plan weighted in the back end will give you this advantage. However, a balanced plan is the fairest of all.

17. There's nothing wrong with receiving a percentage back on product you've purchased. However, some companies use this as a gimmick to try to increase retention by getting distributors to think they're earning commissions in their first month when, in fact, they're just getting a rebate check on product they've purchased. I have people call me all the time and tell me they made $25 in their first week without signing up any distributors or selling any product. I remind them that they only had to spend several hundred dollars to get that rebate check, and that making money when you have not done anything yet in your business is actually a bit alarming. Remember, a rebate is your money that you have already spent, given back to you. Other than the concerns I've outlined, there's nothing wrong with rebates, but I have to ask, why doesn't the company just make the product less expensive, or give a special discount at the point of purchase?

18. The words *infinity bonus* implies that distributors will receive a commission for an infinite number of levels. However, it doesn't take a Harvard math professor to know that you cannot pay infinite levels on any compensation plan or the company will go out of business. Usually infinity bonuses are temporary bonuses

paid on deeper levels until the next qualified distributor takes the bonus away from you. The infinity bonus is the 1990s way of saying the compensation plan has a compression factor. So rest assured, the infinity bonus is not a bad thing to have, but it does not really pay to infinity. If it did, the company would be infinitely bankrupt!

19. Some companies use car and home bonuses to provide performance incentives for distributors. The emotional appeal of owning the car or home of your dreams can be a strong motivator, and these programs have been very successful over all. Distributors should keep in mind that car and home bonus programs pay a bonus to distributors that can be directly applied to a monthly loan payment on a car or home. If distributor performance level drops during the financing of your car or home, you can be disqualified from earning your bonus, but you are still obligated to make payments to the bank. This happens all the time, so try to OVER qualify for your position rather than doing the absolute bare minimum to qualify. Better safe than sorry.

20. It is common knowledge in network marketing that it is illegal to earn commission strictly on recruiting other distributors. In fact, this is one definition of an illegal pyramid. However, some MLMs have devised ways to pay distributors for the act of training other distributors or for selling these distributors training packages. According to MLM law, the training or coding bonuses are illegal. The word coding bonus means *training bonus* and is used to indicate that there are certain training codes assigned to pay out specific compensations to trainers at different qualifying ranks. There are still many companies getting away with giving coding bonus commissions to distributors. But according to top network marketing legal authorities, the companies that are still using coding bonuses are sending up red flags that will eventually be spotted by government regulators (details in later Chapters Ten).

21. Avoid network marketing companies that allow you to sponsor your spouse or another household dependant into your business. When you really understand how most network marketing compensation plans work, there's no benefit to this. If done company wide, it can actually negatively impact the pay plan. Don't join companies that allow you to sponsor yourself back into the pay plan. Exceptions apply when you're dealing

with multiple business centers or reentries in a binary. However, regulators are scrutinizing even these and there's no guarantee that regulators will allow multiple business centers and reentries forever.

22. Some network marketing opportunities get new distributors excited about the fact that all you have to do is make a one-time purchase of product, and then you never have to order again. Companies that do not have ongoing product sales volume requirements are usually doomed to fail. If there is absolutely no standard of performance or activity expected from independent distributors on a month-to-month basis, there will be no activity.

23. Some one-time-purchase plans are not one-time programs at all. They disguise ongoing purchases in the compensation plan by taking a 30–50 percent cut of commission checks that you earn and applying it towards a purchase of product, which they promptly ship to you, kind of like an involuntary auto-ship program. Therefore, since these companies promote their program by touting the benefits of a one-time purchase, the company is not telling new distributors the truth.

24. Some companies have developed creative payout strategies that allow distributors to put product on a kind of layaway plan. A company that collects money for a product or service and then issues payment of commissions before the product or service is delivered is classified as an illegal pyramid. Some companies are still operating these illegal programs right now.

25. Another down payment related practice is the issuing of product vouchers that can be redeemed for products and/or services later. The law states that distributor commissions on money collected in exchange for these vouchers should not be paid until the vouchers are redeemed for real products and/or services. No voucher deal has ever survived government scrutiny.

26. One way a corporation can assure a pay plan will behave correctly is to have a network marketing consulting firm do test modeling with other companies' sales figures. This is a service that can generally be provided by the company that produces your compensation software. Using actual sales volume models as opposed to hypothetical ones can create a very realistic summary of how the plan will pay out.

The Final Word on Compensation Plans

If you're investigating a breakaway, binary or unilevel plan, you may or may not be on the right track, but proceed with caution. Every plan is different. Try to avoid plans that are unproven. Try to find a plan nearly identical to plans that have been used successfully in other companies for years. If the plan is a matrix or a hybrid, your chances are diminished considerably, so use extreme caution. If you're looking at a 1-up, 2-up, 3-up, or any kind of up, or if it's a single-line downline, grab your wallet and run.

While in the process of selecting a network marketing company, do not select a company based on the compensation plan. However, you definitely want to consider disqualifying companies for their pay plans. There are so many other essential criteria for selecting a company. Placing too much weight on the compensation plan can be a deadly mistake. According to Mark Rawlins of MLM.com and author of *Understanding Multilevel Commissions*, selecting a pay plan that has been proven in the real world is critical. "In my consulting career, I've always made a practice of trying to give advice that's grounded in experience. This advice is based on theories that have been tested at enough companies to prove them out. I don't think that you have done well by a company if you bet their financial future on an idea that hasn't been proven out by the marketplace."[14]

Once I know a comp plan is proven in the marketplace, I put about 15 percent of the weight of my ultimate decision on the compensation plan. Any more emphasis is unreasonable; any less is irresponsible.

Chapter Seven Review

1. The most popular compensation plans in network marketing are the breakaway, the unilevel, the binary, the matrix, the hybrid, and the 2-up. Some of these plans are legitimate, and some of them are gimmicks. Study this chapter over and over so you can review pay plans like a pro. Out of the companies we reviewed in detail for our compensation plan study, here's how they break down.
    a. 36% incorporated a breakaway compensation plan (dropping)
    b. 35% use a unilevel or unilevel hybrid (climbing)
    c. 21% use the binary or binary hybrid (climbing)
    d. 6% use a matrix (dropping)

     e.   2% are attempting to survive with the 2-up plan (holding)

     f.   In hybrid plans, there is usually one plan more dominant than the other. I gave credit to the dominant side and tallied it with the rest. The binary/unilevel hybrid was counted as a binary

2.   When someone is introducing their pay plan to you, they will say anything to make their plan look better. Many distributors feel their compensation plan is the best, regardless of whether or not they have compared it to other plans. Picking the right compensation plan can make the difference between success and failure in network marketing. Be sure to review all of the plans on the market and then choose a proven compensation plan.

3.   The matrix plan can be a good plan for certain types of products and services. In network marketing, the matrix has not been accepted as a mainstream plan and it should be avoided.

4.   The breakaway was the most widely used plan in network marketing over fifteen years ago. Recently, the unilevel and binary plans have been rapidly gaining in popularity. The breakaway is still widely used by older, more traditional network marketing companies, but over the last fifteen years it has not been chosen by newer network marketing companies.

5.   The unilevel is a fantastic alternative to traditional breakaway plans. The unilevel does not have the front-end load, fast income potential of the breakaway, but it also does not have the attrition rate. Try to avoid any unilevel gimmicks, like two-level plans and plans that pay different percentages on every level. Compressed plans are ideal for affiliate programs but are not yet proven as mainstream compensation plans. The unilevel is one network marketing payout structure that is here to stay. I rarely hear complaints about the unilevel.

6.   Although the modern binary is constantly evolving, I found it to be a revolutionary plan and a top contender among today's innovative plans. The binary is fair, lucrative, and has an element of synergy and teamwork not found in other plans.

Avoid binary plans that market the compensation plan over the product line. This can lead to trouble and even shutdown. Avoid companies that cap their distributor's volumes too early and force you to reenter your downline for additional streams of income. Don't join companies or organizations that overemphasize joining the powerleg. Remember, many distributors will never have the advantage of being in a powerleg and this can lead to major resentment and massive distributor attrition. The modern binary is here to stay, and it's an exciting alternative to more traditional plans.

7. The 2-up, like the matrix, looks fantastic on paper, but when you put it into practice, it's a disaster. The Australian 2-Up is considered a gimmick compensation plan because no company has ever survived this plan. Just say *no* to the 2-up.

8. The hybrid plan is simply a combination of two or more of the above plans. Hybrid plans are far from proven and generally cause tremendous confusion among distributors. Most MLM experts agree that companies should choose one plan or the other to eliminate confusion and promote duplication.

9. Have a network marketing consulting firm do test modeling on your compensation plan. Using actual sales volume models as opposed to hypothetical ones can give a very realistic summary of how the plan will pay out in the real world.

10. It's illegal to earn MLM commissions strictly on recruiting other distributors. In fact, this is one definition of an illegal pyramid. Also, avoid companies that pay you for getting your distributors to a training meeting.

11. Moderate start-up costs for a network marketing distributorship range from $150 to $1500. If the total start-up is less than $100 and more than $2,000, proceed with caution. If start up is less than $50, including product and distributor kit, or more than $3,000, consult an objective network marketing consultant before proceeding.

12. Distributor commission plans should pay out an actual 33–50 percent on revenue taken in by the company. Companies that

pay less are greedy, companies that claim to pay more are usually lying or ignorant of the actual percentages.

13. Compensation plans may have minor enhancements over time, but the inherent structure should never, ever change.

14. The payout of a commission plan is controlled as much by the rules as it is by the commission percentages.

15. If the corporate leaders are inexperienced, or if they don't understand compensation structures, the initial structure of a company's compensation plan will tell this tale like a crystal ball.

16. If you're already involved in network marketing, don't think your company and compensation plan is the only game in town. You'll never know if your compensation plan is the best until you've looked at all the rest.

17. If you're investigating a breakaway, binary, or unilevel plan, you may be on the right track, but proceed with caution. Every plan is different. Try to avoid plans that are new to the market and therefore unproven. Try to find a plan nearly identical to plans that have been used successfully in other companies for years. If the plan is a matrix or a hybrid, your chances are diminished considerably, so use extreme caution. If you're looking at a 2-up plan (or a 1-up, or 3-up, or any other kind of up) or if it's a single-line downline, grab your wallet and run.

18. While in the process of selecting a network marketing company, do not select a company based on the compensation plan. However, you definitely want to consider disqualifying companies for their pay plans. There are so many other essential criteria for selecting a company. Placing too much weight on the compensation plan can be a deadly mistake. Once I know a compensation plan is proven in the marketplace, I put about 15 percent of the weight of my ultimate decision on the compensation plan.

PART V

The Heart of the Matter

Now we're getting into the company criteria that really divides the pros from the amateurs. Over the next two chapters, we will focus in on scrutinizing the founders and leadership of the company. We'll take a hard look at the company's commitment to legal compliance. We'll also be examining several strategies for breaking down a company's specific products or product line and putting these products through some final evaluation. After applying this process to any large list of company considerations, you'll be able to narrow it down to just a handful of top companies.

Chapter 8

Key #5
Company Leadership:
Partnering with Success

Scrutinizing Corporate Leadership

Investigating a corporate leadership team can be tricky. Some companies will eagerly share their financial numbers with would-be distributors who have genuine interest in doing a thorough investigation. However, these numbers may be inflated or doctored to make the company look more appealing. Experienced corporate teams generally did not get where they are today by opening their books to every Tom, Dick, and Harry who asked to see the numbers. There are ways to get accurate numbers on a company without being related to the founders and without doing any dumpster diving.

More important than reviewing the books of any company is looking at the recent accomplishments and activities of the corporate leadership and founders. The track record of the executive management team, now and prior to launching their current company is one of the most reliable indicators of how a company will do in the future. If a leader had a great track record for inspiring leadership, motivating distributors and employees, dealing with problems and setbacks, and maintaining high standards of integrity, he is likely to display the same behavior as he moves forward. The reverse is also true. Here are some resources that will allow you to do a thorough investigation of your company and leadership team.

Investigation Strategies

1. Company Distributor Agreement and Policies: Every company should have you review and sign a distributor agreement before you're officially enrolled into that program as an independent company representative. Most companies will allow you to initially sign up over the Internet, but you're still obligated to submit a signed distributor application after carefully reviewing

the company's policies and procedures. You must carefully study the company's terms of enrollment as an independent distributor, and company policies and procedures. Most company policies are very similar in today's market; however, some companies will try to sneak by some policies that are absolutely anti-distributor. Also, some companies may be violating their own policies, so you must first know what these policies are.

2. Company Literature: Review all company literature and propaganda. Look the company up online and review their corporate website and any other information that comes up in the search. Don't believe everything you read about a company online. Allow this process to raise questions and concerns about the company. If the company is publicly traded, order a free copy of the company's latest annual report straight from the company itself.

3. Dun & Bradstreet: This is an organization set up to provide accurate and professional news, statistics, legal notices, and other important information about businesses and individuals who do business. D&B is regarded as a reputable and reliable source of information. Their reports can be expensive, but they're worth the cost if you want to make the right choice on a long-term relationship. Visit http://www.networkmarketingbook.com/links for D&B contact information.

4. Attorney General: Check with the state attorney general where the company was founded, where it is located today, and in any states where it is doing a high volume of business. Attorney generals have entire departments dedicated to reviewing business opportunities. When you contact them, remember how busy they are and respect their time. Search for unresolved complaints against companies.

5. Better Business Bureau: Call or go online to the BBB to see if many unresolved complaints are listed with a company. You need to know the main phone line of the company you are investigating, or in some cases, the corporate website. Some of these reports are free, but you might be charged a few dollars for the service in some cases. The BBB will not endorse a company, although you can purchase a superficial seal of approval from them for a substantial fee. The BBB's main job is to log complaints. Even if a company has some complaints on

file, this is generally not a problem. What you're looking for is a pattern of unresolved complaints and problems.

6. Dept. of Consumer Affairs: Check with the DCA in three or four states where the company is doing business, just to make sure there are not some major complaints about the company's business practices in those states.

7. Direct Sales Association: The DSA is a non-profit trade organization that speaks out for direct sales and network marketing. They have established standards of conduct for network marketing companies that must be followed to be an active member. Go to http://www.dsa.org.

8. Annual Report: If the company is publicly traded (more on this later in the chapter), you can request an annual report, which will tell you everything from how much commission is paid to distributors, to what lawsuits they're involved in. You can also document the growth or demise of a company.

9. Resources: Here are some great resources for learning and knowing about network marketing, distributor rights, MLM company rights, and many other topics related to investigating MLM companies.

    a. www.marketwaveinc.com
    b. www.theanmp.com
    c. www.mlmia.com
    d. www.mlmlaw.com
    e. www.themlmattorney.com
    f. *www.mlmatty.com*
    g. www.mlmwatchdog.com
    h. www.mlmlegal.com
    i. www.mlm.com
    j. www.networkmarketingbusinessjournal.com

10. Litigation History: Purchase a litigation history from Corporation Service Company. Find out about everything from major litigation to complaints of unpaid bills. Look for patterns of delinquency and abuse. These reports can require time to review and they can cost hundreds of dollars. Simply call 800-221-0770.

11. Here are some of my favorite investigative strategies taken from some of my favorite gurus and mentors, such as Rod Cook of mlmwatchdog.com, and some I discovered on my own.

Top Internet/Website investigation strategies

Corporate Website Scrutiny
1. Take a good look at the corporate website and trust your initial instincts. If the website has any element that looks unprofessional, cheap, or tacky, then *buyer beware*. A cheesy website is usually the first indication that you have a loser on your hands.
2. Look for company contact information on the websites. PO boxes and 800 numbers are fine, but you also want to see a physical building and direct telephone lines that work. If they don't list these, call the 800 numbers and ask for the direct phone number and the physical address. Not having these posted clearly on the website could be a red flag. If the company only posts an e-mail address for contact information, be afraid ... be very afraid. If the address listed on the Website is PMB (postal mail box), then it is a small postal box rented from a commercial postage service (like Mailboxes, Etc.) and a surefire reason to be suspicious. Are they trying to avoid the U.S. Postal Service?
3. You want to see a summary of the corporate executives, with pictures. Companies that have nothing to hide will want to showcase their leaders. Some leaders have such a spotty reputation that the company is nervous to reveal their names for fear that a simple Google search will uncover the skeletons of past ventures or relationships gone bad.
4. Look for companies that feature images of celebrities at their website, or endorsements and testimonials from celebrities. Find out if these endorsements were ever really given, and if so, if these celebrities still have a legal agreement with the company to endorse the brand. So many of the celebrity pictures on corporate websites and independent distributor sites are simply copied and pasted without permission. This activity is highly illegal and unethical.

Internet Investigation Strategies
1. Visit MLM or network marketing chat boards and forums at AOL, MSN, Yahoo, MLM.com and especially Facebook and Twitter, or anywhere network marketing is being discussed. Don't believe everything you read (as a matter of fact, you should distrust everything you read). However, when bad news

about a company is flowing, it's flowing like a fire hose. I've known distributors who joined a company in the middle of a meltdown, and they didn't know because the company wasn't talking about it. But the chat boards were buzzing. Don't waste your time in the chats or debating on Facebook, but check them from time to time for relevant information.

2. Watch for companies involved in any kind of spam or unsolicited mass e-mail campaigns. Any company initiating spam, or even tolerating the spamming activities of their distributors, will ultimately be shut down. Also, never take seriously any company that tries to recruit you through a mass e-mail campaign.

3. Look up the contact information for the person or company who registered the Website domain name. Go to www.whois.com and try to reach this individual or company through the contact information provided there. I've found out some amazing facts and dug up some big concerns through this simple five-minute process.

4. Look up the company's physical address and do a search for the address with the satellite photo technology at Google Earth. You'll be able to hone in on an actual satellite picture of the building itself. Location is everything. You're not looking for a residence, a trailer park, a crack house, or a desert island. You are looking for an appropriately sized building in an appropriate location. Keep in mind that if the company is a start-up, and the building is new, the image may not be current enough to provide helpful pictures.

Search Engine Investigation Strategies

1. Scour the Internet for information on the company and its founders. Simply go to one of the major search engines like Google, Yahoo, or MSN. Enter the MLM company's name and the executives and owner's/founder's name. Go through these pages! Look for commentary on websites and blogs (blogs are text-based discussion websites with frequent entries). Look for unresolved complaints, lawsuits, and informational articles. Take everything you read with a grain of salt. Most of the anti-MLM websites are very unbalanced in their dissemination of information. Many are just ignorant, or they're even lying.

2. Visit Alexa and use their Website look-up tool to check the traffic rating of the site (like golf, the lower the score, the

better). Some programs that claim huge product sales and enormous recruiting activity have no Website traffic to confirm these claims. The best way to do Alexa traffic tests is to compare the company you're evaluating to a well-established, mature network marketing company, like Herbalife or NuSkin, to see how traffic compares. Traffic is not everything, but it should be substantial and consistent. Scores in the thousands have extremely high traffic. Anything in the 10–50,000 range is very substantial traffic. In the 100,000–200,000 is moderate traffic and likely a newer company. Anything higher than 300,000 is small potatoes. Anything above 400,000 is either a brand-new Website or company or they're not showing substantial traffic. By the way, as for the big boys, Google, Facebook, Yahoo, and MSN are usually rated among the top visited sites online (single digit rankings).

3. Search for advertisements in the search engines that feature the company and its trade names or brand name products. Watch for blatant violations of FDA or FTC laws and policies. Look for inappropriate use of company trademarks and logos, and Websites run by independent distributors that feature the company's name and/or trademarks in the *domain name*. These are all red flags.

Another Perfect MLM Deal

One of the most important things to remember when looking at a company is to not get emotionally wrapped up in the company's product, founders, or story until you've really scrutinized it first. Before you look at this company through rose-colored glasses, look at the company with a skeptical eye. You need to find out what is hiding behind the wizard's curtain. Ask the tough questions so you can find all the skeletons in the closet before it's too late.

As I investigate MLMs, I'm constantly hearing statements from distributors such as this, "Our corporate president, Mr. Peter P. Perfect, graduated from Prestige University with honors and then launched Credibility Corporation, which he took to $100 million in five years. Two years later, he built Incredible Incorporated, which was also a huge success. Now Mr. Perfect is just starting Big Launch Limited. We're already a member of the Better Business Bureau, and we've been honored as company of the year at our local Chamber of Commerce. Our head scientist, who has formulated all of our products, was formerly nominated for a Nobel Prize. He has three patents and has written five books."

Now this story, minus the bogus names, is typical of the stories I hear all the time when being pitched on a new company. This could be the start of another legendary network marketing company. However, it could also be a disaster waiting to happen. Before proceeding with my breakdown, can you spot some of the inconsistencies and red flags in the content of the story? What concerns do you need to follow up on? What questions need answering?

Asking the tough questions

I'd start out by asking questions like, "Did Mr. Perfect really go to Prestige University, and did he really graduate with honors?" Then check it out. You'd be surprised at how many people I've caught being dishonest about their education. If they're lying about their education, they're lying about other details. Next I'd ask about the other two companies Mr. Prestige had launched like, "What happened to these companies? Did they go out of business? Were they sold, and if so, why? If Mr. Prestige started three companies, will he start a fourth company in a few years? If so, what will happen to Big Launch Limited when that happens?" You've really got to get to the bottom of this before falling in love with this program.

Another thing to consider is that some honors and accolades are not necessarily good. For example, to be listed with the Better Business Bureau may simply mean that you have had complaints registered with them. The BBB is simply an organization that registers complaints. Yes, they have membership and anyone can join for a fee. Being honored at your local Chamber of Commerce may mean that you're very involved with your local community, or it may mean you donated a bunch of free product to their annual fund-raising auction. Or maybe Mr. Perfect went to the high school senior prom with Mrs. Popular, the current Chamber president. By the way, anyone can write a book, register a patent, and be nominated for a Nobel Prize. Yes, it shows some discipline to have done some of these things, but it is not necessarily an indicator of the character necessary to lead a major company. I'm not saying that everyone out there is lying about their credentials or embellishing the facts. I am saying, verify, verify, verify. Ask the tough questions so you can gather all the facts.

Start an investigation of your chosen company by interviewing founders, vendors, and top distributors. Although the executives of any top company are extremely busy, they're generally always open to scheduling phone or in-person interviews with prospective distributors, especially if you make it known that you're planning on making a very serious commitment to your new company of choice. If I'm looking at a new company, I'll always travel to the company headquarters to meet the founders in person. This is critical for those who plan on making network marketing their career.

Here are some of the things you'll want to find out in your investigation as you interview executives. Is the company timely on its commission checks to distributors and payments to vendors? Has the company applied for credit? Was credit denied? Is the company having any financial problems? Is the company going through any lawsuits? Is the company keeping anything from the public? How long has the person you're interviewing been associated with the company? How many companies has the person you're interviewing been associated with and at what times? Create a simple timeline. Look for patterns of disloyalty or the constant changing of companies and titles with those you interview. Cross reference your information with the others you interview from the same company and don't be surprised when you see some inconsistencies.

An Ounce of Prevention

No matter how much success, power, and leverage a network marketing company accumulates during hyper-growth, it will always be small potatoes compared to the regulatory bodies that watch over the network marketing industry. Some corporate owners I know let the explosive growth of their companies go to their head. Instead of starting and maintaining a legal compliance department, they start thinking about running for President, buying private islands for distributor retreats, and bucking the legal system. But know this - no network marketing or direct sales company is above the law. Furthermore, companies that are going to last must learn how to work with the government, not fight against it. Here are some guidelines on how to know if the company you're investigating is legitimate and if they're compliant with the laws that govern network marketing.

Things to Watch Out For

As we evaluate network marketing companies, it's critical that we check and cross check our work to avoid mistakes. Here's a fantastic list of things to avoid in a company. Be sure to double check this list with every company you scrutinize.

1. Avoid companies that do not appear to have bona fide products or services. Never join a program where the product is simply thrown in the mix as an attempt to legalize the process of mass sponsoring. For every top distributor earning $10,000 per month or more in commissions, there are literally thousands of customers purchasing product month after month. If the product cannot stand on its own, these checks will not last long.

2. Avoid companies that focus on rewarding you for the mere act of recruiting. Commissions are earned through the sales of product, not distributor sign-ups.

3. Avoid companies where the product price is inflated beyond what is reasonable in the marketplace. Compare the price of the product to other top networking products that have been selling successfully for 10-20 years or more.

4. Avoid companies that don't control all revenues. All revenues associated with product sales and commissions paid to distributors should be collected and dispersed by the company, not the distributors.

5. Avoid companies that make, or allow their distributors to make, unrealistic earnings claims. Any earnings statements of any significance must be substantiated through strict guidelines set forth by the FTC. It's better to just avoid income claims.

6. Avoid companies that allow inaccurate or misleading advertising. Aggressive promotion is fine. Deception or exaggeration on any level is intolerable.

7. Avoid companies that make illegal medical claims. FDA and FTC attacks against careless network marketing companies are becoming more and more frequent. Companies and distributors must be increasingly cautious about the statements they make about health products. All companies planning on sticking around must be proactive in self-regulation and should have an aggressive program in place to stop any improper product claims. Good management teams will not hesitate to reprimand distributors for making improper medical claims and will even cancel distributorships for repeat offenses. After all, the company can be held liable for claims made by independent distributors.

8. Avoid companies that do not keep distributor testimonials in check. Testimonials of health benefits, lifestyle benefits, or other

product benefits can easily be counted as product and income claims. Make sure the company you're investigating has guidelines for testimonials, which they are proactively teaching to distributors.

9. Avoid companies that send commission checks late or not at all. Avoid companies that send product shipments late, have frequent back orders, or fail to send product or perform services in a timely manner.

10. Avoid companies that make the distributorship seem like a job offer. Independent distributors are just that, independent contractors. They own their own business and do not draw a salary or benefits from the company like an employee.

11. Avoid companies that have an unfair or non-existent refund policy. Most companies offer at least the standard 90 percent unconditional buy-back policy on unopened product which means they'll unconditionally refund 90 percent of your purchases, holding 10% with the company for a restocking fee. Some exceptions exist in the various states. Make sure your company is confident enough in their product to offer a refund without question.

12. Avoid companies that pay commissions on sales aids, distributor kits, distributor training, or anything other than the company's legitimate product or service.

13. Avoid companies that encourage distributors to make a large purchase of inventory when joining the company. Generally anything over $1500 can send up red flags. Pyramid laws state that you must sell 70 percent of your product inventory before making another purchase.

14. Avoid programs that require substantial investments in tools like brochures and sales aids. Most companies can be started for $20–200 in tools and a $50 distributor kit. Why would you need thousands in tool inventory when shipping only takes three days? Distributor kits should be sold at or near cost.

15. Watch out for companies that require the purchase of peripheral items, accessories, or other services.

16. Avoid companies with no requirement of purchasing products to maintain activity as a distributor. These opportunities are usually short-lived.

17. Avoid companies that do not encourage the retail selling of your product or service. You should be able to document retail sales

to at least five to ten customers per month who are not a part of the commission plan.

18. Avoid companies that claim you can succeed without recruiting distributors or selling product. These programs are scams preying on the ignorant.

19. Avoid programs with too many complaints filed against the company. Most regulatory agencies keep track of complaints. Looking into these complaints can be helpful. By the way, even the legitimate companies are going to have some complaints from a few disgruntled distributors. There are countless ways to offend people in modern society. What you don't want to find is frequent litigation, many unresolved complaints, or criminal activity.

20. Avoid companies that allow spouses or even dependent children still living at home to sponsor under each other. This type of sponsoring is illegal in many states and is a great way to attract the attention of enthusiastic regulators. At the very least, it's a manipulation of the compensation plan and can disrupt the natural flow of earned commissions.

21. Avoid companies that offer to sign you up in multiple MLM programs. These companies are called *portfolio programs* and they usually don't even have permission from the companies they are promoting to do what they are doing, even though they swear they have written contracts. No portfolio program has ever survived.

22. Avoid companies that have not raised sufficient start-up capital. You'll generally be able to find out about financing when you interview the company's CFO, top distributors, and company vendors. Avoid companies that are using a prelaunch to raise money for the start-up of the company. Lack of start-up money is one of the top reasons that companies go out of business. Start-up companies often use profits from today's sales to operate the business, hoping that they can pay distributor commissions out of next month's profits. Soon, products start to back order and commission checks arrive late, or not at all. Most undercapitalized companies can't maintain this juggling act for long and end up filing bankruptcy.

23. Avoid companies that agree to build your downline for you in exchange for you investing in the company. Don't believe them for a second. These programs usually take your money and build their own downlines, leaving you high and dry months later.

Report any of these programs to your local state attorney general's office.

What is a Pyramid Really?

A pyramid, or I should say illegal pyramid, is simply a game involving people and money. It usually starts with some ignorant, greedy person who gets the *original* idea that if he or she removes the product or service out of the MLM deal, it would allow the program to replicate faster and he or she wouldn't have to ship or fulfill anything. Money itself becomes the product. A typical pyramid will have you pay a fee to join, and then you go out and get others to pay this same fee. Then you teach them to go get more people to pay the fee. Once this scenario has replicated several generations, you get a payout. Then you jump back into the pyramid with a bigger investment and start the process again. This time, as you fulfill the requirements for a payout, the prize is even bigger. Once you've cycled through this process several times, you could be earning tens of thousands of dollars or more without delivering any kind of real value or merchandise.

While I was in high school, I was exposed to my first pyramid. A friend of mine asked me to meet him in the school library. He proceeded to explain to me that if I could come up with $100, I could join him in what he called *an airplane investment.* He explained that when you invest the $100, you purchase a seat on the very back of this virtual airplane. As you get others to invest the $100, you get to move up a seat. You move farther and farther up the airplane until you're eventually the pilot of the airplane. Once you've filled the entire airplane with passengers who have invested $100 each, you get a handsome payout. When you've filled three airplanes, this payout becomes tens of thousands! It seemed a bit unusual, and certainly too good to be true, so I decided to ask my father about it when I got home from school. I diagramed it out on a piece of paper for him, and without hesitation he said, "Son, this is a pyramid scheme."

My father graciously volunteered to call my friend with me and explain it to him, which he did. I was impressed with how my dad was able to break it down for my friend without making him feel totally stupid that he'd fallen for a scheme like this. Unfortunately, my friend's father was one of the ringleaders in the scheme, and so I'm not sure if my dad's message was taken very seriously. But a few weeks later, the local attorney general did take it seriously and shut down the scheme and exposed all of its founders. I remember feeling so relieved that my dad had prevented me from getting involved. Sure $100 was difficult to lose as a high school student, but more importantly, I couldn't imagine how embarrassing it would have been to have to go back to the people I got involved and tell them it turned out to be a scam and they would not be getting their money back. Would you risk your integrity and reputation for a few hundred dollars, or a few thousand?

Ponzi Schemes and Why to Avoid Them

A Ponzi scheme is simply a type of pyramid investment deal with a little twist to trick people into believing it is legitimate in the beginning. The Ponzi scheme is named after Charles Ponzi, who became famous, or should I say infamous, for his little mathematical game. Back in the 1920s, Charles Ponzi developed an investment program that would allow people to earn a healthy 50 percent return on their money. If someone invested $1000, they would earn back $1500 for a $500 profit. Let's say Ponzi's first three victims were Adam, Bill, and Carl. Ponzi would get Adam and Bill to both invest $1000. Ponzi would then take $500 from Bill's investment and pay Adam back $1500, artificially proving to his future victims that his investment system actually worked. Ponzi would earn money on transaction fees. With $500 remaining from Bill's investment, Ponzi would then bring on Carl as a $1000 investor, to create a total of $1500, which he used to pay Bill back. By constantly expanding his investor base, Ponzi was able to accumulate massive profits in transaction fees. However, he could not keep up on this charade forever, and before his death, Ponzi's scheme came crashing down and many people lost their $1000 investment. Any investment scheme that is designed to rob Peter to pay Paul is now referred to as a Ponzi scheme.

So what is the lesson for network marketing companies? The survival of a network marketing company from month to month should not be dependent on sponsorships, but the sale of products of true value. Recruiting can expand a company's distribution base, but recruiting should not fuel the compensation payouts.

Public vs. Private

Researching a public company (a company traded on the stock market) is as simple as pulling a Dun & Bradstreet report through your banker or attorney. These reports usually cost a few hundred dollars and are very reliable. Also, request an annual report from the company itself.

Most network marketing consultants agree that going public is a Pandora's Box. Once opened, it can't be closed and it can lead to problems. Trying to please both distributors and stock holders at the same time is tricky business. Still, a handful of companies have made this work over the years. Companies go public and sell stock in order to raise money for growth and expansion. I like to see companies raise their money through investors, or better yet, self-fund the venture with capital raised from previous business successes. As Len Clements, author of *Inside Network Marketing,* says so well, "Going public is great when everything's beautiful, but when it turns ugly, you can't wear makeup."[15]

It is more difficult to scrutinize a private company since they do not have to release any financial information. Any information that is released by a private company may or may not be accurate since the giver does not have any incentive to be 100 percent accurate and objective. Therefore, it is even more critical with a private company to get to know the backgrounds, personal mission, and motives of the corporate officers. You can still order a Dun & Bradstreet report on the company and on all of the founders. The best and most objective information I've ever received about a company was gathered from people who had worked with the founders of the company before the company was founded. Again, you're looking for a history of performance, integrity, experience, and resourcefulness. You must be able to answer yes when you're asked if you really trust the people who are running your company.

Keeping Up With Growth

Most companies that go out of business do not go under because of lack of growth, but because they grow much too fast. In a popular MLM article, Len Clements discusses the issue of exponential growth. He states, "Consider what is involved with keeping up with a company's growth curve. The difference between 'keeping up' and 'catching up' in this industry is usually the difference between life and death from a corporate standpoint. If a MLM company gets even one month behind the growth curve it can be like letting go of the reins of a wild horse."[16]

Start-Up and Maintenance Requirements (SUMR)

One of the most important decisions a management team must make deals with what I call start-up/maintenance requirements, or SUMR. The term

SUMR is used to describe the financial commitment level that is expected of each distributor at the point of start-up and the ongoing financial commitment necessary to maintain active status from month to month. The trick is to find a balanced package. In order to understand the importance of balance, we must first look at the two extremes of the SUMR spectrum.

High-end SUMR companies

There are three types of SUMR: high-end, low-end, and medium-range. Companies that opt to go with a high-end structure typically encourage or require $2,000–10,000 down at start-up and a $500–5,000 per month group volume requirement to maintain active status. These are fees required by the company itself and may not include additional fees for marketing tools and advertising. These companies are characterized by fast growth and high attrition rates. Many companies tolerate and even sometimes support front-end loading and encourage distributors to go full-time immediately, as this is the only way to have a decent chance of maintaining the heavy group volume requirements. High-end companies attract charismatic individuals who are generally excellent public speakers and very persuasive. There are a handful of distributors who have the ability to make $50,000–100,000 per month while thousands of others struggle to make less than minimum wage for their efforts. Many distributors end up with credit cards maxed and garages full of product.

On the up side, high-end companies tend to attract higher caliber individuals, who treat the business like a business. Also, the possibility, no matter how remote, for reaching millionaire status within as little as twenty-four months is possible with high-end companies. Almost all of the high-end SUMRs are typically characterized by having breakaway compensation plans.

FTC Start-Up Limitations

The FTC has warned network marketing companies about unreasonable start-up costs and the stocking of unnecessary amounts of product. They have created laws like the *70 percent rule*, which encourages the industry to eliminate overstocking and front-end loading. But if this isn't enough to convince you not to stock up too much in your first order, nearly two dozen state attorney generals have set a start-up cost threshold at a maximum of $500. This means that many states will not allow initial purchases of over $500.

Low-end SUMR companies

Low-end companies deal with the exact opposite issues. They do not have any group volume requirement and have very low personal volume requirements ranging from $10–50 per month. These companies also grow quickly because of low personal volume requirements. But it takes many thousands of people to produce enough product volume to provide good commissions to distributors. Even a downline of one thousand distributors could equal only a few hundred dollars per month. Low volume requirements attract lazy distributors and/or distributors who have failed at other programs and want to do something that doesn't require as much time and money commitment.

Low-end SUMR companies have the highest percentage of inactive distributors of any type of plan, because sponsoring strategies focus so heavily on the ease of starting the business and not on moving large volumes of product. On the up side, low-end SUMR companies are more user friendly than the high-end companies. Low-end companies are fairer to the average person and allow everyone to participate. Most low-end companies are typically characterized by having a unilevel compensation structure.

Medium-range companies

Balance, as was stated earlier, is the key. A medium-range company, or balanced company, has just enough initial start-up cost to cause distributors to make a solid financial commitment, yet not enough to be considered front-end loading. Initial start-up costs range from $100–1,000. Half of this cost should be for purchasing your product and distributor kit from your company, and the other half should be for business-building tools and/or leads. Maintenance should consist of a moderate personal volume requirement of around $100 per month (the industry average). If your volume requirement is five times higher, the opportunity becomes five times less duplicable. If the requirement is half as much, the distributor's income potential drops in half. The distributor's average level of commitment drops way below average. Middle-range companies tend to find a healthier balance, attracting a high caliber individual while maintaining reasonable commitment levels.

What can the average person do?

In network marketing, the average distributor typically sponsors less than a handful of people and does an average of $100 per month in personal product purchases. Many of the top management teams in MLM companies now realize that in order for the company to succeed, they must design a marketing plan catered to the average person, not the below or above average person. Some companies, realizing the tough economic times our country is in, have provided various options for autoship ranging from $50 to $300 per month, giving distributors various options. This can be very constructive if marketed correctly.

Is cheaper better?

There is one particular company offering a program that keeps you active for $40 per month and they are saying, "Join us; we're less!" Now if less is better, why not appeal to even more people by going even lower. I know programs that require $20 and even $10 per month to stay active. Why not go with these? The answer is obvious! The more the company lowers the requirements past the average expectation, the less commitment the company requires and the less income potential exists. You begin attracting mostly couch potatoes. No duplication occurs. In addition, the payout begins to wither to the point that you need to sign-up half the population of Asia to produce a full-time income.

A particular friend of mine is a prime example of this mentality. He is constantly bouncing from program to program, looking for the deal with the least amount of commitment and with the same lucrative payout. My friend found a program just a few months ago that requires only a $20 per month maintenance. What has happened? He has attracted several like-minded individuals, who have all come in with the minimum investment and are doing $20 per month in volume. It's a generic unilevel structure and the payout is 10 percent. None of them are making more than a few dollars per month. Six months from now, he will be in a new program with another pay plan that requires only $10 per month to stay active. He's cut his income in half again and start attracting people with half the ambition of those he attracted to his previous company. Less is not always more.

The Sponsor Sets the Standard!

The sponsor is the only one who can set proper standards for his/her downline team. Even after choosing a medium range company, the sponsor has the choice of following the recommended start-up plan or doing their own thing. The sponsor must set standards high, but they shouldn't be so high that they discourage distributors. Investing $1,000 in a business upfront is very reasonable if the distributor is able to purchase everything, including product, training materials, and a good amount of prospecting supplies. After all, even an inexpensive franchise costs over $40,000 in start-up capital with all of the same risks, enormous overhead, and less income potential. Compared to the cost of a franchise or a traditional business start-up, starting a network marketing distributorship is a drop in the bucket. Furthermore, spending as much as $200–500 per month on business-building tools and leads is quite common in the beginning of any network marketing distributorship. Invest in your business but try to maintain a healthy balance. Don't invest too much or too little.

Product Value Is the Answer

In an article entitled "The Preeminence of Value," Network Marketing Attorney Kevin Grimes made the following statement: "Any network marketing opportunity is *ONLY* as good as the value of the products. Where there is no value, there is no opportunity and there is no future. Where there is tremendous value, there is tremendous opportunity and a tremendous future."[17]

Grimes further stated, "Value is the ultimate determiner of a company's profitability, viability, and future. A company can make a lot of mistakes, but if it offers substantial value, the market and distributors can be quite forgiving. No amount of hype, excitement, trips, cars, dream houses, cruises, or even money will overcome poor value, nor will they sustain a company or your business for the long term. *Long-term* success and growth flow *only* from products that are a good value. The magic is in the value of the products!"[18]

I couldn't agree more with Kevin Grimes' statements. As someone who works directly with dozens and dozens of network marketing companies on a daily basis, he should know. As a matter of fact, Grimes has come up with a formula for determining the value of a product.

$$\frac{\underline{Quality + Benefits}}{Price}$$

The formula is the sum of Quality and Benefits divided by Price. For a full explanation of this formula, visit http://www.mlmlaw.com and click on "Articles." Look for the article entitled "The Preeminence of Value."

The Lure of the Scam

Prominent MLM Attorney Jeffery A. Babener comments on the importance of offering quality products or services in his popular article, "Dot Com or Dot Scam?"

"Periodically, the network marketing industry is faced with a phenomenon in which distributors leave legitimate product or service companies in droves to partake in a feeding frenzy in a 'façade' MLM opportunity. The industry has seen this in overpriced phone cards, diet cookies, garage loads of water filters, high priced training fee telecom programs, gold bullion contract programs, travel and discount buying service packages, and a host of others. Such programs are short lived, but the industry suffers as individuals jump on the latest MLM junkie 'pyramid train'." [19]

Government Regulation on Health Products

The dietary supplements industry is constantly changing. New discoveries are being made every year, and new products are constantly introduced to the market. The demand on supplements is growing, and more and more entrepreneurs are being attracted to the health and wellness industry. To help protect consumers against unfair business practices and scams in the United States, the government has created two major organizations, the FTC and the FDA. Similar organizations exist in Canada and other countries across the globe.

The FTC, or Federal Trade Commission, plays the role of watchdog. It enforces laws outlawing "unfair or deceptive acts or practices." The FTC's mission is to ensure that consumers get accurate information about dietary supplements so that they can make informed decisions about these products. The FTC also has responsibility for claims in advertising.

The FDA, or the Food and Drug Administration, has responsibilities over dietary supplements and foods. The FDA is responsible for claims on product labels, packaging, inserts, and other promotional material. The FDA works closely with the FTC in monitoring advertising related to supplements and foods.

In 1994, the Dietary Supplements Health and Education Act (DSHEA) significantly changed the FDA's role in regulating supplement labeling. Although DSHEA does not directly apply to advertising, this act has compelled the FDA and the FTC to become more specific with their policies on advertising of supplements. In essence, advertising for any product (including dietary supplements) must be truthful, not misleading, and substantiated.

In general, the FTC gives great deference to an FDA determination of whether there is adequate support for a health claim. Furthermore, the FTC and the FDA will generally arrive at the same conclusion when evaluating unqualified health claims. As the Food Policy Statement notes, however, there may be certain limited instances when a carefully qualified health claim in advertising may be permissible under FTC law, in circumstances where it has not been authorized for labeling.

However, supplement marketers are cautioned that the FTC will require both strong scientific support and careful presentation for such claims.

Network marketing distributors should be familiar with basic FTC advertising principles. The FTC has taken action not just against supplement manufacturers, but also, in appropriate circumstances, against ad agencies, distributors, retailers, catalog companies, infomercial producers, and others involved in deceptive promotions. Everyone who participates in marketing dietary supplements has an obligation to make sure that claims are presented truthfully. They must be able to support any claims with documentation.

The FTC and FDA's advertising compliance policies are listed in detail on their respective Websites. Make sure the companies you're investigating comply with these standards. For more information visit http://www.ftc.gov and http://www.fda.gov

Conclusion

Be sure to take the time to scrutinize every company you're evaluating. It may seem like a big job, but believe me when I say that it is much less pain, suffering, and sacrifice than what you'll experience if you don't. This chapter is worth reviewing over and over until you memorize the content.

Chapter Eight Review

1. The track record of the executive management team, now and prior to launching their current company, is one of the most reliable indicators of how a company will do in the future.

2. Standard Investigation Strategies
   a. Review the company distributor agreement and policies
   b. Review company literature
   c. Order a Dun & Bradstreet Report*
   d. Check with the attorney general in several states
   e. Check for unresolved complaints at the Better Business Bureau*
   f. Check for unresolved complaints at the Department of Consumer Affairs*
   g. Check on membership status and standing at the Direct Sales Association*
   h. If the company is publicly traded, order an annual report

   i. Review industry resources and visit the websites listed in this chapter.

   j. Purchase a litigation history from Corporation Service Company*

3. Top Internet/Website Investigation Strategies

  a. Corporate Website Scrutiny
   i. Scrutinize the corporate Website for design or content
   ii. Look for full company contact information on the Websites
   iii. Look for companies that feature images or endorsements of celebrities, and verify authenticity

  b. Internet Investigation Strategies
   i. Look for company news on forums, chat boards, and blogs*
   ii. Watch for companies involved in any kind of spam
   iii. Do a Google Earth search on the company's physical address*

  c. Search Engine Investigation Strategies
   i. Scour the Internet for information on the company and its founders
   ii. Visit Alexa and use their Website look-up tool to check the traffic rating of the company's site*
   iii. Search for ads online that violate governmental regulations *

4. One of the most important things to remember when looking at a company is to not get emotionally wrapped up in the company's product, founders, or story until you've really scrutinized it first. Before you look at the company through rose-colored glasses, look at the company with a skeptical eye.

5. No matter how much success a network marketing company has during hyper-growth, it's still no match for the government. No network marketing or direct sales company is above the law.

6. Be sure to review my detailed list of twenty-three things to watch out for when investigating a network marketing company.

7. Avoid companies that:
    a. don't have bona fide products
    b. reward recruiting only
    c. price gouge with inflated products
    d. don't control all revenues
    e. allow or make illegal earnings claims
    f. use misleading advertising
    g. make illegal medical claims
    h. don't monitor distributor testimonials
    i. send commission checks late or not at all
    j. make the distributorship seem like a job offer
    k. have an unfair or non-existent refund policy
    l. pay commissions on sales aids, kits, or training
    m. encourage distributors to make a large purchase of inventory when joining the company
    n. require substantial investments in tools
    o. require the purchase of peripheral items
    p. no requirement of purchasing products
    q. do not encourage retail selling
    r. claim you can succeed without recruiting distributors or selling product
    s. have too many complaints filed against the company
    t. allow you to sponsor household members
    u. offer to sign you up in multiple MLMs
    v. have not raised sufficient start-up capital
    w. agree to build your downline for you

8. An illegal pyramid is a type of company with a multilevel compensation structure and no product. Money itself becomes the product. Just remember that this kind of pyramid structure is illegal, and they never stay in business. Eventually everyone loses money, credibility, and reputation.

9. Ponzi schemes are disguised as legitimate investments that pay out substantial returns, but the money isn't really invested. Eventually the scam is exposed and it crashes.

10. Researching a public company (a company traded on the stock market) is as simple as pulling a Dun & Bradstreet report through your banker or attorney. These reports usually cost a few hundred dollars and are very reliable. Also, request an annual report from the company itself. Going public is a great way for companies to raise cash for growth and development, but it usually causes many more problems than it solves.

11. It is more difficult to scrutinize a private company since they do not have to release any financial information. With a private company, get to know the backgrounds, personal missions, and motives of the corporate officers. Try to get information from trustworthy people who were previously associated with company founders. You must be able to trust the people who are running your company.

12. Sometimes being debt free can actually be a red flag. Some of the individuals applying for a loan to finance their network marketing start-up have such a poor track record that creditors might laugh them right out of the bank.

13. Most companies that go out of business do not go under due to lack of growth, but because they grow much too fast. Find out what kind of plan a company has, the amount of financing they're starting with, and the resources a company has in place to deal with hyper-growth.

14. Retention studies show that distributors should not be required to purchase more than $100–200 per month in product to remain active and about the same amount in business-building tools and marketing expenses.

15. Investing $500–1,000 in a business up front is very reasonable if the distributor is able to purchase everything, including product, training materials, and prospecting supplies. A few states will not legally allow companies to solicit start-up expenses in excess of $500.

16. The foundation of any network marketing company is based in the value of its products. No MLM company has ever stood the test of time without offering a quality service or product.

17. To help protect consumers against unfair business practices and scams in the United States, the government has created two major organizations: the FTC and the FDA. Similar organizations exist in Canada and other countries across the globe. Visit http://www.ftc.gov and http://www.fda.gov to learn the laws and regulations associated with network marketing and the various consumer industries, such as health and nutrition.

Chapter 9

Key #6
Product Integrity: How to Scrutinize a Product

Your Opinion is More Important than the Expert's Opinion

Many seminar participants and students have asked how I was able to effectively evaluate and compare such diverse product fields as nutritional supplements, personal care products, household products, and telecommunications services without a specific background in each of these industries. Well, the truth is I do have backgrounds in many of the industries I have studied, although I don't have any professional credentials or degrees. However, there is something even more powerful than specific expertise in a field of study. I'm speaking of a very special power that is exclusive to the human animal—the power to read, research, and reason.

I have applied these *special powers* in my efforts to find out what to look for in a nutritional supplement, how to analyze a tube of toothpaste, and what to avoid in a bottle of shampoo. I may not be a scientist or a PhD, but I can study and cross-reference what top scientists and doctors are saying. In the end, I find my methodology more effective and objective than the methods used by most top scientists. My philosophy is simple. I call it "research the research." Then I simply determine what the experts agree on, and what they don't agree on.

Step One: Researching the Research

If I were to read the top twenty most respected and universally recognized books on the subject of antioxidants, it would be quite clear what points these scientists, doctors, and researchers agreed upon. Any topics that were not agreed upon could be great theories, but there's really no reason to draw any conclusions from research that is isolated to one scientist. However, if most of these scientists agree that antioxidants can reduce the incidence of disease in the human body, you can be quite certain that this is a true finding.

A great example of this truth versus theory idea can be drawn from some of the most recent new therapies in weight management. Therapies such as HCG injections, Hormone Replacement Therapy, and Weight Loss Hypnosis are all very controversial topics among weight loss authorities. Since there is disagreement and controversy associated with these theories, they must remain theories until more experts agree one way or the other, and thus tip the scales to one side or the other.

When you're selecting a product to represent in network marketing, learn how to research the research. Find several of the best authors and the most credible scientist on the subject and read what they have published. Gathering information from multiple sources will help you stay honest and objective with your decisions.

Step Two: The Acid Test

The next question you must ask yourself when selecting any specific network marketing product is, "If people did not receive any kind of monetary incentive for promoting this product or service, would people still buy this product or service at this price? Would the product still be in high demand?"

In Chapter Five, I revealed the characteristics of high-demand products. As you may recall, I created a statement that will help you remember the acronym for these seven steps. It goes like this: Each Criterion Unlocks The Vault To Success! E.C.U.T.V.T.S

Again, a product needs to be ...

1. Emotional
2. Consumable
3. Unique
4. Traditional
5. Valuable
6. Timely
7. Stable

Step Three: Getting Specific

As we learned in Chapter Five, nearly every type of product or service is sold through direct sales. Here's the list in review.

The A List: Top network marketing product industries
- Nutritional Supplements and Health Products
- Personal Care Products (Skin Care, Hair Care, Body Care)

The B List: Other popular, less profitable, less stable industries
- Household Products (if products are very unique and environmentally friendly)

The C List: Alternative MLM industries with some exposure and appeal, but not yet proven over the long term in more than one company.
- Telecommunications (residential and commercial long distance, cell phones, VOIP)

- Financial Programs (financial planning, debt elimination, investments, asset protection)
- Travel and Vacation Programs
- Legal Services (identity protection, pre-paid legal services, wills)
- Buying Clubs and Catalog Shopping
- Greeting Cards/Gifts
- Video Email/Online Video Advertising
- Internet Advertising

The D List: Industries with extremely limited exposure in network marketing
- Computer Hardware and Software*
- Internet Access and Services (hosting, broadband, websites)*
- Books, Reports, Newsletters, and Publications
- Water and Air Filters
- Buying Clubs and Catalog Shopping*
- Lead Generation Programs
- Jewelry, Gold, Silver, and Collectibles
- Satellites (Hardware and Service)
- Automobile and Auto-Care Products
- Home and Personal Security Products
- Electronics and Appliances
- Grocery and Coupon Programs
- Information Services*
- Clothing, Fashions, and Lingerie

*Up-and-coming industries with future potential, yet absolutely not proven in today's market

Research reveals that there are only two A-list industries (nutrition and personal care), which make up a vast majority of the success stories in network marketing. I will also cover the one B-list industry (household consumables) since many A-list companies have diversified into household products. Even though it is a limited appeal industry ranking on the C-list, I've thrown in an exposé on the telecom industry simply because it was a large part of the last edition of this book. Although the telecom industry is no longer much of a contender, it's still present.

Nutritional supplements

Even though we narrowed the bulk of our research down to wellness and nutrition products, we still had quite a job in front of us. How can anyone possibly review all of the following products?

Elixors, Pills, Tablets, Capsules, Magnets, Coral Calcium, Body Balance, Lavie, Primorye, StemCell, VitaOne, Appetizer Diet, Xanthone Factor, Vitale, Magestic Earth, Immunocal, Transfer Factor, Riovida, Healthy Coffee, Xooma, Vitalee, Fruta Vida, Vibe, DoTERRA, Versativa Products, Qore, Scensy, Protandim, Sibu, XanGo, Seasilver, Tongan Limu, Tahitian Noni, Hawaiian Noni, Goji, Calorad, BiosLife, Pyruvate, Pycnogenol, Ambrotose, MSM, Soy Products, Soygenol, Melatonin, DHEA, Blue-Green Algae, Parasite Cleansers, Manapol, Juice Plus, Colloidal Minerals, Skintastic, Double X, Chocamaca, Vemma, Ageless Extra, SeaAloe, Monavie, Xocia, TruChocolate, Zrii, Max GXL, Hoodia, Opuntia, MOXXOR, O3World, MAXeGEN, Zurvita, FORM, FIXX, OceanBreakers, Nopalea, Essential D, Subligual B-12, Verve, Bod-e, Thirst, Next, SmartMix, XM, Transfer Factor, GoVera, Xtra, PRIME, Whey Protein Shakes, Probiotics, Cleansers, and many, many more products.

These are just a few examples of over one thousand name-brand products I have in my database. Keep in mind that many companies have more than one focus or flagship product, and new product lines are popping up daily. How can we possibly even begin to sort them all out? Again, we have to apply our "research the research" philosophy and come to the table armed with knowledge so we can intelligently sort and sift through these different lines. Here are some of the principles I discovered as I worked on this process.

Picking a Winning Nutrition Product

While it's true that a vast majority of the companies I reviewed were nutritional companies, top economists agree that health and wellness is the most viable industry in direct sales. *"Wellness industry products and services have perhaps the strongest legs of any product or service, as people immediately notice when someone has a wellness experience and are anxious to duplicate their results."*[20]

Paul Zane Pilzer, *The Wellness Revolution*

With the Baby Boomers entering their fifties, this industry will continue to explode for the next twenty years. It's important to note that the Baby Boomers are very wise consumers. They demand quality and value, and they are tough to fool. Here are some important points to think about while scrutinizing and comparing nutritional product lines.

Philosophies behind nutritional product lines

Before reviewing a product line, it's important to find out the company's philosophy behind its products. There are several basic product philosophies adopted by nutritional product lines on the market today. Some of these philosophies are in conflict with each other, as you will learn. I'm going to review the pros and cons of each philosophy as I go through this material, and as I do, I will give a short summary and offer some observations and opinions. You can decide which ideas match the way you think. Then try to match the philosophy with the product line. If you don't, you run the risk of joining a company you don't believe in.

Treating Symptoms with Herbs Philosophy

First, we have the herbal medicine product lines. To understand an herbal medicine line, you must first understand traditional medicine and drugs. When we go to the doctor, the doctor examines our symptoms and prescribes a drug. The purpose of the drug is to take care of the symptom as quickly as possible. If you have a headache, you may receive a prescription painkiller. You take the painkiller and the pain goes away. Is the problem cured? Probably not, since we really don't know what was causing the symptom. For convenience and comfort, the symptom was simply masked. If the symptom is gone, that's all that matters, right? Some doctors seem to think so.

Herbal medicine companies believe in treating health issues with all-natural solutions. Think of the native villagers living in the heart of the Amazon basin. They do not have access to hospitals or HMOs. They have to deal with any kind of health condition or emergency with the plants and botanicals growing around them. And generally speaking, they do so quite remarkably. If they have an infection, they use plants. If they have pain, they use plants. They use the whole plant, not just an extract or a concentration of one ingredient from many plants. This is the holistic approach that herbal medicine companies swear by, and it seems to work quite well.

Now on the flip side, herbal medicine companies claim to disagree with the "American medicine philosophy." However, the first thing you do when you join an herbal company is purchase a book on herbs and then you look up all of your ailments in the index to determine which single herbs, herbal combinations, and vitamins you should be taking. Is this not the same allopathic approach used by Western doctors? For example, if you have a headache, the herbal book says to take White Willow Bark or various other herbal combinations that act as natural pain relievers. Again, we are just putting a mask or a bandage over the symptom. If you have multiple ailments, you could be taking different combinations of herbs that are mixing together to cancel each other out or react to each other. Many herbal medicine combinations, like drugs, can be highly toxic or even deadly.

The power of herbs and herbal medicine is undeniable. In fact, millions of people consume herbal products daily, including me. What most herbal supplements enthusiasts have a problem with is the philosophy of treating the symptom rather than treating the cause. After all, symptoms are the final manifestation of illness and the first thing to go away with treatment. Even when symptoms go away, sometimes the root cause of the symptom still exists.

Regardless of how you feel about using herbs to fight symptoms, most people today would agree that the natural approach is still preferred to taking prescription drugs. The natural cure is still the best cure.

Full Meal Deal Philosophy

Consumers want peace of mind, knowing they're getting everything the body needs for optimal health. Science has taught us most of the critical vitamins, minerals, antioxidants, enzymes, acids, and other substances that are needed in the body daily. Some product lines are designed to offer a complete spectrum of nutrition. It's always a great idea to try to cover all of your bases. Be sure to know the ingredients in your supplements. Find out where the nutrients are derived and why these sources are better than the competitor's sources.

Some companies do a fantastic job of providing the essential nutrients in proportions that most researchers agree are ideal for the human body on a daily basis. However, many companies will claim to have every nutrient necessary for optimal human health when, in fact, their product is quite deficient. Beware of claims that seem too good to be true. It has been proven many times that companies that claim to have all of the active ingredients of the top brands in their one flagship product are generally blowing smoke. Most of these products are discovered to contain only trace amounts of the nutrients required for optimal health. I've seen dozens of products pulled off the market for illegal or misleading advertising claims. This can throw any company into a tailspin.

Also, keep in mind that it can become quite cost prohibitive for individuals to be taking every beneficial nutrient known to modern science. So it may be necessary to control your spending and stay within a reasonable budget for your daily nutritional supplements. For example, at least a dozen nutritional lines I have studied carefully would have you believe that an individual looking to achieve optimum health could spend as much as $1000 per month just on their own full-spectrum nutritional system. This does not account for the rest of the family's nutritional needs.

Immune System Philosophy

Another type of nutritional product is what I call an immune system product or a product line that focuses on building the body's immune system. The immune system is your front line of defense against infections, diseases, and other illnesses, and it is regulated by nutrition. If we give the body's cells everything they need for optimal health, the body can take care of itself, with a strong immune system to ward off disease and maintain optimal health. As a result of this philosophy, immune system companies have developed products that do not treat symptoms. These products are developed to assist the body in getting to the root of the problem by helping the body correct its nutritional balance and eliminate any deficiencies.

Hypothetically speaking, if you were to take a product designed to boost the immune system and your headache were to go away, you might conclude that it wasn't a mask designed to temporarily cover up your symptom. Your body may simply be getting the nutrition necessary to take care of itself. Sadly, in our study we only found a handful of companies with a preventative philosophy and a focus on the immune system. However, based on product sales and retention figures, this is probably the most consistent, sound, and popular philosophy on the market today.

Even though the immune system products seem to provide the best overall solution to human health challenges, sometimes consumers simply need a specific herb, herbal combination, or a special nutrient designed to address a specific problem or ailment. In these situations, a product designed to treat the whole body is not sufficient. However, in most cases, a healthy immune system is all that is required to keep people in optimum health. From a marketing and sales perspective, this philosophy seems to generate optimal sales and retention.

Be aware of products that claim to be a silver bullet, but are simply over-hyped, standard ingredients. Do the research to find out if the products you're taking have an adequate dosage and are the right potency necessary to do your body good.

Science vs. Testimonials

Presently we are moving from an era of salesmanship into an era of science. Some call it the information age, and it is changing the way people are selecting a nutritional product line. In the 1980s, people attended opportunity meetings and were pitched on the latest new products or services. Then, a handful of distributors would get up on stage and tell about how this nutritional product had helped them lose 100 pounds, re-grow hair, and get off of antidepressant medication in one week (I'm attempting to sensationalize a bit, if you weren't picking up on that). The decision to buy the product and to get involved with the distributorship was purely emotional.

During the 1990s, although many people were still making their decisions based on emotional factors, many others started to do their due diligence when investigating a product line. People were getting tired of the hype associated with only testimonials and no scientific backing. As studies on nutrition became more scientific, people became more analytical in their approach to selecting a good product.

It's very clear that people in the twenty-first century are more concerned with scientific validation rather than hype and sensationalism. While companies of the '80s and '90s relied on emotional hype, companies launching after 2012 are prepared to spend millions of dollars on product research and technology. Network marketing is now big business and companies that are competing are investing in scientific validation.

All-Natural, Whole Food Philosophy

Ten years ago, I was much more critical of the whole foods sales pitch. Almost everyone who was making a big deal about whole foods was more concerned about saving endangered naked mole rats than they were about saving human lives. But I must now admit that the hippies were really on to something. Today, the whole food movement is not only scientifically validated, but it has moved into the mainstream. Everyone is going all natural. Everyone is eating whole foods and touting incredible benefits. People are getting wise to the dangers of genetically modified foods. From a sales and marketing perspective, if you're not focusing on whole food nutrition, you're behind the times and your sales will suffer for it.

Frankenstein's Monster

What does it mean to be whole food, and what does it mean to be synthetic? Even the whole food products industry is confused about this one. A whole food product is simply a product delivered in its natural, whole state while a synthetic product is man-made or put together in a man-made formula. Even though some products are a sampling of many different nutrients derived from whole food sources, they're still synthetically formulated. In other words, some human being decided how much of each nutrient goes into the product as a standard for that product or they fill the product with extracts from a natural source. It's hard to claim your product is a whole food when it has a breakdown of how many milligrams of beta-carotene are in the product, and how many international units of vitamin C are in each bottle —especially when these amounts are the same in every bottle. How can a whole food product have perfectly defined amounts in neat little portions, perfectly measured and then pressed into pills or encapsulated? I call these products Frankenstein's monster. Dr. Frankenstein believed in assimilating parts and pieces of once organic, living matter and trying to breathe new life into them. All of the parts were from natural sources, but they were put together in unnatural ways. Scientists who try to second-guess nature or improve upon it are truly distinguishing themselves in a way that other scientists fear.

Real whole foods don't necessarily rely on itemized labels. They may tell what plant or botanical is in the product, but to break down the amounts of beta-carotene, calcium, and zinc is to admit that some human being manufactured this product to their specifications. With a whole food, you get what you get the way nature intended. True, there are some very smart scientists out there. But can scientists really improve on an all-natural, whole food formula? That's a question you can only answer for yourself. I admit to leaning toward the philosophy of "you can't improve on God's formulas." Is it because I'm a spiritualist? I assure you that I'm more of a scientist than a spiritualist. My conclusions are strictly based on the numbers. Product reorder rates for whole food products are off the charts.

One day it may be required that whole food products that are not really whole food formulations to at least come up with a fancy new marketing term such as "scientifically enhanced" so the rest of the marketplace wouldn't get so confused. This way, the products derived from whole food sources, but then scientifically reengineered into a specific formulation, could distinguish themselves from the synthetic products that are actually man-made, laboratory-produced nutrients designed to mimic nature. The lab-produced product lines would probably need a fancy name as well, because no one cares for the word *synthetic*.

By the same token, having some synthetic vitamins and minerals in a product is better than nothing. Especially when you compare the natural products you're consuming with the chemical and toxin laden garbage that you'll find in most grocery stores and convenience stores. Almost all direct sales/network marketing products are better than what you'll find in the stores. Most food manufacturers are off the ranch when it comes to quality human nutrition.

Scientifically Enhanced

Other voices claim that based on the depletion of nutrition in the soils and other environmental concerns, no products or ingredients in their natural state have enough nutritional value to supplement a fruit fly, much less a human being. This group feels that God has given humans the intelligence to enhance human nutrition through scientific methods. I must admit that I do agree with this philosophy to an extent. After all, so many manufacturers of nutritional supplements feel that offering whole food, all-natural, or organic products take the place of good science. They feel that no studies are necessary to validate the benefits of their product. Their belief in their natural products supersedes all rational thought.

My research points me to this conclusion: all-natural, organic, whole food products validated through scientific studies will retain more long-term customers than any form of synthetic products. They also produce the best sales, reorders, and retention of customers and distributors.

Taking The All-Natural Theme Too Far

Some people get so caught up in the all-natural battle cry that they disregard all practicality. After all, if you really wanted to start a business that supplied organic, unaltered whole food botanicals to consumers, you'd have to hand-gather herbs from some virgin rainforest and then hand-deliver them to your clients—no processing, no packaging, and you'd better figure out how to clean the bacteria off your hands without using harmful chemicals so you don't contaminate the goods. No one can really claim to market all-natural products when they have to process them into tablets or liquids. No nutritional supplement manufacturers can downplay the role of technology in the mass production, distribution, and storage of highly effective supplements. Even the all-natural products are encapsulated, pressed, freeze-dried, pasteurized, or processed in some other high-tech manner to allow for safe, mass distribution. Some things are lost in mass production, but so much is gained when you can standardize the process. You want to be able to touch the four corners of the globe with your product. You must be able to trust that your product will be stable and effective once it reaches the other side of the country, or the other side of the world.

First, Do No Harm

Some products sold through direct sales today are ticking time bombs. Not because there's any risk that the product will explode (although it has been known to happen on occasion), rather, the product has not been protected against bacterial outbreaks or other stabilization issues. No company likes processing that can affect the contents of the product. No one says, "I wish we could add more preservatives to this product." No one in his or her right mind would go through the costly and tedious process of filtration or pasteurization if it could be somehow avoided without increasing risk. When you're dealing with human lives, an ounce of prevention is definitely worth a pound of cure. In fact, it's not even an option. If you're marketing a product that is not protected in any way against the risk of bacterial outbreak or other dangers, you might be better off not going into business with that product. It's only a matter of time before you have an outbreak on your hands, and that means instant death to your product brand and reputation. Don't risk it. Find a safe and effective preservative or preservation process and use it.

Beware of Junk Science

Like any good researcher, I enjoy reviewing any scientific study I can get my hands on. However, as of the publication date on this book, the network marketing industry is going through a junk science phase of epic proportions. Never in the history of direct sales have so many companies chosen to participate in, or allow their independent distributors to participate in, junk science wars.

Let's first define *junk science* as it relates to the network marketing industry. When you're attempting to market a nutritional product through direct sales in the twenty-first century, competition is fierce. Distributors are always seeking new technologies, tools, and information that will help them compete on a higher level. At the same time, with our employment crisis, many scientists who were trained to never violate the scientific code of integrity and objectivity are starting to compromise their standards to get work. It seems that many scientists today would rather eat than maintain any form of objectivity. Can you blame them? They're just trying to survive like everyone else. If you have a few hundred thousand dollars and the right connections, you can hire a laboratory to conduct experiments on your product and on your competitor's products to try to create a comparison that will make your product shine. These scientists understand the age-old saying, "If you torture the numbers long enough, you can get them to say anything."

If you don't believe me, go to the Internet and review the various Websites set up by network marketing corporations and their independent distributors. Try doing a Google images search for "ORAC charts." If you scroll through just a few pages of these search results, you'll find dozens and dozens of ORAC charts, most of them contradicting each other. ORAC is an acronym that means Oxygen Radical Absorption Capacity. It's basically a scientific testing system designed to measure the nutritional value of a product and its ability to absorb free radicals.

As you take a closer look at these sites, you'll find that they contain bar graphs and charts detailing studies done at some laboratory that no one has ever heard of—except for the company paying for the experiments. They'll go on and on about how this laboratory is the most respected in the world. Then they'll publish their findings, placing their new Product X at the tip top of the scale, while lining up the competition (Product Y and Product Z) at the bottom of the scale. Then, you can go to another Website featuring the competition's famous study and now you see Product Y at the top of the chart, totally eclipsing Product X and Z. Then repeat the process for Product Z. It's ridiculous! Surprisingly, most of the network marketing wannabes will never even verify these numbers and will take them at face value because they're either too unintelligent to verify the facts or, more likely, they don't want to know the truth. They'd rather blindly accept someone else's conclusion since it will help them sell more of their product and condemn their competitors. They take great confidence in their product by believing bogus research projects conducted by sell-out scientists. What a great way to select a product.

Numbers Don't Lie

You might be wondering, "Who can I believe"? This is an excellent question considering the fact that you'll eventually have to trust somebody if you want to build a successful business. Here's a foolproof method for determining if a company truly has a powerful and effective nutritional product line or if they're just blowing smoke. First, find out how long the company has been in business and attempt to acquire the annual sales figures for every year they've been in business. Obviously you're looking for an upward trend, not a downward spiral. But you're also looking to see significant sales. Substantial increases in sales indicate explosive growth in a product line. Small incremental improvements show that a company is hanging in there and could someday be a contender. A downward trend is a sure sign of trouble. Once you find a company with a substantial growth trend (maybe the company started out doing millions in sales and is now doubling every year), then you want to look at retention rates. A company must be experiencing substantial reorder rates over years of marketing activity. The company should also have a very high customer and distributor retention level. Retention of customers and distributors is even more important than growth rates.

Next time someone tries to shove a study down your throat, demonstrating the superiority of their product over the leading competitors, ask them to produce some numbers. Ask them for growth rates, reorder rates, and retention rates. If they don't have these numbers, they're flying blind. They have no way of knowing how their product is doing in the marketplace, and they have demonstrated a certain level of incompetence. If they do produce numbers which aren't impressive, then their study is meaningless. If their numbers are impressive, you should continue to research that company, verifying that the numbers they're giving you can be validated. You should also start looking at the other criteria for selecting a top company. If the numbers are too impressive, be wary. They might be fabricating the numbers just to impress you.

By the way, all of the sales numbers you're seeking can be found either through company reports and literature, or by consulting with top distributors associated with these companies. Don't just accept numbers from one person. Verify these numbers with several top leaders who are in different legs of the company. Sometimes I get different numbers from every distributor I go to. This does not instill confidence. I get some of my most objective reports from distributors who are retired or on their way out of a company. If they don't have an axe to grind with that company, these are usually the most honest and objective figures you can find. You can also talk to the many network marketing consultants available for hire. Believe me, it's worth the money to get the real facts before joining.

Copycats

I've had different thoughts and opinions about copy cats over the years and I'd like to present both sides of this issue. First of all, if you build your career on waiting for others to become a category creator for some new herb, or botanical, or formula, and then you copy their idea and run with it, it could work, but you'll develop a reputation as a copy cat and you likely will not develop any real traction with your own brand. On the other hand, if you're fast, innovative, and original, you can learn how to do what I advise my clients to do. I call it *copying the trend, not the product*. It's obvious that the industry goes through cycles. We've seen the nutritional field cycle from a focus on herb remedies in the early 1980's to antioxidants and minerals throughout the 1990's to functional beverages during the 2000's and now going into the 2010-2020 decade, we're seeing a huge emergence in the fitness/weight management craze. Building a strong immune system has also stayed steady and sure throughout this time. These are trends that are solid and secure and if you can find your own unique approach to capitalizing on it, you can compete with the big dogs. *Copy the trend, not the product*, and you'll be on the right track. Bring your own unique talents and people to the table and build a brand that addresses the major trends of the times, that no one can duplicate.

Products Don't Formulate Themselves

To close out this section on nutrition, it's important to review the basic philosophy of researching and comparing nutritional product. Again, one of the best ways to scrutinize a nutritional line without a PhD in biochemistry is to research the people behind the products. These individuals should have many past accomplishments that will give you an indication of their experience, competence, and effectiveness in their respective fields. By reviewing *all* of the popular books on cutting-edge health and nutrition research, you can get a fantastic feel for what is developing in the world. In your studies, find out what the experts agree upon, and there you will find the most reliable, scientifically documented answers.

Personal Care Products

Now we'll have a discussion on the philosophies behind selecting a great personal care line. Since personal care products do show up among the top 30 companies in network marketing (listed at www.networkmarketingbook.com) and since they represent the second most popular industry next to nutritional supplements, we need to discuss the basics of evaluating a top product line.

All of The Good; None of the Bad

Many companies have adopted this philosophy with their personal care products. The idea is very simple. Take all the ingredients that have been known to be good for the skin, hair, and body and add them to the product. Take all the ingredients known to be bad and leave them out of the product. Be sure to check the labels on all of the company's personal care products.

Natural and Organic

Another popular philosophy that goes along with the "all of the good" philosophy is the idea of using all-natural and organic ingredients. This philosophy is gaining in popularity every year as people are becoming more sensitive to the environment around them and the products they consume.

Hypoallergenic

Allergies have become one of the biggest concerns in healthcare today. Topical allergies and even reactions to scents and aromas can be debilitating. Be sure the product you research has been thoroughly researched for its potential to cause allergic reactions.

Alternative Strategy – Replace the Bad with the Good

One of the best marketing strategies I have seen with personal care products is the *alternative* strategy. Look for a company that markets its personal care products as a safe and effective alternative to the products on the market that contain harmful ingredients. *Natural*, *safe*, and *effective* are the operative words.

Here are some of the controversial ingredients commonly found in store bought personal care items. Go check your shampoo bottles and skin care products for the following:

- Mineral oil is a mixture of refined liquid hydrocarbons derived from petroleum. It is the stabilizing ingredient of many skin formulas. Mineral oil forms a film on the skin, blocking the pores and interfering with normal skin respiration. Therefore it may dry the skin and also be a contributing cause of blemishes and even stop the development of skin cells altogether.
- Petrolatum is found in products, such as Vaseline, that do not penetrate the skin, but sit on the surface, blocking natural respiration, excretion, and absorption of other nutrients. Petrolatum is derived from petroleum, a dark, oily, flammable liquid used in gasoline and kerosene.
- Propylene Glycol is a known skin irritant. It dries the skin from the inside out while clogging pores and causing blemishes. This is the primary ingredient in brake fluid and antifreeze! Use it in your car, not on your skin.

Many other controversial ingredients exist; however, the ingredients I mentioned are commonly promoted as harmful.
Is It Marketing Hype?

No one but an esthetician with a background in biochemistry and a knowledge of cosmetics could really know if these ingredients really harm the body. Some say that these ingredients have never been known to cause any problems. Some say there is no documentation to prove such. However, as a marketing strategy, this alternative ingredients strategy has been proven to build tremendous brand loyalty and attachment.

Unique Ingredients

Another powerful marketing strategy is to promote a unique ingredient that no other product has. Maybe the ingredient is very rare or difficult to acquire. The ingredient may be accompanied by some new research or study. If a company is first to include an ingredient in their product that could be used by other companies, and that product becomes a top seller, copycat products may follow. However, if the company is strong and well financed, being first to market can distinguish that company as the market leader, and the leader will generally capture a majority of the market share. Some of the unique ingredients that are used in personal care products include citrus, aloe vera, tea tree oil, mint oil, essential oils, alpha-hydroxyl acids, OPCs, algae or spirulina, fruit rind, fruit husk, unique and safe emulsifiers, humectants, and even human placenta.

Unique Formulator

Many companies have incorporated the strategy of hiring a well-known expert or celebrity who has a background in personal care products. Leveraging the name and reputation of this individual, they're able to successfully launch and build a new product brand.

Household Products

Now it's time to review household products. Household consumables have been one of the most traditional product industries represented through network marketing over the years. Here are some ideas top companies are incorporating to add more to their bottom line.

Environmentally Friendly

Network marketing is filled with companies that market environmentally friendly household products. These companies offer alternatives to products that contain chemicals toxic to the environment. Consumers are even willing to pay more to buy the non-toxic products. Make sure to only look for environmentally friendly products.

"We can't turn our backs on the web of life that sustains us ..."
-Paul Hawken, *The Ecology of Commerce*[21]

Safety

Another great selling point for many household products is safety. For example, some companies have household cleaning detergents that will not harm a child if swallowed. You usually can't say that about most store-bought brands. This is an excellent selling point and something to look for.

Unique Features

Color, scent, texture, taste, and packaging can all act as unique features to set a brand apart from the pack. With repeat use, so many consumers will develop a strong brand attachment based on any of these simple factors. They could even develop a lifetime product attachment.

Telecom: Long-Distance Service/Cell Phones/Calling Cards/VOIP

When considering a network marketing industry, telecommunications can be an attractive choice at first glance. After all, where else can you find a product or service where you don't have to stock inventory, don't have to collect money, and don't have to convince people about the need for the product? I must admit that marketing long distance and other telecommunication services seemed so attractive to me that I tried it twice. It took close personal involvement to help me realize how difficult it is to create residual income in today's telecommunication market and how much more difficult it will be in the future. If you are interested in pursuing a MLM career with telecommunication services, please read the following with an open mind and you might be able to avoid some of the challenges that caught me by surprise.

Thousands of Customers Required

Did you know that in the average telecom MLM, if you wanted to make a good full-time residual income, you would need over ten thousand customers in your downline within the first seven pay levels? Since nearly everyone has a phone, there are plenty of potential customers, so don't let this number scare you off. But you will never hear about this at an ity meeting. Make sure you are ready to dedicate yourself to this venture. A half-baked effort will not do when trying to these numbers.

Take time to study the compensation plan before you sign on the dotted line. Make sure the plan you are reviewing offers plenty of residual income from the products and services, not just commissions on linear (non-residual) training bonuses. Traditional network marketing plans offer over five percent commission on six to seven levels of product volume. Most telecom companies offer an average of less than two percent commission on six to seven generations of long distance customers and sometimes as low as half a percent. That's why you need so many more customers and distributors to make a telecom program work.

Many New Telecom Companies - No New Market

This low payout is due to the competitive nature of the telecom industry. The long distance market is limited in its size. Almost everyone in North America already has a phone and already has long-distance service. The number of new long distance users is not expected to double, triple, or quadruple over the next several years. As a matter of fact, while technology is growing by leaps and bounds, the long distance market is not. New long distance companies are flooding the market, but the market is not growing to match the demand. Make sure the company is diversifying to remain competitive.

Now the cell phone market is another story, but so far I have not see a MLM take on cell phones in a big way. The profit margins seem to slim to support a MLM. We'll see if any of the new cell phone companies can pull it off over the next few years.

Deregulation and Price Wars

Since the deregulation of long-distance service in the 1980s and 1990s, hundreds of new long distance companies have entered the market, trying to compete for AT&T's scraps (almost everyone who has long distance is, or at least was, using AT&T). Since competition is so fierce, prices are rock-bottom. With the heavy increase in competition, the long distance phone rates in the United States have dropped from ten cents per minute, to five cents per minute, to a penny per minute and less. Now with flat-rate long distance made possible through Internet services like VOIP, you can spend $20–40 per month and receive unlimited service in North America. Yes, it's a great value to the consumer, but it leaves virtually no profit margins for the companies to cover overhead, payroll, and commissions to sales representatives. Most distributors for long distance telecom MLMs are only receiving about 1–2 percent residual income on an average phone bill of less than $30 per customer, seven levels deep. That's about 7–14 percent payout total. Most other top companies pay from 30–50 percent in distributor incentives. This brings us to a dilemma. Does the company hold onto high rates to pay higher commissions to independent distributors, or does it match the market by dropping rates, thus leaving very little for ς? This problem exists in all competitive service markets, ↲elecommunications.

↲ıl phone prices are also plummeting. We may start seeing the ↲ɔt offerings of flat rate cell phone minutes, more cell phone VOIP options like Skype mobile apps, and some MLM texting packages. Margins are still an issue and must be addressed in MLM.

Creative Commissions

When telecom companies went MLM, they realized that they would either have to go with premium prices and give good commissions to their distributors, or go with discounted prices and pay horrible commissions. Needless to say, everyone chose to offer deep discounts since they could not seem to take business away from AT&T and the other large providers any other way. Consequently, these MLM telecom programs have had to come up with some fairly creative ways of paying their distributors.

Coding Bonuses

The most popular and controversial way of dealing with the lack of profit margins in telecom programs is a little thing called a *coding bonus*. This is a bonus paid to distributors for something other than the product or service being offered by the company. In the case of most telecom programs, these coding bonuses are paid on trainings. Technically, they could be called *training bonuses*. Why is paying override commissions for trainings controversial? It's not necessarily the act of paying someone for teaching a training class that is taboo. It's the act of paying someone in the downline for enrolling a person into that training class that is illegal in most states. Coding bonuses are simply a creative way of rewarding distributors for recruiting new agents. However, these coding bonuses are highly controversial and technically illegal.

In an article written by Spencer Reese, a prominent and respected network marketing attorney, the dangers of coding bonuses are exposed. Mr. Reese states, "Paying commissions based on enrollments into a training program can easily be viewed as a headhunting operation that compensates participants for signing up new participants. This is simply the operation of an illegal pyramid."[22]

Service Charges

Other telecom companies have chosen to charge a monthly fee just for the privilege of calling long distance at a great discount. When customers factor in the extra $20–50 per month to their phone bill, they don't get too excited about their phone rates. Most people will spend more with the new pricing structure than they were paying previously. Many of these companies are now out of business.

Pre-Paid Phone Cards

Several years ago, pre-paid phone cards were the big craze. No doubt they will cycle back around soon, offering cell phone minutes, international dialing, remote Internet access, and other modern features. These cards are usually ridiculously overpriced. However, the rational is "as long as your customers sign up two, who sign up two, who sign up two, then their calling cards are free!" So rate per minute is not an issue. Get the picture? The more the minutes cost, the more you make. Watch out for pre-paid anything, including cell phone minutes, texting, and mobile data. It's a great way to pre-pay for a failing business.

Wrapping It Up!

Telecommunications is still a very exciting and dynamic industry. There are a handful of charismatic people at the top of several main telecom companies, making millions and beckoning to the masses to hop on the bandwagon. Still, telecom is one of the most difficult industries for the average distributor in today's market. If you have your heart set on telecommunications, check out the specific criteria for evaluating a telecom company located in the next section.

What Are the Experts Saying About MLM Industries?

For fear of sounding like I have an axe to grind with certain industries, I thought I'd throw in some comments made by a former industry insider, and oldie but a goody, Chuck Huckaby, which was written over a decade ago and is still true today.

In an article in *NetWork Marketing Today*, Mr. Huckaby states, *"On the technology front, while many are gobbling down one pill after another, the Age of Competition has also produced a mentality in another sector of the market that says 'pills, potions, and lotions are bad.' In a sense, this is a natural response to all the hype in the marketplace surrounding nutritional products and beauty treatments that will supposedly grow hair on doorknobs and, applied to Cleopatra's mummified body, restore her good looks. These people are sorely tempted to promote high-tech products and services or at least non-nutritional products and services like legal insurance. Some recent non-events have been online services, long distance MLMs, phone cards and personal computers. This is not to say that some companies haven't had some success in these fields, but most haven't (to say the very least). This is because all these things are mere commodities to be hawked at every Walmart and Costco from here to Kalamazoo, the criteria for selection mainly revolving around price. While discount chains with massive purchasing power can adjust prices regionally or even locally on a regular basis, the relatively small purchasing power of a MLM tends to keep prices high and unresponsive to the marketplace."*[23]

The Company with the Best Branding Wins!

No matter which industry you're marketing, a company's overall performance comes down to how well a company can brand their product in the competitive marketplace. To understand branding, I'd like to turn to the most successful and innovative branding experts in the world, Seth Godin, Al Ries, and Laura Ries.

"What do Starbucks and JetBlue and Krispy Kreme and Apple and Dutch Boy and Kensington and Zespri and Hard Candy have that you don't? How do they continue to confound critics and achieve spectacular growth, leaving behind former tried and true brands to gasp their last?"[24] Seth Godin, *Purple Cow: Transform Your Business by Being Remarkable.*

Although experts agree that a network marketing product must be a traditional, mass-market product, it must also have something that sets it apart. Rosser Reeves coined the phrase *USP,* or a unique selling proposition, in his book, *Reality in Advertising,* in 1961. A product must have a powerful USP. Seth Godin calls it a *purple cow* in his book of the same title, which he describes as that special something that sets your product apart from the competition. No matter what you call it, your product must have a unique, exclusive twist that is recognized by the masses as such. It needs to have something very special or remarkable. *"Successful branding programs are based on the concept of singularity. The objective is to create in the mind of the prospect the perception that*

there is no other product on the market quite like your product." Al Ries and Laura Ries, *The 22 Immutable Laws of Branding*[25]
Women Don't Buy Brands; They Join Them

Since women make up a vast majority of the decision makers in any purchase, it's important to understand what women are looking for in a product. Women don't just purchase product brands, they want to feel some kind of connection to them. Once a woman becomes impressed with a product brand and develops an attachment over time, you can't pry the product out of her cold, dead fingers. Women will take their loyalty with them to the grave. Trend expert and economist, Faith Popcorn, says it best in her book *EVEolution*: *"A customer of the moment is the one who buys your brand; a customer for life is the one who joins it. Think about it. The things we join—clubs, political parties, organizations, even religions—are the institutions in our lives that really matter. The ones we stick with through thick and thin. The ones we cherish and value and grow old with."*[26]

A Commitment to Branding

Within the past few years, some of the most insightful texts and presentations on the power of branding have been released into the marketplace. It's no wonder that intelligent business owners are truly starting to understand these principles. Never before have we seen so many powerful marketing campaigns designed to create lifetime product loyalty and a culture of satisfied, repeat customers. Be sure the company you select not only understands these principles, but has also mastered the art and science of branding.

Chapter Nine Review

1. You have the power to research and the power to reason your way to the truth in network marketing. By researching others' research, you can become an armchair expert in dozens of fields of study and create a well-rounded base of knowledge and wisdom.

2. Read the most respected and universally recognized books about the products in your industry of choice. If most of these scientists agree on certain points and findings, you can be quite certain that this is true doctrine.

3. Ask yourself, "If people did not receive any kind of monetary incentive for promoting this product or service, would people still buy this product or service at this price? Would the product still be in high demand?" If you can answer yes to this question, you've passed the acid test.

Nutrition Industry

4. While it's true that over 65 percent of the four hundred companies I reviewed were nutritional companies, top economists concur that health and wellness is the most viable industry in direct sales.

5. With the Baby Boomers entering their fifties, this industry will continue to explode for the next twenty years. It's important to note that the Baby Boomers are very wise consumers. They demand quality and value, and they are tough to fool.

6. Here are some of the philosophies behind popular nutritional lines. Be sure you can define all of these philosophies before moving on.

    a. Treating Symptoms with Herbs: Many holistic practitioners still treat their herbal formulas like conventional doctors treat drugs. You must decide where you stand before you select a nutritional company.
    b. Full Meal Deal Philosophy: Some product lines are designed to offer a complete spectrum of nutrition. However, many companies will claim to have every nutrient necessary for optimal human health when in fact their product is quite deficient.
    c. Immune System Philosophy: Everyone agrees that when the body's immune system is functioning optimally, every system of the body is improved. Some conditions or symptoms can actually go away without you ever knowing what was really causing the problem. When you help the body help itself, more areas of the body can be affected in a positive way.

d. All-Natural, Whole Food: Today, the whole food movement is not only scientifically validated, but it has moved into the mainstream. Everyone is going all-natural. Everyone is eating whole foods and seeing incredible benefits. From a sales and marketing perspective, if you're not focusing on whole food nutrition, you're behind the times and your sales will suffer for it. The bottom line: product reorder rates for whole food products are off the charts.

e. Scientifically Enhanced: Although we've seen strong evidence to suggest that all-natural products tend to sell better, some companies have more of a scientific slant. Many scientists feel that based on the depletion of nutrition in the soil and other environmental concerns, it is necessary to scientifically enhance nutritional products for maximum assimilation.

7. Science vs. Testimonials: Personal health experiences have been, and always will be, a powerful way to introduce potential consumers to excellent products. However, people in the twenty-first century are now more concerned with scientific validation rather than hype and sensationalism.

8. Beware of Junk Science: Right now, network marketing is going through a junk science phase of epic proportions. It's not wise to trust any study that is not backed up by many objective, unrelated parties.

9. Numbers Don't Lie: Next time someone tries to shove a study down your throat, demonstrating the superiority of their product over the leading competitors, ask them to produce some numbers. More important than any scientific study is the comparison of two or more companies' sales, growth, and customer/distributor retention. These numbers tell the whole story.

10. Ounce of Prevention: When you're dealing with human lives, an ounce of prevention is definitely worth a pound of cure. In fact, it's not even an option. If you're marketing a product that is not protected in any way against the risk of bacterial outbreak or you're

using ingredients that are controversial or even dangerous, you might be better off not going into business with that product.

11. Copy the Trend, Not the Product: It's better to start with an original concept than try to steal someone else's thunder. However, if you can spot a strong trend, build your own unique brand around it and thrive. Learn how to copy the trend, not the product.

12. Research the people behind the latest product discoveries. By reviewing all of the popular books on cutting-edge health and nutrition research, you can get a fantastic feel for what is developing in the world and how you can leverage these discoveries in a distributorship.

Personal Care Industry

13. Find a company that markets personal care products with safe and effective ingredients. These products are great alternatives to the products on the market that contain harmful ingredients.

14. Mineral oil, petrolatum, and Propylene Glycol are just a few of the more common ingredients labeled "harmful" by some personal care product companies. They would have you believe that these ingredients could cause serious health problem. True or not, it's a powerful marketing strategy.

15. Another powerful marketing strategy is to promote a unique ingredient that no other product has. The ingredient could be very rare or difficult to acquire. The ingredient may be accompanied by some new research or study.

16. Many companies have incorporated the strategy of hiring a well-known expert or celebrity who has a background in personal care products. By leveraging the name and reputation of this individual, they're able to successfully launch a new product brand.

Household Products

17. Environmentally friendly household products offer alternatives to products that contain chemicals toxic to the environment. Consumers are even willing to pay more to buy the non-toxic products.

18. Another great selling point for many household products is safety. This is an excellent selling point and something to look for.

19. Color, scent, texture, taste, and packaging can all be unique features to set a brand apart from the pack.

Telecom Industry: Long-Distance Service/Cell Phones/Calling Cards/VOIP

20. When considering a network marketing industry, telecommunications can be an attractive choice at first glance. But there are some serious hang-ups that everyone should know about before getting involved.
    a. Typical telecom MLMs pay out a fraction of one percent per level on five or six generations of commissions, which is not enough to support distributors on telecom usage alone. Most MLMs pay five percent per level on average.
    b. Training bonuses are considered illegal in the United States, but they are still being used by most telecom companies to supplement usage commissions.
    c. Price wars caused from the deregulation of the telecom industry have led to virtually free long distance and no profit margins for distributors.
    d. Pre-paid phone cards are a dying industry. Just say no.
    e. Telecom consumption for Baby Boomers is not increasing with time.
    f. Even though there are still a handful of charismatic individuals at the top of several top telecom companies making millions and beckoning to the masses to hop on the bandwagon, telecom is one of the most difficult industries

for the average distributor in today's market. It's a dying breed.

21. No matter which industry you're marketing, a company's overall performance comes down to how well a company can brand their product in a competitive marketplace.

22. Although experts agree that a network marketing product must be a traditional, mass-market product, it must also have something that sets it apart. Some marketers call it a USP, or a unique selling proposition. No matter what you call it, the product must have a special something that is recognized by the masses as such.

23. Since women make up a vast majority of the decision makers in any purchase, it's important to understand what women are looking for in a product.

24. Within the past few years, some of the most powerful texts and presentations on the power of branding have been released into the marketplace. It's no wonder that intelligent business owners are truly starting to understand these principles designed to create lifetime product loyalty and a culture of satisfied repeat customers.

PART VI

Conclusions

Finally, we're nearing the end of our long journey—hopefully a little wiser and more prepared to make a decision that will lead to opportunity and ultimately prosperity. Now it is time to use the information we have acquired to test our knowledge, and then use that knowledge to select a top company. Although I will offer some recommendations, I will not do your thinking for you. This book is simply a resource and a tool to help you scrutinize and select a company. After you've taken the test and reviewed the lists, please take time to debrief using the follow-up materials at the back of the book. This book is a doorway to your future.

Chapter 10

Company Testing: Which Companies are the Best?

In my seminars, I test my audiences to see if they are thinking like pros or thinking like novices. I ask them to repeat back to me the six important criteria for selecting a company. They tell me mindset, product industry, timing, compensation plan, management team, and product integrity. They always seem to get that part right. But when I ask them, "Which *one* criterion is the absolute most important of all?" I always get a split decision. I get six different answers every time! Do you want to know the real answer? Well, the truth is that they are *all* important, and you can't be missing even one piece of this puzzle if you want a whole company.

Do you remember the story of the six blind men from Chapter Three? The six blind men each felt a different part of the elephant and although they were all touching an elephant, they thought they were each touching something completely different. As I mentioned before, a company is just like the elephant. It's not whole and complete without all six of these vital parts or keys. Make sure you understand the importance of all of these criteria and how they make a company complete.

However, choosing the best company management may be the most important criterion of all for selecting the right company. After all, isn't the management team responsible for making the products, designing the compensation plan, and making the decisions? It's the people running the company that affect the longevity and viability of the company. And if you have great people, you're always going to have great products, a great pay plan, growth, and stability. Just like Jim Collins says in his best-selling book, *Good to Great*. Before you worry about which direction the bus is going, you must first get the right people on the bus, and then the bus will start going the right direction.

Selecting a Company Report Card

Here are the six criteria used in my previous study. I designed a comprehensive testing procedure to help you assign letter grades to each company in each of these six areas.

Final Exam Overview: Six Criteria for Selecting the Best Company

Key #1 Test: Profit Mindset

Learn to think like a marketing pro, to acquire and keep customers. This test will determine whether or not you were paying attention in Chapter Three. This test is pass/fail, and if you fail, you need to go back to Chapter Three and study it again before proceeding.

Key #2 Test: Product Industry

Which product or service should you represent and why? Which industries should you avoid altogether? See how each industry scored in my evaluation and the letter grades assigned to each. Apply this grading system to the product industries represented by the company you're evaluating.

Key #3 Test: Timing

What are the phases of growth in a direct sales/network marketing company? During which phase of a company's product life cycle should you join that company? Here's a refresher on *when* to join a company. Check to see where the company you're evaluating fits in.

Key #4 Test: Compensation

What are the most common distributor compensation plans on the market today and which plans are the best (and the worst)? Which compensation plan does the company you're evaluating have, and can you identify any red flags associated with the compensation plan?

Key #5 Test: Company Leadership

How do I effectively evaluate a company and its corporate leadership/ownership? Also, discover how legally compliant the company is with governmental regulations. Spend some quality time with this test. Be honest with your answers. If you don't know enough about the management team to do a thorough evaluation, take the time to find out, or hire a reputable network marketing consultant.

Key #6 Test: Product Integrity

What makes one specific product or product line better than another? How can you select the best product for your home-based business without having expertise in that product industry? Use this in-depth evaluation process to score the product you're evaluating. Take the time and do the work necessary to thoroughly evaluate the product and search for red flags.

By assigning values to each of the possible options in each of these top six categories, I've created a rating system for network marketing companies based on my preferences among each category. Simply select the company you want to evaluate and put that company to the test. Produce your own report card for each of the companies you are evaluating. The results may surprise you.

Key #1 Test: Profit Mind Set

Are you prepared to choose the *best* network marketing company? Have you acquired a profit mindset? Answer the following questions to find out. This test is all or nothing. Any incorrect answer will disqualify you from continuing on. You must pass this section to move on.

Questions:

1. There's only one reason for starting and operating a business. What is it?
2. What is the difference between self-employment and business ownership?
3. Fill in the blank: Most people would rather be _____ than rich.
4. Fill in the blank; One of the greatest secrets to becoming a master marketer is to learn how to pay attention to the _____.
5. True or False: When selecting a product, it is critical that you have a very powerful, personal experience with that product right away.
6. Fill in the blank: By studying successful _____, we can determine what the market is demanding today and what it is not.
7. Fill in the blank: To know if something is the _____, you have to look at all the rest.
8. Please name the *Six Keys* used in selecting a top MLM distributorship.

Answers:

1. The purpose of any business is to *make a profit* through the acquisition and retention of customers.
2. Self-employment is *owning a job*, business ownership is *controlling a money machine* that does not require you to be there. You work IN a job, but ON a business.
3. Most people would rather be *right* than rich. They're more concerned about pride and ego than profits.
4. Learn how to pay attention to the *marketplace*.
5. It's great to have a profound personal experience with your product, but it's not a requirement for massive profits. *FALSE* is the correct answer.

6. By studying successful *models*, we can determine what the market is demanding today and what it is not.
7. To know if something is the *best*, you have to look at all the rest.
8. *Mindset, Product Industry, Timing, Compensation Plan, Management Team, Specific Product*

If you failed, go back and study Chapter Three very carefully one more time and then come back and try again. If you passed with 100 percent correct answers, congratulations! You're ready to finish the exam. Give yourself 12 points and move on.

Points Subtotal: _____

Key #2 Test: Product Industry

If the company you are evaluating markets products or services through one of the following industries, apply these values accordingly. Please do not select more than one industry for each company. Select the industry that best describes the company's product focus. Then, move points to the subtotal line.

Product Industry Report Card

Industry Grade Points	Grade	Number Score
• Nutritional Products (consumable)*	A	11
• Personal/Skin Care (consumable)*	B+	9
• Household Items (consumable)*	B-	7
• Energy Programs	C	5
• Travel Programs	C-	4
• Pre-Paid Legal Services	C-	4
• Telecommunications	C-	4
• Financial/Debt Elimination	C-	4
• Wholesale/Catalog Clubs	C-	4
• Jewelry/Collectibles	D	2
• Sales Lead Generation	D	2
• Filters (water, air)	D	2

Points Subtotal: _____

Key #3 Test: Timing

The following table documents the seven phases of a company's growth. I assigned values to each phase. Find out the annual sales volume over the past several years for the company you are evaluating. Apply the following points scale to the company's annual sales volume. Remember, what you are interested in is the phase that the company is going through in the country that you are building in. For example, a company may be forty years old in the United States, but you may live in New Zealand where the opportunity is brand-new. Pick the phase of growth that applies to the country in which you are building your business.

Keep in mind that you are selecting the best time to *start your distributorship* within that company. If you've established a large organization in a top company and you're now in the advanced stages of maturity, you're in an ideal situation. Congratulations. Don't let this chart discourage you from remaining in a good program. This is strictly a guideline for distributors launching a new opportunity.

Here's a breakdown of the different phases of growth in a company's momentum lifecycle.

Major League Company Momentum Cycle

Timing Report Card

Phase of Growth	Annual Sales	Grade	Points	League Ranking
1. Pioneering	$0–5 million	D-	1	Little League
2. Concentration	$5–10 million	C+	6	Minor League
3. Pre-Momentum	$10–20 million	B	8	Minor League
4. Momentum	$20–100 million	A	11	Minor League
5. Advanced Mo.	$100-500 million	A-	10	Major League
6. Stability	$500 mil –2 bil	B	8	Major League
7. Maturity	$2 billion +	C+	6	Major League

Points Subtotal: _____

Note: If a company's growth has leveled off, it automatically defaults to a C grade. If a company's sales are sliding backwards annually, the company scores an automatic D- and distributors should proceed with extreme caution.

Key #4 Test: Compensation Plan

I ranked compensation plans with the following values. The point spread is varied based upon the many variations within each pay plan. For example, a high-ranking breakaway plan will score a B grade based upon maximum benefits and limited restrictions within that plan. Another breakaway plan can score a D+ grade based on limited payout, limited levels, or high quotas. Top pay plans ranked high based on fairness to distributors, immediate and long-term payout potential, and the team-building incentives built into each plan. Remember, no pay plan is perfect. You won't see any pay plans that score a perfect A+ grade. In fact, my highest grade possible is an A-, and the averaged high grade is a B. However, some plans are better than others. I assigned the average of the high and low score as an overall grade for the plan. Here are the six plans and how they scored.

Compensation Plan Report Card

Name of Plan	Grade Variance (low/high)		Ave. Grade/ Points	
Binary	Low = C- (4)	High = A- (10)	B-	(7)
Breakaway	Low = C- (4)	High = B (8)	C+	(6)
Standard Hybrid	Low = D- (1)	High = B- (7)	C-	(4)
New Binary Hybrid	Low = C+ (6)	High = A- (10)	B	(8)
Matrix	Low = D- (1)	High = B- (7)	D+	(3)
Two-Up	Low = F (0)	High = D (2)	D-	(1)
Unilevel	Low = C- (4)	High = A- (10)	B-	(7)

Points Subtotal: _____

Key #5 Test: Management Team and Company

This test is divided into two categories: things to look for and things to avoid.

Management Team Report Card

Test 5.1: Things to look for in a company and management team

In the "things to look for" category, all management teams and companies can earn half their points (6 points) towards a perfect score of 12 possible points. We proceeded to take points off if the company lacks any of the following positive features. Below is a listing of the features or benefits all companies should have. Start with 6 points and take off points for every feature or benefit listed below that is not present in your company.

Look for visionary leadership, extremely high integrity, mission-driven company and management, corporate business experience, network marketing experience, great track record, great credit, strong financial backing, professional and functional facilities, long-term vision, strict compliance to MLM laws and regulations, proactive regulation of company and products, distributor recognition program, responsive and courteous customer service, drop ship capabilities, a variety of product order options (phone, fax, Website), prompt shipping (delivered two-four days in most countries), timely commission checks (never late), moderate business start-up and maintenance requirements, professional packaging, well-researched product line, quality control program, continuing product research, product enhancement, verification on company headquarters building, and sufficient employees and management to run the company.

Also look for the following business building tools: High-tech computer system (shipping, commissions, downline tracking, order tracking); weekly conference calls; corporate-sponsored national and regional conventions, trainings, distributor retreats, and vacations; professional promotional materials produced by the company at reasonable prices (audios, videos, brochures, magazines, and newsletters); professional Website with full company contact information and corporate officer profiles; online ordering; product profiles; and more.

Test 5.2: Things to avoid in a company and management team

In the "things to avoid" category, all management teams and companies were given 6 more points. Then we proceeded to take points off for any of the following concerns. Below is a list of the concerns that resulted in a loss of one or more points. Start with 6 points and take off points for every negative feature.

Watch out for past or present criminal activity; numerous bankruptcies; inexperienced management team; lack of past successes; unethical activity of any kind; tolerance of unscrupulous staff or distributors; unprofessional conduct (foul language around distributors, harassment); poor personal money management; poor communication; dominant personalities (meet the founders and interview people who have worked with them); apathy; short-term vision; company association with unscrupulous activities or people; excessive hype; false science, product, health, or medical claims; no ownership of products (some other company owns the brand); overemphasis of compensation plan over products; company endorsed slandering of other MLMs; unethical company recruiting campaigns; income claims; one time pay plans; paying on product vouchers/down payments; the promotion of "no sales"; extreme start-up expenses (too high/too low); constant backorders; high attrition rate; low re-order rate; low start-up capital; high start-up capital (front-end loading); heavy debt; poor money management, stagnant growth; drastic changes in product line; drastic changes in compensation plan; sweetheart placement deals and/or special favors, privileges, or rewards to distributors that are not directly tied to performance; corporate employees with downlines; promises from upline to build your downline; promise of spillover from upline; promise of free leads; lack of professional-looking promotional materials such as audios, videos, brochures.

Points Subtotal (both categories):   _____

Key #6 Test: Selecting the Best Product or Service

This test is divided into two categories for each of the four industries: nutritional supplements, personal care, household products, and telecommunications. The two categories include "things to look for" and "things to avoid." On the "things to look for" side, I gave each company points for every criteria that was present in that program, with a maximum of 12 possible points (A+). On the "things to avoid" end, I started each company with a perfect score of 12 points, and then I began eliminating points as I ran into concerns. Add up points from all eight categories and average them at the end. Please review each category.

Selecting a Product Report Card

Test #6.11: Things to look for in a nutritional product line

Product potency (combination of strength and freshness)*, synergy (ingredients work together as a team)*, solid research and documentation on product, simplicity (easy to take, simple dosages), strong nutrition focus (not just herbal), focus on immune system, 90–100 percent unconditional return/refund policy, solid sales growth from month to month and year to year, solid retention and reorder rates.

Test #6.12: Things to avoid in a nutritional product line

Incomplete line, herbal medicine focus rather than nutrition focus, undocumented product claims, exaggerated testimonials, inexperienced scientists formulating products, unsafe ingredients, no results using products, bad results on product, inaccurate labeling*, too much or too little of key nutrients*, low quality/cheap ingredients and formulations*, complicated product line, no return/refund policy, lack of sales, poor customer retention, products proven to be gimmicks (thigh cream, Ma Huang weight loss pills, diuretics, spray vitamins, parasite cleansers, etc.).

*Please note: Without becoming a microbiologist, it may be difficult to evaluate some of the criteria for selecting a high-quality nutritional supplement. Therefore, you must rely on documentation provided by the company and from independent sources to determine the effectiveness of these products.

Test #6.21: Things to look for in a personal care product line

Quality ingredients, such as aloe vera, alpha-hydroxy acids, antioxidants (vitamin A, vitamin D, vitamin E), botanicals (most popular: chamomile, fennel, ginkgo biloba, ginger, ginseng, gotu kola, hops, sage, rosemary, St. John's wart, and others), essential oils (most common: rose, lavender, mint, chamomile, calendula, and tea tree oil), natural ingredients, unique formulations, unique scents (not too overpowering), hypoallergenic, consistency from order to order, appealing packaging, functional packaging,

Test #6.22: Things to avoid in a personal care product line

☞ Harmful ingredients, such as beeswax, collagen, harmful artificial colors and fragrances, lanolin, mineral oil, petroleum (or petrolatum), propylene glycol, sodium laurel/laureth sulfate, sharp exfoliants that cut the skin, anything causing an allergic reaction, anything causing breakout or acne, anything that causes pain or itching.

Test #6.31: Things to look for in a household products line

☞ Quality, environmentally friendly, highly consumable, good pricing, safe, traditional product types, unique formulations, quality packaging

Test #6.32: Things to avoid in a household products line

☞ Extreme pricing, requirements for quantity or bulk purchasing, "concentrated soap" gimmicks (justify high pricing by claiming that soap/detergent is concentrated), false science (like the laundry ball/disk, proven to be hype), cheap quality, ineffective products, cheap packaging

Test #6.41: Things to look for in a telecommunications service MLM

☞ Company provides monthly statement, accurate billing, prompt billing, flat-rate service at competitive market pricing, calling cards with easy calling requirements and competitive market pricing, good international rates, financial commitment to hardware (not just reseller), cell phone packages with current models and plans.

Test #6.42: Things to avoid in a telecommunications service MLM

☞ Large monthly billing charges, high activation fees, circuit's busy signals, drop outs, static or noise on calls, programs dedicated mainly to marketing pre-paid calling cards, one minute or thirty second billing increments, coding bonuses and/or large training fees,

Only take the test for the primary product industry represented in the company you're evaluating. 12 points possible.

Point Subtotal (all categories): _____

Overall Company Grade

Test #1   _____

Test #2   _____

Test #3   _____

Test #4   _____

Test #5   _____

Test #6   _____

TOTAL _____ ÷ 6 = GRAND TOTAL _____

Now take the grand total and apply the following grading scale to give the company a letter grade:

12 points = A+
11 points = A
10 points = A-
9 points = B+
8 points = B
7 points = B-
6 points = C+
5 points = C
4 points = C-
3 points = D+
2 points = D
1 points = D-
0 points = F

Overall Company Grade:

Chapter 11

Best MLM Companies Review

Thank you for studying this book. By doing so, you have proven that you are genuinely interested in becoming educated about network marketing. Hopefully, this book has helped you to better understand emerging trends in network marketing. I also hope that you learned some valuable techniques for selecting the right network marketing company for you.

Using the criteria in this book, I reviewed over four hundred of the most popular network marketing companies. This was quite an undertaking. I gained valuable insights about the industry that have helped me continue to evaluate opportunities more accurately and objectively. Although many companies scored highly in testing, many did not. Some programs didn't make the top ten, top twenty, or even the top four hundred. Some didn't make any list other than my black list. Although many of the following programs have significant flaws that would keep them from being recommended as top opportunities today, they are worth listing. The top ten opportunities are worth evaluating seriously, and only the top five scored high enough to be considered superior companies. I update this list as new information becomes available. However, these updates are only accurate at the date of publishing. I realize that there may be companies that were doing fantastic at the date of publishing, but within as little as two weeks, a company can get into big trouble. So please excuse any information that has become inaccurate. Be sure to check http://www.networkmarketingbook.com for updates, corrections, and additions.

One of the reasons I conducted such a thorough study of over four hundred programs was to pick the number one company in network marketing for the purpose of pursuing an independent distributorship. Although I believe in developing multiple streams of income, I truly believe that you should commit to *one* network marketing opportunity at a time and give it your heart and soul. Please review the following pages to find a list of the top programs in network marketing today.

The following is a list of my top picks in North America for 2012. It's no coincidence that none of these companies are start-ups. In fact, all of these companies are 2-50 years old. Be sure to study Chapter Six again to understand why start-up companies are to be avoided. You see that there is a strong focus on health and nutrition products among these top companies. I spent a lot of time in Chapters Four and Five explaining why health and nutrition is the most viable industry today. It's also interesting to note that although many of these companies have 100-1000 products or more in their line, nearly half of these thirty companies utilized less than a dozen products to produce momentum growth.

Over one third of these companies still produce a majority of their revenue through 1-4 flagship products. Most of these companies feature a unilevel, breakaway, binary, or binary hybrid compensation plan. Be sure you study Chapter Seven carefully so you can understand the pros and cons of each before making your ultimate choice.

In Chapter Eight, I outlined many strategies and tools for scrutinizing the company's management team. Although we don't have room to comment on each below, know that this is the most important criterion of them all. The experience, integrity, and ambition of the founders of these top thirty companies is as varied as their product lines, but these companies have all shown some level of determination to get where they are. Be sure to carefully check out each of the founders on your own. This is the key to a long, successful career in network marketing.

Finally, every company featured in the top thirty has phenomenal products or they would not have made the list. You can rest assured that these are some of the best products in the world, and I would use and recommend all of them (and I actually do use and recommend many of them).

Success leaves clues, and so does failure. Make sure you study this book inside and out so you can understand why some companies survive in network marketing and some don't. Being featured on this list of the top thirty companies in network marketing for 2012 is an honor but there are no guarantees that these companies will continue to grow and thrive. Odds say that several of these companies will make poor choices over the next five years and sabotage their existing momentum, and possibly even go out of business. Continue to apply the strategies for scrutinizing network marketing companies outlined in this book and you'll drastically increase your chances for selecting a solid, long-term winner every time.

Daren's Top Company Choices

Due to the ever changing MLM environment, and the constant cycling of companies and products, I have chosen to keep a current Best MLM Companies List online at www.networkmarketingbook.com.

This list will give you the most accurate and up-to-date information. However, the page is password protected. To get on my mailing list to receive updates, articles, and special offers, visit www.networkmarketingbook.com and submit your contact information. Check your email for the username and password after you submit your contact information. Thank you.

Subject to Review and Change

You may have followed my criteria for evaluating a top network marketing company. You may have selected one of my top picks for network marketing today. Please keep this in mind: no program is perfect. In fact, I discovered concerns associated with every single company in network marketing today, including the companies listed among my top picks and even the company I'm currently associated with. I recommend that if you are considering any of these companies, please do your homework. The names on my top companies list and their ranking can change every few months. First of all, make sure you are looking at a current copy of this book or look at my updated list of companies at my Website, www.networkmarketingbook.com. If the company you are researching did not make my list, please proceed with extreme caution. Don't be foolish in selecting a company. Picking a start-up program is a great way to lose time, money, and the respect of your associates.

One of Many

I'm the first to admit that the companies I have selected for my clients and the companies I have selected to personally build are not the only games in town. To be listed among the top companies in network marketing is an accomplishment, considering the fact that few companies survive more than three years. However, even if a company did make the list, there is still a considerable amount of risk attached to each opportunity. We will continue to see companies in the top one hundred go out of business every year. If a company is less than five years old, the company is still at great risk of going out of business. If the company is over thirty years old and financially strong, the company should stay around but the momentum phase may be so advanced that the opportunity is not as great as it once was in your state or country. If a company is not listed among the top thirty, my advice is to proceed with extreme caution. For legal purposes, I will not mention names of companies I have strong reservations about, but be careful. I don't want your first or next experience in network marketing to be your last.

Best Network Marketing Companies - Updated 2012

Rising Stars (2012 Momentum Companies)

Our rising stars are the new, progressive, fast growth companies that are generally at least 2-10 years old. These companies have recently caught their momentum. Some companies take a little longer to catch momentum than others, but there's no better time to build a MLM company than during the momentum phase. Here's this year's picks for Rising Stars listed by date-of-launch:

Yoli	2009	Nutrition, Weight Loss	Binary/Unilevel Hybrid
NuCerity	2009	Skin Care	Binary/Unilevel Hybrid
Qivana	2009	Nutrition	Binary/Unilevel Hybrid
Doterra	2008	Essential Oils	Unilevel
Zija	2006	Nutrition, Moringa	Unilevel
MXI (Xocai)	2006	Nutrition, Healthy Chocolate	Binary/Unilevel Hybrid
Visalus	2005	Nutrition, Weight Loss	Unilevel

Industry Icons (Top 20 Established Companies)

Our industry icons list consists of network marketing's powerhouse companies. Most of these companies have weathered their initial momentum cycle and lived to tell about it. These brands are solid, sound, and most of them are still growing mostly in international markets. Here are the top 20 listed alphabetically:

4Life	1998	Nutrition	Unilevel
Arbonne	1975	Skin Care	Breakaway
ForeverGreen	2003	Nutrition	Unilevel
Forever Living	1978	Nutrition, Skin Care	Breakaway
Herbalife	1980	Nutrition, Skinl Care	Breakaway
Isagenix	2001	Nutrition, Skin Care	Binary/Unilevel Hybrid
LifeVantage	2003	Nutrition, Skin Care	Unilevel
Mannatech	1992	Nutrition	Unilevel
Market America	1992	Household, Variety	Binary
Monavie	2005	Nutrition	Binary/Unilevel Hybrid
NuSkin	1984	Nutrition, Personal Care	Breakaway
Scensy	2004	Candles, Gifts	Breakaway
SendOutCards	2004	Greeting Cards, Gifts	Unilevel
Tahitian Noni	1996	Nutrition, Personal Care	Unilevel
Trivita	1999	Nutrition	Unilevel
Univera	1999	Nutrition	Unilevel
USANA	1992	Nutrition, Personal Care	Binary
Veema	2004	Nutrition	Binary
Vitamark	2002	Nutrition	Unilevel
XanGo	2002	Nutrition, Skin Care	Unilevel

Honorable Mention (Foundational Companies)

I never want to forget to give a shout out to the companies that originally established the network marketing industry. Without the blood, sweat, and tears of the founders, staff, distributors, and vendors of these fine companies, none of us would be where we are today. To be considered a foundational company, you must be at least 20 years old, and be well established as a brand. Here are the companies that deserve to be honored as foundational companies:

Company	Year	Category	Type
Amway	1859	Household, Variety	Breakaway
Avon	1886	Cosmetics, Personal Care	Breakaway
Fuller Brush	1911	Household Products	Breakaway
Golden Neo-Life	1958	Nutrition	Breakaway
Mary Kay	1963	Cosmetics, Personal Care	Breakaway
Nature's Sunshine	1972	Nutrition	Breakaway
NSA	1970	Nutrition	Breakaway
Nikken	1975	Nutrition, Health Magnets	Breakaway
Legal Shield	1972	(Was PPL) Legal Services	Breakaway
Primerica	1977	Financial Services	Breakaway
Reliv	1988	Nutrition	Breakaway
Shaklee	1956	Nutrition	Breakaway
Sunrider	1982	Nutrition	Breakaway
Watkins	1977	Household, Variety	Breakaway

101 Popular (or Formerly Popular) Network Marketing Companies – Updated 2012

Please note that I do not necessarily endorse or recommend any of these companies. This is simply a list of the 101 most popular and recognized network marketing companies as of 2012, or companies that were formerly popular and are still in existence today. I will say this, if the company you're investigating did not make this list, beware. Here they are:

Company Name	US Phone #	Corporate Website
1. 4Life Research	888-454-3374	www.4life.com
2. Acai Plus	858-514-8271	www.acaiplus.com
3. ACN	248-699-4000	www.acninc.com
4. Advantage	800-867-1891	www.welcometoadvantage.com
5. AdvoCare	972-478-4500	www.advocare.com
6. Agel	801-563-3366	www.agel.com
7. Amazon Herb	800-835-0850	www.rainforestbio.com
8. Ambit	877-282-6248	www.ambitenergy.com
9. AmeriPlan	972-702-9856	www.ameriplanusa.com
10. Amigo Health	866-455-1185	www.amigohealth.com
11. Ampegy	855-267-3491	www.ampegy.com
12. AMS Health Sciences	405-842-0131	www.amsonline.com
13. Amway	616-676-6000	www.amway.com
14. Arbonne	949-770-2610	www.arbonne.com
15. Avon	212-282-5100	www.avon.com
16. Beach Body	800-998-1681	www.beachbody.com
17. Big Planet	801-345-7000	www.bigplanet.com
18. Body Wise	801-466-8300	www.bodywise.com
19. Cambridge	831-373-2300	www.cambridgedietusa.com
20. Care Entrée	800-820-6474	www.careentree.com
21. Cognigen	206-297-3900	www.cognigen.com
22. Cyberwize	941-371-1010	www.cyberwize.com
23. DWG	702-262-5555	www.dwginternational.com
24. EcoQuest	800-989-2299	www.ecoquest.com
25. eCosway	949-453-0888	www.ecosway.com
26. Eniva	763-795-8870	www.eniva.com
27. Enliven	800-548-5746	www.enliveninternational.com
28. Essentially Yours	604-759-5000	www.eyicom.com
29. Forever Green	801-655-5500	www.forevergreen.org
30. Forever Living	800-309-2057	www.foreverliving.com
31. ForMor	501-336-0077	www.formorintl.com

32.	FreeLife	203-882-7250	www.freelife.com
33.	Fruta Vida	512-266-1944	www.frutavida.com
34.	Fuller Brush	620-792-1711	www.fullerbrush.com
35.	Gano Excel	626-338-8081	www.ganoexcel.biz
36.	Golden Neo-Life Diamite	510-651-0405	www.gnld.com
37.	Goldshield Elite	866-218-8142	www.goldshieldelite.com
38.	Herbalife	310-410-9600	www.herbalife.com
39.	Heritage Health	970-484-7120	www.heritagehealthproducts.com
40.	Ignite	866-447-8732	www.igniteinc.com
41.	Immunotec	450-424-9992	www.immunotec.com
42.	Isagenix	856-983-6900	www.isogenix.com
43.	Kaire	877-603-1710	www.kaire.com
44.	Legacy For Life	800-557-8477	www.legacyforlife.com
45.	Life Force	800-531-4877	www.lifeforce.net
46.	Life Plus	870-698-2311	www.lifeplus.com
47.	Lifestyles	800-461-3438	www.lifestyles.net
48.	Mannatech	972-471-7400	www.mannatech.com
49.	Market America	336-605-0040	www.marketamerica.com
50.	Mary Kay	972-687-6300	www.marykay.com
51.	Matol (Univera)	800-363-6286	www.matol.com
52.	Melaleuca	208-522-0700	www.melaleuca.com
53.	Momentus	403-815-9623	www.momentusenergy.com
54.	Monavie	801-748-3100	www.monavie.com
55.	Morinda	801-234-1000	www.tni.com
56.	MXI/Xocai	866-469-4267	www.xocai.com
57.	NHT Global	604-533-4425	www.nhtglobal.com
58.	Nature's Sunshine	800-223-8225	www.naturessunshine.com
59.	Neways	801-423-2800	www.neways.com
60.	Nikken	949-789-2000	www.nikken.com
61.	NSA	901-366-9288	www.nsaonline.com
62.	NuSkin	801-345-1000	www.nuskin.com
63.	Omnitrition	972-702-7600	www.omnitrition.com
64.	Orenda	480-889-1001	www.orendainternational.com
65.	Oxyfresh	800-333-7374	www.oxyfresh.com
66.	Pharmanex	801-345-1000	www.pharmanex.com
67.	Pre-Paid Legal	580-436-1234	www.prepaidlegal.com
68.	Primerica	770-381-1000	www.primerica.com
69.	Reliv	636-537-9715	www.reliv.com
70.	ReVita	904-269-3240	www.re-vita.com
71.	Royal Body Care	972-893-4000	www.royalbodycare.com
72.	SeaAloe	800-299-8256	www.seasilver.com
73.	Scent-Sations	866-207-2368	www.scent-team.com
74.	Shaklee	925-924-2000	www.shaklee.com
75.	Sibu	801-542-7500	www.sibu.com

76.	SimpleXity Health	800-800-1300	www.simplexityhealth.com
77.	Somalife	250-491-5090	www.somalife.net
78.	StemTech	541-850-1700	www.stemtechhealth.com
79.	Sunrider	310-781-8096	www.sunrider.com
80.	Symmetry	800-796-6387	www.symmetrydirect.com
81.	Synergy	801-431-7600	www.synergyworldwide.com
82.	The Limu Co.	866-852-4832	www.thelimucompany.com
83.	Trivita	800-991-7116	www.trivita.com
84.	Unicity	801-226-2600	www.unicitynetwork.com
85.	Univera	877-627-4749	www.univeralifesciences.com
86.	Usana	801-954-7100	www.usana.com
87.	Veema/NewVision	480-927-8999	www.vemma.com
88.	Vitamark	281-220-1240	www.vitamark.com
89.	Waiora	866-699-2467	www.waiora.com
90.	Watkins	651-776-7632	www.watkinsonline.com
91.	Wellness (WIN)	972-245-1097	www.winltd.com
92.	World Fin. Grp	319-369-2877	www.wfg-online.com
93.	World Ventures	972-805-5100	www.wordventures.com
94.	XanGo	801-816-8000	www.xango.net
95.	Xtreme Health	909-420-0222	www.xtremehealthformulas.com
96.	XPI	301-315-0626	www.xpionline.com
97.	Xooma	888-865-6687	www.xoomaworldwide.com
98.	Yoli	888-295-9009	www.yoli.com
99.	Young Living	801-418-8900	www.youngliving.com
100.	Youngevity	800-982-3189	www.youngevity.com
101.	Zurvita	713-464-5002	www.zurvita.com

Now What?

I've Selected My Company ... Now What?

Now you might be thinking, "Okay, I have done my due diligence, paid my dues, applied the research in this book, and I have finally selected my company. My job is done! Right?" Wrong. There are several additional steps you must take in order to avoid the four most common reasons for failure in network marketing. Let's review these reasons briefly to show you what you are up against, and then I'll give you some ideas on how to get around these obstacles. Let's start with the one we've been spending so much time on already.

The Four Reasons for Failure in Network Marketing

1. Wrong Company: When distributors select the wrong company, they will likely fail for one of two reasons. First, the distributor could fail because he/she does not have a good experience with the company. If the distributor does not get along with the company's management, if the product is ineffective, or if the compensation plan is not fair, the distributor will most likely leave the company within the first one to two years. Second, sometimes the distributor believes in the company 100 percent. However, due to poor management, bad finances, ineffective products, or lousy compensation, the company goes out of business, leaving the distributor high and dry.

2. Wrong Upline: Even when distributors find a great company, it is nearly impossible to build a successful network marketing business without a supportive upline offering weekly training and support. Without training and support, new distributors are left to their own devices and will likely fail.

3. No System: Most beginners in network marketing are very excited about getting started. However, even very determined individuals will usually fail within their first year if they're not working a proven system.

4. No Commitment: It's simply human nature. Most people want to take the easy road. It's hard to find people with the

determination to stick to it. Lack of commitment is the number one reason for failure in MLM. Without a solid commitment, even a great company, upline, or system will not help you.

How You Can Increase Your Chances For Success

1. Find the Right Company: This book was designed to help you understand the criteria for selecting the best company in MLM. After reviewing the research contained in this book, thousands of people (including myself) have been able to select the best company ... but don't take my word for it. Read this book and find out for yourself which company is the best. Then join that company with confidence and don't look back.

2. Select the Best Upline: Make sure your upline is truly committed to their success and to your success. If the person who wants to sponsor you is known to be flaky, lack integrity, or become overwhelmed easily, you might want to carefully evaluate the situation before moving forward. If your upline is extremely successful, make sure that they will have time for you. If your upline is brand-new to the business, make sure they or someone in your immediate upline has the same commitment you have. Selecting a sponsor and an upline is a lot like getting married. You have one shot, and you want to make the right choice or it could end in heartache and despair. Seek relationships that will last with people who will help you be all you can be.

3. Utilize the Right System: It is the sponsor's responsibility to refer you to a proven system for success and to assist in your training. New distributors should be able to plug into this system within their first week in the business. Top network marketing systems incorporate the advantages of traditional marketing with cutting-edge advancements in new, high-tech marketing. Your system should include information on how to create a local marketing campaign, how to do three-way calls, how to utilize weekly conference calls, and how to prospect and recruit through direct mail and the Internet.

4. Make a Commitment: Commitment is essential for success in any field of endeavor, especially network marketing. What does it mean to be committed? It means doing whatever it takes to be

successful, with no excuses. Before you look for a company, you must ask yourself, "Am I committed to doing whatever it takes to make this work?" Then surround yourself with people who share that same commitment.

The Final Step!

I hope you benefited from the information in this book. Now you have one last step to take. It is time to take action! As I mentioned in the beginning of this text, this book was designed to teach you how to generate wealth in network marketing. But this message has only been told halfway. Step one is selecting the best company. Step two is selecting an able and ready support team within that company and building your own momentum. Please get in touch immediately with the person who referred this book to you. Request specific information about the company this person is promoting and then apply the principles outlined in this book to make sure it matches the profile of a top network marketing program. Don't settle for second best; join the best company you can find and then get moving in that company. I want you to be a main character in one of my upcoming books.

I want to hear from you!

Collecting success stories of top network marketers is my passion. If you've achieved extraordinary success in network marketing on any level, please contact me. I'm writing two different books showcasing these success stories and maybe you can be featured in my new book or on my new Website. Also, I would love to get your feedback on this book and learn how it has helped you select a top network marketing company.

Good luck, and I hope to see you featured as a top distributor on the cover of your new company's monthly newsletter or magazine soon. Best of success!

Daren

P.S. To order additional copies of this book, go to http://www.networkmarketingbook.com

Afterword

Thank you for reading *How to Select a Network Marketing Company*. The purpose in developing this book was two fold. First, it was designed to provide an objective analysis of the many companies that make up the network marketing industry. Second, it was designed as a resource to help aspiring network marketing leaders scrutinize and select a network marketing company while, at the same time, learning how to spot and avoid scams.

This book was not intended to slander any legitimate network marketing program and should be used only as a reference guide. The comments, evaluations, and comparisons contained in this book are the educated opinions of Daren C. Falter. Any other companies or individuals mentioned or quoted in this book are not necessarily endorsing this book or my opinions. All quotes made by individuals in this book have been selected from reliable sources by the author. Those being quoted are not responsible for any inaccuracies in this text.

How to Select a Network Marketing Company was written with careful attention to accuracy. With this amount of information, this book may contain inaccuracies that have escaped my scrutiny. If you feel you have discovered any false or misleading information, please email me at daren@networkmarketingbook.com. These matters will be taken very seriously and I will immediately implement any needed corrections. Please provide me with specific details and documentation to back up your findings. Hearsay and conjecture is not tolerated.

A word about objectivity

Please note that when research began on this book, I had no special connection or relationship with any of the over four hundred companies I've now reviewed. I'd previously been involved with several network marketing programs as an independent distributor. Before conducting my study, these distributorships were dissolved. After scrutinizing the first two hundred companies, I became involved with one of the companies I selected as one of my top five choices for 1995. Over a three-year period of time, I built a large and successful independent distributorship with this company. As of the publication of this book, the other four companies that I selected as top programs in 1995 are still in business today and thriving in the marketplace.

From 1995 to 1998, I developed a manuscript, which eventually became the first paperback version of *How to Select a Network Marketing Company* in 1998. Since the publication of the first version of this book, I have reviewed another two hundred top companies and have continued to revise and update this book. This book is the fifth such revision. Although I have thousands of names of network marketing and direct sales companies in my database, I have specifically reviewed over four hundred popular programs and I will continue to research more companies every week.

Having access to the most detailed research and statistics, I have successfully selected and built several streams of residual income through Internet affiliate programs and network marketing opportunities. As of 2003, I again became involved as an independent distributor in one of my preferred network marketing companies, and I now have a downline organization numbering in the tens of thousands of independent distributors in over a dozen countries. My success in network marketing allows me to continue to research, speak, and write about network marketing. The companies I represent now as an independent distributor or as a consultant do not necessarily agree or disagree with my findings.

I will continue to strive to remain extremely objective in my writing and will continue to scrutinize my research so I can provide useful and truthful information to my readers. The truth is out there, and I'm dedicated to helping you find it.

Daren C. Falter
http://www.networkmarketingbook.com

Endnotes

Chapter Two

1. Billings, *The Dictionary of Humorous Quotes,* 32.

Chapter Four

2. Upanishad, *The Upanishads,* 207.

3. Billings, *The Dictionary of Humorous Quotes,* 33.

Chapter Six

4. Ries, *The 22 Immutable Laws of Branding,* 38.

5. Nichols, *The Ideal Business,* 52.

6. Pilzer, *The Wellness Revolution,* 40.

7. Popcorn and Marigold, *The Popcorn Report,* 66.

Chapter Seven

8. *King James Bible,* Ecclesiastes 3:1.

10. Shakespeare, *Julius Caesar,* Act IV Scene III.

9. Hedges, *Who Stole the American Dream?* 130–1.

11. Ibid, 131–2.

Chapter Eight

12. Nichols, *Successful Network Marketing for the 21st Century,* 6.

13. Rawlins, Binary Plans, 1.

14. Rawlins, *Understanding Multi-Level Commissions,* vi.

Chapter Nine

15. Clements, *Inside Network Marketing,* 82.

16. Clements, Facts & Myths of MLM.

17. Grimes, The Preeminence of Value.

18. Ibid.

19. Babener, Dot Com or Dot Scam?
Chapter Ten

20. Pilzer, *The Wellness Revolution*, 11–2.

21. Hawken, *The Ecology of Commerce,* 31.

22. Reese, MLM & The Law, Coding Bonuses.

23. Huckaby, Key Trends for Evaluating an MLM Opportunity.

24. Godin, *Purple Cow,* inside jacket cover.

25. Ries, *The 22 Immutable Laws of Branding*, ix.

26. Popcorn and Marigold, *EVEolution,* 4–5.

Bibliography

Babener, Jeffery. 2001. Dot Com or Dot Scam?
http://www.mlmlegal.com/, 10/8/06.

Billings, Josh. *The Dictionary of Humorous Quotes.* Dorset Press, New York, NY, 1989.

Clements, Len. 1998. Facts & Myths of MLM: The Useless Questions Distributors Ask. *NetWork Marketing Today*, 1998.

Clements, Len. *Inside Network Marketing.* Prima, Roseville, CA, 2000.

Godin, Seth. *Purple Cow: Transform Your Business by Being Remarkable.* Portfolia, Hudson Street, NY, 2003.

Grimes, Kevin. 2002. The Preeminence of Value.
http://www.mlmlaw.com/, 10/8/06.

Hawken, Paul. *The Ecology of Commerce.* HarperBusiness, New York, NY, 1993.

Hedges, Burke. *Who Stole the American Dream?* BFH Productions, 1992.

Huckaby, Chuck. 1998. Key Trends for Evaluating an MLM Opportunity. *NetWork Marketing Today.*

King James, *The Holy Bible*, The Church of Jesus Christ of Latter-Day Saints, Salt Lake City, UT, Ecclesiastes 3:1.

Nichols, Rod. *Successful Network Marketing for the 21st Century.* Oasis Press, Central Point, Oregon, 2002.

Nichols, Rod. *The Ideal Business.* Morris Publishing, Kearney, NE, 2005.

Pilzer, Paul Zane. *The Wellness Revolution.* Wiley, New York, NY, 2002.

Popcorn, Faith, and Lys Marigold. *EVEolution: Eight Truths of Marketing to Women.* Hyperion, New York, NY, 2000.

Popcorn, Faith, and Lys Marigold. *The Popcorn Report.* HarperBusiness, New York, NY, 1992.

Rawlins, Mark. 2002. Binary Plans: Taking our industry to new heights, or the beginning of the end. http://www.mlm.com, 10/8/06.

Rawlins, Mark. *Understanding Multi-Level Commissions.* Mark Rawlins, Salt Lake City, UT, 2002.

Reese, Spencer. 1998. MLM & The Law, Coding Bonuses: Is There Trouble Ahead? http://www.mlmlegal.com/, 10/8/06.

Ries, Al and Laura. *The 22 Immutable Laws of Branding: How to Build a Product or Service into a World-Class Brand.* HarperBusiness, New York, NY, 2002.

Upanishad, Shvetashvatara. *The Upanishads.* Translated by Eknath Easwaran. The Blue Mountain Center of Meditation, Tomales, CA, 1987.

Index

About the Author

Daren C. Falter launched his direct sales career in 1990, and has since become a passionate student and advocate of network marketing. He wrote the first manuscript edition of *How to Select a Network Marketing Company* in 1995-96 and published it as a paperback for the first time in 1998. Daren has served as a top MLM consultant, master trainer, popular convention speaker, and a full-time independent distributor in network marketing building downline organizations into the tens of thousands of distributors. Daren has recently become a corporate owner of a Utah-based network marketing company. Daren maintains a close connection to the industry and keeps his finger on the pulse of the network marketing industry by continuing to conduct monthly interviews with MLM's most successful leaders.

Daren lives in Olympia, Washington, with his wife Sandy and their six children. More than anything, he loves dates with his wife, supporting his children's activities, church and community service, time with friends, playing guitar & piano, basketball, skiing, camping and hiking, travel, and meeting new people.

16168180R00167

Made in the USA
San Bernardino, CA
21 October 2014